LADY HESTER

Born into the age of revolution, Lady Hester Stanhope had a radical spirit. Following the death of her uncle the Prime Minister William Pitt in 1806, she chose the excitement of travel and adventure over the life of a spinster in polite London society. And she never looked back.

Surviving a terrible shipwreck and the scorn of Lord Byron ('that dangerous thing – a female wit'), Lady Hester adopted male Arabic dress, became the Queen of the Bedouin and was the first European woman ever to enter Palmyra. Recovering from the heartbreak of a passionate love affair, she became a political force in Lebanon. In defiance of despotic war lords she offered sanctuary to an oppressed minority, creating a fortress which became a focus of both gossip and awe.

Told with all the verve of its subject's life, based on much new source material and extensive travel in Hester's footsteps, *Lady Hester* traces this extraordinary life from Downing Street to an isolated monastery in the hills of Lebanon – a stunning evocation of a unique and pioneering figure.

Lorna Gibb grew up in Bellshill, Scotland and worked as a professional dancer in Italy before studying at London University. She took her PhD at Edinburgh, lectured at Helsinki and Sheffield University, and was a guest lecturer at the University of Salzburg. She lives in London with her husband. *Lady Hester* is her first biography.

Further praise for *Lady Hester*:

'Gripping and readable . . . [Lorna Gibb] has a talent for vivid, detailed descriptions of places and climates.' *Independent on Sunday*

'[Gibb] writes with sympathy, warmth and some style . . . The shadowy figure of the earlier chapters begins to gain substance and Gibb, who clearly admires her, does ample justice to an extraordinary personality who, almost always, got her way.' Miranda Seymour, *Sunday Times*

Lady Hester
Queen of the East

LORNA GIBB

faber and faber

First published in 2005
by Faber and Faber Limited
3 Queen Square London WC1N 3AU

This paperback edition first published in 2006

Typeset in Minion by Faber and Faber Limited
Printed in England by Mackays of Chatham, plc

A CIP record for this book
is available from the British Library

ISBN 978–0–571–21754–0

2 4 6 8 10 9 7 5 3

For my parents,
And for my husband.

Contents

Map of Hester's travels viii
Acknowledgements xi
Prologue xv
1 A Chapter of Endings 1
2 Private Sorrow and Public Opinion 13
3 First Love and Escaping 21
4 Childhood 25
5 Departures 45
6 Anticipation and Arrival 57
7 Change and Beginnings 79
8 Triumph and Belonging 99
9 Sadness and Sickness 119
10 Treasure, Reunion and Revenge 137
11 Of the East and of the West 155
12 Passion and Political Unrest 175
13 Families 195
14 Final Farewells 211
15 Aftermath 225
    Epilogue 231
    Select Bibliography 235
    Endnotes 239
    Index 253

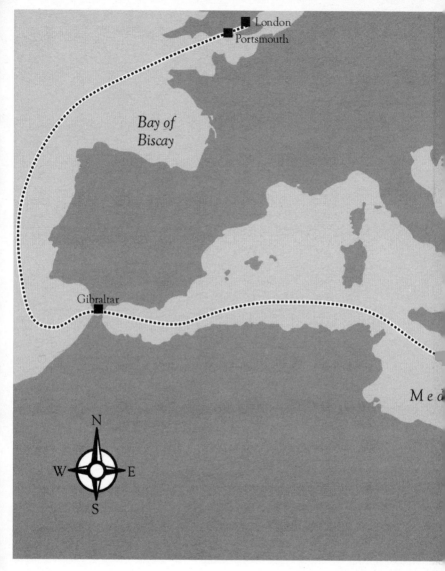

The travels of Lady He.

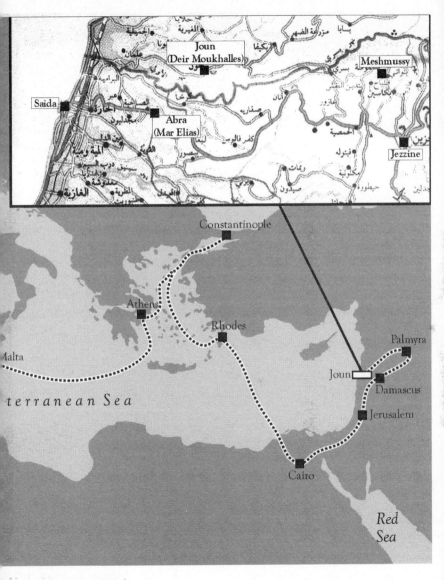

Joun
(Deir Moukhalles)

Meshmussy

Saida

Abra
(Mar Elias)

Jezzine

Constantinople

Athens

Rhodes

Palmyra

Malta

Joun

Damascus

terranean Sea

Jerusalem

Cairo

_Red
Sea_

er Stanhope, 1810–1839

Acknowledgements

I have had a lot of help and encouragement from people while research-ing this book. Thanks are due to the staff of the British Library, especially Marcus Langley-White in Rare Books and Manuscripts, the staff of the Public Record Office, Herefordshire Record Office, Centre for Kentish Studies, Westminster Archives and West Sussex Record Office; the Wellcome Foundation, the London Library, Christine Penney at Birmingham University Special Collections, The Royal College of Physicians, Jane Weeks, the Victoria and Albert and the Bodleian Libraries. My first trip to the Lebanon was made financially possible by a generous award from the Society of Authors; I am very grateful to them.

Sally Mewton Hynds and Rowena Shepherd allowed me some time alone in Pitt's dining room in Walmer Castle as well as giving a wonder-ful and informative tour of the whole building. Colonel Richard Brook has been incredibly supportive, not only finding some letters and photos for me, but also allowing my husband and I to pass a really special day at Chevening with him. Caroline Carty welcomed me into her beautiful home in Montagu Square, then made me coffee till the rain stopped. Simon Weager at Ian Hodgkins very kindly sent me a photocopy of a letter by Hester which they were selling but which I could not afford. Another private collector who wishes to remain anonymous did the same with two letters in her possession.

One of my dearest friends, Paul Coombs, soothed and encouraged, providing support with everything from computer programmes to proof-reading and finding possible covers, while another, Leo Marshall, seemed always ready with sympathy and boxes of chocolate. The writer, Charles Palliser, has helped many fledgeling writers; I am lucky not only to be one of them but to have had his friendship for more than 20 years. The intrepid Chris Burkinshaw was a fantastic travelling companion in Palestine and Israel. Lee Sands read and commented on various chapters, giving me the benefit of his wisdom and insight, while Sarah Luznat made careful German translations of Puckler Muskau for me. My friend and university colleague, the late Ylmas Vural, first introduced me to the East during long spring and summer months in his magical Istanbul flat overlooking the Bosphorus. He is sadly missed. My former students Mustapha, Karim and Milgo helped in a variety of ways, including discussions about Islam, Arabic translation and fantastic Somalian food; it was a selfish pleasure to teach them as it enabled me to learn so much. Grant Glendinning from City & Islington College helped me through a difficult time with understanding and support. Liz Sommerville, my excellent secondary school Latin teacher, gave me enough skill to be able to decipher Meryon's jokes and asides. Dr Michael Newton commented on this manuscript patiently and constructively; I am grateful for his expert advice, for the benefit of his talent and, most of all, for his friendship throughout the years.

Many, many people have helped me on my travels. In Greece, Amalia and Odysseus Korkanitou gave me the advantage not only of their wonderful hospitality but also their expert knowledge of the sea and sailing. In the Lebanon, Nanette Ritter and Nora Jumblatt all gave generously of their time. Particular thanks are due to Drs Roget and Dolly Jawish, now very dear friends, for so many favours and pleasures and help that I cannot begin to list them all here but wish that I could. At Masmoushy, Jamil Joseph Jabr and Sabir Abi Atme spent a magical evening with us and allowed us to share in the history of their talented family. Mohammed Chamseddine welcomed me on my first visit to the Lebanon both into his home and to his country. The staff at the Mir Amin Palace Hotel were kind and welcoming. Many of them used their own time to talk to us about being Druse as well as share family folklore about Hester. Chris Poole MBE and his wife Lynne were obliging in their pursuit of information for me. On my last visit to Lebanon, the British Ambassador, HE James Watt, made me very welcome in his home, while the Lebanese Ambassador H.E. Jihad Mortada delighted me yet again with the extent of Lebanese hospitality and generosity. The Hon. William Stanhope helped in many direct and indirect ways; it is a pleasure to know him.

Dr Borre Ludwigson of the University of Oslo deserves a special acknowledgement for the e-mails, pictures, anecdotes and maps which have so helped me picture Hester's life in the East.

Julian Loose, my editor at Faber, and his assistant, Henry Volans have been charming and constructive. Working with them has given me a great deal of pleasure. Special thanks also to Ron Costley for making the book look so beautiful. Paul Marsh at the Marsh Agency has been a fantastic agent and I am indebted to others there, particularly Leyla Selmi.

Throughout all of the process of writing and researching three people have loved, supported and believed in me: my husband, Alan Wesselson, and my parents Ian and Jessie Gibb. Alan was the perfect travelling companion when he came with me, and a joy to come home to when he did not. His patience, faith and, perhaps most of all, his ability to make me laugh carried me through the difficult times, and his pleasure in my happiness made the good times so much better. My mother and father brought me up in a household full of books where learning and love were valued above all things. I thank them for these, the most precious gifts of childhood; without them I would be unable to do now the work that I most enjoy.

Photographs and illustrations are reproduced by kind permission of the following organisations and individuals: private collection (plates 1, 19); The Board of Trustees of the Chevening Estate (2, 3, 5, 6 and the illustration on page 188); The Royal College of Physicians (8, 20); The Bodleian Library, Oxford (9, 11); Alan Wesselson (15, 16, 17, 18); Professor Roget Jawesh (the illustration on page 231). The map on pages viii–ix is reproduced by kind permission of Paul Coombs.

Prologue

Lady Hester Stanhope is a figure who provokes. A woman who was at the pinnacle of British politics at the side of her uncle, William Pitt the Younger, she spent most of her life in the Middle East dressed as a man, took at least two much younger men as lovers, yet died destitute and alone in an isolated Lebanese village.

The journey of her life, from drawing room to desert, was marked by scandal and intrigue; the power of her adventures such that, in the decades immediately following her death, she featured in the consciousness of Western artists and intellectuals.

James Joyce and W. H. Auden wrote of her; even Picasso claimed that he first planned to come to England solely so he could meet 'such a breed of women' as Lady Hester, while a town in Iowa, USA, was named Stanhope in honour of her exploits.[1]

It was not only in the West that Hester's name was posthumously associated with such strong emotions. Around the villages of the Chouf in Lebanon where she spent so much of her life, people vacillated between awe at her defiance of two local despots, and hatred because of her cruel treatment of their ancestors who worked for her. There was a great sense of pride that she had chosen to live in their country. And, among some of the religious minority called Druse, there was gratitude for her protection from persecution during some of the many wars that ravaged the region at the time.

While the Middle Eastern picture of Hester was largely created from collective memory, family history and local myth, the European version primarily originated from two trilogies of books, written by the physician, Dr Meryon, who accompanied her on her travels for many years. The generally accepted accuracy of these books meant that until recently many of the original documents, scattered literally around the world, were ignored. Some of these letters are in open conflict with the published volumes, although there are others which substantiate and complement them. Taken altogether they create a kaleidoscopic image of Hester which, while it does not deny the strange Garbo-like reclusion of her later years – that favourite subject for inclusion in late-twentieth-century anthologies – is also a glimpse at a teenage girl who danced all night and a reminder of a woman who loved not wisely but with a great deal of passion; the same Hester who carefully packed her little blue baby dress and carried a brave, dead soldier's bloodstained glove for thousands of miles through shipwreck and plague.

Early in the twentieth century, Hester's legend certainly prevailed: great writers were intrigued; articles were written. But then, as decades passed, so did the splendour of the story. Now, just after the beginning of the new millennium, the power of the woman who was at the right hand of Britain's prime minister and returned to glory as protector of an Eastern minority seems largely disregarded by the country of her birth in favour of anecdotes about her eccentricities and religious delusions.

But it is not so in the Middle East, especially in Lebanon. Here still there remain dramatic characterizations, not always flattering, to be found: Hester was the tyrant with a tireless spirit, a fearless lady who instilled terror, desecrator of villages, saviour of the faithful, defender of the few.

In London, where her house in Montagu Square does not even carry a blue plaque to show that she once lived there, it is far too easy to forget how important and wonderful the Queen of the East once was.

Do not try to convince people anymore 'I am this – I am that': time, please God, will prove what I am; I think I have been a true prophet in all things.

Lady Hester Stanhope

1

A Chapter of Endings

A poor gentlewoman, doctor, is the worst thing in the world.
Lady Hester to Meryon

William Pitt the Younger

IT WAS A TERRIBLE WINTER. And for the friends and family, now waiting together in the splendid Putney house, the weather of the preceding weeks, its unrelenting severity, had been a harsh backdrop to the slow, sad days of dying. A short time ago, in the closing months of 1805, there had been some hope. The Prime Minister, William Pitt the Younger, was sick, troubled by a complaint that had recurred for many years, which rendered him unable to hold down any food and racked his body with sudden, agonizing pains. His niece and companion, Lady Hester Stanhope, tended him and worried, filled by a sense that this bout was somehow more serious than the others had been. She joined her own pleas to those of his doctor, the renowned Walter Farquar, and urged him to take the water at Bath, a restorative cure that had helped him in the past. Tucking a quilt around him as he sat in the carriage, she bade him farewell, settling to wait at Putney for news of change. But the change that came was not for the good. When Farquar joined him at the spa he was shocked. Pitt's weakness and pallor were accentuated by emaciation, the consequence of constant, violent vomiting. Both Pitt and Farquar accepted the reality that Bath was having no beneficial effect, and after further consultation with a local physician, Pitt returned home. The changes in Pitt's physical state had happened gradually over the weeks, and while both doctor and patient had helplessly witnessed the deterioration in health, Hester had not. As his carriage approached and his arrival was announced, Hester rushed from one of the upstairs parlours. Pitt's voice greeted her from the landing below, so that even before she saw him, Hester was shocked and overcome by the change in his voice. She realized then, 'It is all over with him.'[1]

As January progressed the sickness grew worse.[2] Pitt threw up all solid food, with the exception of a concoction made up of egg yolk beaten with brandy, which only brought temporary respite but exacerbated the alcoholism which was the main cause of his illness. Within a week even the egg was too much for him; his footman muttered to other servants about the folly of doctors who insisted on 'giving him the egg; for he brings it up every time'. Yet Pitt refused to admit the severity of his condition, and when parliament requested that the celebration of Queen Charlotte's birthday, bizarrely set on 18 January although her birthday was not until May, be postponed in deference to the Prime Minister's health, he insisted that it should not, that Hester would attend on his behalf. In what would be her last great appearance in English society, Hester reluctantly, but splendidly, left Putney for the ball: wearing a costume of black and green velvet embellished with gold and embedded with rubies, she was praised by the newspapers for the tasteful elegance of her diamond studded headdress and the courteous grace of her conduct. But she spent the evening in a daze, impatient for it to be over, relieved only when she arrived home to find that her youngest half-brother, James Stanhope, had arrived to help her care for their uncle. With the arrival of James and the imminence of death, the attendant doctors forbade Hester to see her uncle again in the belief that the excitement of a visit from her could only hasten the inevitable. Hester asked again and again to be allowed to see him, only to be refused until, distracted with worry, characteristically but understandably disobedient, she sneaked into the room late at night while they conversed downstairs. It was Wednesday, 23 January. Earlier that day the doctors had said that Pitt would not live beyond twenty-four hours. With little hope of being acknowledged, Hester crept to his bedside. Her uncle tossed and turned, burning with fever, delirious and rambling. Yet, on seeing her, there were a few moments of lucidity and his eyes focused. Suddenly aware, he 'immediately recollected her, and with his usual angelic mildness wished her future happiness, and gave her a most solemn blessing and affectionate farewell'.[3] The stunned stupefaction of the previous days when Hester had been unable to cry gave way and, with his recognition, Hester collapsed in tears by his bedside. The noise brought others and she was led away. Still coherent, Pitt continued to call restlessly for his niece after her departure: 'Dear soul, I know she loves me, where is Hester? Is Hester gone?'

Hester's hysterical weeping was seen as a relief. George Canning, her uncle's adviser and friend of many years, believing that Hester's quiet, intense grief might bring her to the verge of insanity, would later write, 'it certainly saved her reason, or perhaps her life'.[4] After the reunion, Hester's exclusion was more carefully enforced. Thus it was James who sat with Uncle William in the last hours of a bitterly cold, pitch-black January night, until at half past four in the morning, in a final fit of delirium, Pitt cried out, 'Oh my country; how I leave my country', and was dead shortly after.

Ever careless with his personal finances, Pitt had borrowed extravagantly to satisfy his taste for beautiful houses as well as to make extensive improvements and modifications to those which he already owned. The Prime Minister, whose reputation for successfully managing the nation's finances was unsurpassed by his predecessors, left only debts. Unmarried and childless, his last thoughts were of Hester and her sisters; he requested that the nation, as a gesture of thanks for his service, provide for the three young women. Parliament obliged and Hester, the eldest unmarried niece, was left £1,200 a year, while her sisters received £600 each, just enough to provide for a moderate, comfortable life. Without it, as the malicious society gossip and Hester's earlier rival in love, Countess Bessborough, was quick to point out, 'poor Hetty' would have been destitute. Pitt's political rival Charles Fox thought it insufficient and in a generous gesture offered Hester a further allowance. But a mixture of pride and political loyalty to her own and her uncle's conservatism prevented her from accepting, so that she settled with two of her three half-brothers, Charles and James, in Montagu Square.

The house in Montagu Square was neither very big nor particularly remarkable. Mayfair was a fashionable district of London, but only in parts, not this far west where large areas around the square were little more than busy, noisy building sites where Portman Estates, buoyed by the success of Portman Square, supervised the building of yet more elegant houses. Number four was by no means the most expensive house either. The rent was £120 a year, a modest sum. With the remains of her allowance, Hester made an elegant home for Charles and James and began a quiet and reclusive existence, her outings infrequent both because she was in mourning and because her new reduced circumstances meant she could afford to keep neither animal nor carriage. A hackney cab was not a fitting way for a titled woman to travel, and because prostitutes often plied for trade by walking with a footman in attendance, that too was out of the question. Going out alone made her the brunt of pitying and curious remarks from former friends. Alienated from her father, the sole relative with whom she might have sheltered, Hester's situation was not an easy one. She was almost thirty-one, unmarried and without wealth or position. She was tall and graceful, with flawless pale skin of which she was inordinately proud, but, and her contemporaries were unanimous on this point, not beautiful. Without a husband or protector, Hester's future in London society was an uneasy one. Features of her personality which had been so valued by her uncle – her intelligence, her political acumen and amusing, if at times cruel, wit – were not fashionable qualities in a woman whose only real importance lay in her past. Missing her uncle and the life they had shared, Hester declared, 'A poor gentlewoman is the worst thing in the world.'[5]

Hester's two younger sisters, Griselda and Lucy, were married, as was her eldest half-brother, Philip, Lord Mahon. But while staying with Lord Mahon at his home might have seemed a welcome alternative to the difficulties of meeting society's expectations on a limited income, the relationship between him and Hester was far from amiable. Their affiliation was subject to a continuous succession of highs and lows, but the differences that sprang from events immediately following Pitt's death proved irreconcilable. They arose from more than one source, and were undoubtedly exaggerated by the distress of recent events. As he lay dying, Pitt obtained a promise from Mahon that he would honour some small debts incurred by Mahon's two brothers. But after Pitt's death, when a tradesman applied for the recovery of his money to Mahon, he refused to keep his word, thus incurring his sister's wrath. In fury she confronted him, 'Why, what's the meaning of this? Did you not promise Mr Pitt you would pay their bills for them?' Hester thought his reply was unforgivable: 'I might,' answered Mahon, 'but Mr Pitt is now dead and the promise is void.'[6] Disgusted by Mahon's 'cold-blooded sensibility' and determined to protect the reputation of his brothers, Hester sent James off to a longstanding close friend of Pitt, the peer Lord Lonsdale, who gave him £2,000 for his debts, which James later dutifully repaid. Hester did not forget Lord Lonsdale's kindness and rewarded him many years later with the gift of a statue from Syria.

The other cause of the enmity between Hester and Mahon had its origins in earlier times. The last years of the eighteenth century were rife with political unrest. The English aristocracy adjusted to the torn and bloodied remains of the French Revolution, nervously clutching at its own precarious position and drumming up patriotic fervour against France with unparalleled ferocity. Nelson's spectacular defeat of Napoleon in 1798 had spurred on the formation of a new coalition between Britain, Austria and Russia. But it was an uneasy alliance. By September 1800 the Tsar was angry at the British acquisition of Malta, a blow to his plans in the Mediterranean, and changed sides. At home the issue of Catholic emancipation was dividing Pitt and George III. While Pitt supported the rights of Catholics and dissidents to be admitted to parliament and to office if they agreed to take an amended oath, the King was adamant in his objection.

In contrast to the national turmoil, the winter of 1800 heralded the beginning of the most halcyon period of Hester and Mahon's relationship, without the slightest indication that it would deteriorate into the dissension and differences of their later lives. While it was a time of relief for Hester, who had just left the difficulties of the family home at Chevening, in Kent, to live with her maternal grandmother in Somerset, it was a time of stress and anxiety for her eldest half-brother.

Chevening was a magnificent estate whose origins went as far back as the end of the twelfth century. Hester's great-grandfather James Stanhope, who had made the first marital connection to the Pitts with his marriage to Lucy Pitt in 1713, extended the house to the form it had in the eighteenth century and for the most part still has today. Projections were added to the east and west side, and the two pavilions were built and joined to the main building so that they form three sides of a rectangle. Hester's father Charles, the third Earl, made many changes to the garden while Hester's mother, Hester Pitt, was alive, cultivating it as a landscape in accordance with the fashion of the time, creating a lake and planting an unusual double hexagonal kitchen garden.

But with her death, and in spite of his second marriage to Louise Grenville and the three sons it produced, the Earl's obsession with science and politics gradually, over the years, came to fill his life to the exclusion of all else. Even the carefully created garden ran wild, so that by the time

Mahon inherited it in 1816 it was described as 'a house standing in a hay-field'.[7] The estate suffered directly from the Earl's twin occupations. Although he was a scientist of some success and reputation, his constant experimenting was a strain on the family wealth. Politically, the Earl was a staunch republican, a supporter of the revolution who styled himself as 'Citizen Stanhope' and consequently rejected his aristocratic heritage. The estate, a physical emblem of that heritage, was a sign of everything he most despised. His plan was to sell it, thus, in one move, ridding himself of the hated trappings of his aristocratic heritage while raising sufficient funds to finance his latest venture: to design a ship powered by steam. The problem with this plan was that it involved the co-operation of his eldest son, whose right to the estate as an inheritance was protected by entail. The Earl began a steady battle of coercive bullying against Mahon, who became more and more desperate to escape his father's aggressive wheedling. Mahon appealed again and again to his father to allow him to go to university in vain, as Stanhope kept his son a virtual prisoner in Kent, where he could best overturn his refusal to agree to a sale.

It was Hester, from the countryside retreat of Burton Pynsent in Somerset, Lady Chatham's lovely, rambling, haphazard house with its strangely added architectural features and its much talked-about room filled with plants and trees where colourful birds flew and sang, who devised a plan to help Mahon escape from the stifling atmosphere of Chevening. In the calm engendered by the wintry countryside, Hester schemed to protect her brother's inheritance, writing letters prolifically to friends and relatives to gain their support and interest. As a result, she managed to procure the services of several notable men of the time, all prepared to help her with her intrigue: Pitt, also estranged from Lord Stanhope, his erstwhile brother-in law, gave his full backing, as did Sir Francis Burdett, related by marriage to the Coutts banking family, who were Hester's own bankers, and Francis Jackson, a diplomat whom she had met and befriended during a London season.[8] Money was essential to any successful operation and Burdett's role was to acquire some; Jackson had lived on the continent for many years and was able to provide a passport under a false name and letters of credit; and one of Mahon's long-standing personal servants engineered the practicalities of the physical escape from Chevening Manor.[9]

Late at night, after Mahon had purportedly retired for the evening, the manservant dangled twisted sheets from his bedroom on the first floor, which Mahon precariously slid down to the estate garden. This ploy meant that some time would pass before his absence was noted and aroused suspicion in the house. Past the huge iron gates of Chevening, which had been stripped of family crests and emblems and were no longer decorated with gold as a consequence of Lord Stanhope's political stance, another of Mahon's servants waited, in a post-chaise, for the escapee. Together, the young Lord and his accomplice made for the Channel at full speed. A few hours later, the Earl, possibly tipped off by someone else in the house, realized his eldest son was missing and immediately sent a search party off in pursuit. Hester's clandestine and devious plan was not so easily spoiled: her uncle's support guaranteed fashionableness for her project and her apparent unselfishness endeared her to those who already regarded her as a friend. The ring of secrecy around her, her family and friends was tight; no one was prepared to help the Earl recover his son. Mahon was well on his way to Erlangen, where he would become a student of Professor Beyer, a man of considerable academic standing, renowned in Europe for his teaching. In a final gesture of support, the cosmopolitan Jackson provided letters of introduction and recommendation to local society, including the highly popular circle of the Margravine of Brandenburg-Bayreuth, a lady for whom Hester had the highest respect and who kept a little court.[10]

Mahon took up his assumed identity with enthusiasm and revelled in the delights of his new life, writing often to his sister that he was now as happy as he had been miserable before. Filled with gratitude to her, in the spring he wrote a letter bursting with thanks and admiration which was accompanied by a small present of a portrait. It was the closest that half-brother and -sister would ever be, and Hester, enchanted by his delight and her own success in arranging it, wrote to all who had been involved of her 'charming, charming, incomparable Mahon'.[11]

Correspondence between brother and sister was frequent and affectionate until a chance meeting for Hester, in Weymouth a year later, made a reunion a realistic prospect.

Weymouth was a thriving town in 1801, with an excellent reputation as a place to 'take the water'. The King had four houses there and often went to convalesce during his recurring bouts of illness.[12] Gratified by her reception from the royal family, and reassured that her father's much discussed eccentricities had not damaged her own reputation, Hester eagerly accepted an invitation from the Queen to join the royal party in the 'inner room', where she met up with Mr and Mrs Egerton, a well-connected elderly couple who were planning a trip to the continent.[13]

Impressed by Hester's manners, and undoubtedly by her lineage, the Egertons begged her to join them on their forthcoming trip. Inviting them back to Somerset to meet her grandmother, she wrote to Lady Chatham in advance to warn of her plans. Her choice of travelling companions was not an obvious one. They were a mature and sedate couple. Mrs Egerton was a 'good and sensible person' of somewhat shaky health, while her husband was a shy, bumbling gentleman. But they allowed Hester to influence their itinerary; she would be able to meet up with both Mahon and her friend, Francis Jackson. The demands of propriety were met in that the Egertons were unquestionably chaperones of suitable rank and moral disposition, but their great advantage as far as Hester was concerned was the licence they seemed prepared to afford her. When she advised Jackson of her trip she wrote enthusiastically that, while the Egertons might not be the most dashing company, she would have more independence than she otherwise might. 'I shall have perfect liberty to act in all respects as is most pleasing to myself. They want a companion,' she said, 'and I want a nominal chaperone.'[14]

Preparations began in the autumn. A large and commodious travelling carriage was commissioned and built, servants engaged, letters sent out for advice as to the best routes and destinations. The Treaty of Amiens between England and France the following March brought an uneasy peace that would prove short-lived. But while the resumption of war, just two years after the agreement was signed, would curtail Hester's European tour, the signing of the treaty nevertheless opened up the continent for the travellers in the meantime.

En route to join her travelling companions, Hester visited Pitt at Walmer. Shocked to find him ill, she delayed the trip, remaining by his side to nurse him. Finally, in October 1802, Mahon and Hester were reunited in Italy. The romantic descriptions of their idyll, which found their way back to England in letters, seemed to show a continuation of the solidarity that had existed between them before their parting. They lunched together on fresh trout at the scenic summit of Mount Cenis, laughing conspiratorially at their own enjoyment, while the Egertons grumbled about the difficulties of the mountainous ride and lack of suitable facilities. The camaraderie was far more strained than it appeared. Mahon's pet poodle, which accompanied him everywhere, barked incessantly, driving Hester to distraction, and in more revealing correspondence she admitted her dismay at Mahon's 'continental manners', which she found foppish and affected: 'I am sorry to find him inclined to be too old for his age, and approaching a quiz in manner and dress.'[15]

Mahon, for his part, described his sister's lack of apparent interest in museums and culture as shocking, and her overall manner as bossy and overbearing. When their journey took them in separate directions there was relief on both parts. However, Hester's unhappiness in her stepbrother was not matched by displeasure at his choice of wife, and his marriage in June the following year seemed to bring the possibility of reconciliation. Catherine Smith was pretty and popular. The fourth daughter of Robert, first Lord Carrington, Catherine was a sweet and amiable woman who encouraged Mahon to effect a reconciliation with his father – which Mahon duly did by writing to ask for his blessing on their betrothal. The reply was cordial, even familial, but stressed that Mahon's 'close connection with Mr Pitt and certain other persons of his description will certainly prevent our being reconciled'.[16] Hester approved of Catherine's attempts to restore familial relations, and despite her frequent dislike of other women, lavished praise on her sister-in-law: 'She knows what is right nor is she the least likely ever to encourage what is otherwise; she is admirably well disposed, lively to a degree, and a great deal of temper.'[17] But the affection that Hester had for her sister-in-law did not extend to Mahon, who she believed despised 'everybody's opinion but his own' and who showed no gratitude for the help she had given him, so that she was 'far from satisfied with him in any one respect'.[18] Any hope that a friendship between Catherine and Hester might improve relations was finally lost with Mahon's attempts to keep them apart. As he wrote to his father-in-law, Lord Carrington:

I hope that Catherine does not see Hester much alone; this intimacy can be productive of no good consequences, but probably of much mischief. I have endeavoured this week to prevent it by painting with truth and sincerity and I trust with candour and impartiality what Hester's character was and the evils that too great an intimacy might occasion.'[19]

While Mahon was pleased to take, and try to control, a spirited wife, he was determined that she be kept away from his commanding half-sister.

Private Sorrow and Public Opinion

Slowly and sadly we laid him down,
From the field of fame fresh and gory;
We carved not a line, and we raised not a stone,
But we left him alone with his glory.
From 'The Burial of Sir John Moore after Corunna', by Charles Wolfe

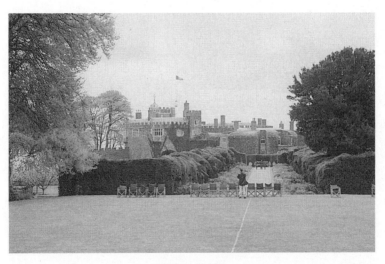

Walmer Castle

During her period of mourning for Pitt, Hester remained conscious of the importance to her younger stepbrothers' prospects of retaining some semblance of rank in her new home. Two bedrooms and breakfast rooms in Montagu Square were fitted out for Charles and James in a fashionable way, with private libraries. Concerned that their careers did not suffer from their reduction in circumstances, Hester attempted to create a sophisticated and welcoming environment where they could bring friends and colleagues. Yet their life, in the months after Pitt's death, was a quiet one, with socializing mostly restricted to visits from their military friends or to close friends of their dead uncle. George Canning remained in close contact with Hester in the first days, and Sir John Moore was a frequent visitor to the house, initially as Charles's General, but increasingly to spend time with Hester. As it turned out, within the year, Hester's regard for Moore would lead to the dissolution of her friendship with Canning.

Moore was a tall, good-looking Glaswegian with dark hair and hazel eyes. In his younger days his face was 'filled out and ruddy', but in later years, unsurprisingly in the light of his battle experience, it became gaunt and weather-beaten. In spite of his reputation for strength and bravery, he had a tendency to blush when spoken to by anyone he deemed to be important, a trait both Hester and her uncle believed was symptomatic of his modesty.[1] Hester found him handsome, as did her brother Charles, who openly discussed his appearance in their home, much to Hester's amusement. One afternoon Charles, half teasing, asked Hester whom she thought better looking, Moore or another acquaintance, and she replied that the former was 'certainly, very handsome'. Charles replied that if she were 'only to see him when he is bathing' she would know that 'his body is as perfect as his face'.[2] Hester later said her brother's naivety both charmed and amused her. The nature of her relationship with Moore was unquestionably close. Hester, more than a decade later, would say that they had been betrothed, and although no evidence of an official announcement exists, the notion of a more personal understanding between them is borne out by the slightly flirtatious and gently concerned remarks with which the habitually restrained and undemonstrative Moore filled his letters to her.

The couple had met, for the first time, at the barracks in Shorncliffe where, as a result of his distinction at the Battle of Alexandria, Moore was appointed to command an assembled force. Pitt, who resigned as prime minister over the question of Catholic emancipation, had not yet taken up office for the second time. He was living at Walmer Castle on the Kent coast, with his niece, and oversaw the training of recruits while carrying out his duties as Warden of the Cinq Ports to establish and maintain the defences along the English coast. Pitt was impressed by Moore, to the extent that when he did return to parliament he made him a Knight of Bath. Even early in their acquaintance Hester was taken with Moore and frequently praised him, commenting on her uncle's respect and fondness.

But in the years following Pitt's death, Moore's fame, like Hester's, was ebbing. He failed in a diplomatic mission to co-operate with the King of Sweden, so much so that he had to return to England, in disguise, when King Gustavus IV threatened to imprison him. On his return, he was ordered to proceed to Portugal, under the command of Sir Hew Dalrymple and Sir Henry Burrard. Napoleon was gaining control in southern Europe and had established his brother, Joseph, as King of Spain. Moore asked Charles to accompany him as his aide-de-camp. As a general with an outstanding reputation, used to holding chief command, it was a bitter insult to be placed under two other officers. In the drawing room at Montagu Square, just before his departure, Hester listened, reacting with furious indignation. And Canning was the subject of her wrath. She referred to Moore's new commanding officers as the 'Volunteer Colonel and Buttonhole Bore', quarrelling bitterly with Canning, who refused to intervene for Moore.

Wellington, at that time still Arthur Wellesley, who was also under their command, shared Hester's scorn, giving the two commanders his own nicknames: 'Dowager Dalrymple and Betty Burrard'. Moore was less vitriolic in his concern but later wrote to Hester admitting that, while his actions in Sweden had been fully considered and were not regretted, he had acted in a way he would not have had to under the Pitt government. 'Had Mr Pitt been minister, I should have remained, knowing that he would have sent a squadron to Stockholm to demand me.'[3] He believed that the administration of the new prime minister, Grenville, did not have the 'spirit to act as they should'. Moore carried out his orders and by the autumn was able to write to Hester that Sir Henry (Burrard) was, in fact, 'the most liberal of men' and had agreed to let him have Charles's regiment, the 50th, march with him to Salamanca. While Burrard remained in Portugal, his eldest son followed Moore as a second aide-de-camp to Spain. Moore was constantly worried about the weather, which needed to be dry for the roads to remain passable, and he wrote to Hester:

> I wish you were with us. The climate now is charming; we should give you riding enough and in your red habit, à l'amazone, you would animate and do us all much good.[4]

Hester continued her campaign of criticism against the government, and by early October, Wellesley too was writing letters to try and improve the relationship between Moore, whom he held in high esteem, and the government. Hester's youngest half-brother James felt he was missing out on the action and, as Charles's regiment marched to join with Moore, he entreated his half-sister to use her influence with Moore to see if he too could receive orders to act as aide-de-camp to the General. This she did, and Moore acquiesced, saying that even though it meant he would have too many, his regard for her half-brother and wish to refuse her nothing were more important. But the letter was full of foreboding. Moore was pragmatic. Realizing that his force was vastly inferior to the enemy, he warned that James would arrive too late: 'I shall already be beaten.' Hester was in 'a wretched state of anxiety', worried for her half-brothers and her friend, angry 'beyond measure'[5] with her erstwhile friend Canning, and resenting the apparent indifference of other family members such as Mahon and her uncle, Lord Chatham. Her worries and Moore's prediction would be realized.

In late November, Moore wrote what was to be his last letter to her. Neither Charles's regiment, one of the last to leave Lisbon, nor James, had arrived. Close to Napoleon's army with only a third of his fighting force, within just two weeks of writing the letter and in spite of truly terrible odds, he managed to push forward from Salamanca and defeat the French cavalry, only to discover that Napoleon was advancing with a massively superior force. Across the bleak winter mountains Moore, with his already tired and sick soldiers, led the awful retreat to Corunna. Thickly falling snow and icy cold gave way to heavy rain, and with the rain came dysentery. Hester waited in vain for news over the Christmas and New Year festivities. When finally it arrived it was all that she had feared: General Moore was dead. Grieving again, sick with fear for James and Charles, Hester nevertheless wrote to the new prime minister, Lord Grenville, to ask that Moore be given 'every tribute of public respect due to his talents', arguing that the unlimited confidence Pitt had had in him was justified and fearing that the present ministers, guilty of his 'ill-treatment', might stoop so low as to 'persecute him beyond the grave'.[6]

The first visitor admitted to Montagu Square after Hester received the terrible news was Colonel Anderson, an officer who had served with Moore for many years and who was held in high esteem by James and Charles. He brought Hester the story of Moore's death, some personal mementoes and yet another painful shock: Charles Stanhope was dead, having fallen within minutes of Moore.

Anderson was wounded and worn out, but he sat with Hester and recounted the story of the last hours of Moore and her brother, while she, desperate to learn everything that had passed, urged him to stay in Montagu Square and be nursed back to health. The sixteenth of January had been a day of carnage and Hester was not by any means the only one to have suffered loss. Even Burrard's eldest son, Moore's enthusiastic follower, sustained fatal injuries and was dead in a matter of days. Charles Stanhope's end was sudden. Shot through the heart, he died instantly. But Moore's was slow and agonizing. For three hours he struggled with a vicious wound in his side, his men rallying together to try to carry him back to his lodgings, blood gushing out over them as they did so. In his pain, Moore constantly asked if the French were beaten. When finally a messenger arrived with the news – that, against all odds, the enemy was in retreat – his only concern was that his own death would be soon: 'I feel myself so strong, I fear I shall be long dying; I am in great pain.'[7]

Hester's youngest brother came to his side, and just before he slipped into unconsciousness, Moore grasped James's hand and said, 'Stanhope,

remember me to your sister.'[8] They were his last words and Hester treasured them. For weeks following Anderson's arrival, her only conversations were of the two men she had lost. A gauntlet, stained with Moore's
dying blood, was one of the few things she kept with her, through shipwreck, plague and many years of journeying, until her death.

There were still further days of anguish before Hester heard that James
was safe, but wounded. It was a miraculous escape. As he broke line to
catch a final glimpse of his dead brother, a cannon ball fell, killing the four
men who had stood beside him. Clinging to the scrap of comfort that was
the safety of her youngest brother, she awaited his return, misery alter-
nating with rage as parliament began to criticize Moore's conduct. In
spite of their earlier rift, Canning wrote a letter of condolence to Hester,
only to receive a torrent of abuse in return. Castlereagh was the minister
jibing at Moore, but it was Canning who was the brunt of Hester's hatred.
His crime was to remain silent. Canning was known for his great elo-
quence, and Hester could not stand to see him say nothing in Moore's
defence. He was not the man she thought he was and she would accept no
consolation from him. Lord Chatham broke his long silence to write a letter of condolence to his niece, but Hester, sickened by his earlier neglect,
tinged her reply with bitterness. Anderson returned to active service and
James came home. Drawing together in their bereavement, Hester and
her brother rarely left the house, their alienation from other company
only aggravated by their double tragedy.

Twenty years later she recalled that the greatest, perhaps only, kindness
shown to her in that bleak time was by a dressmaker she had patronized for
some years, Miss Stewart. This woman called on Hester to offer sympathy
and they conversed in the front room. Hester was fond of her but eager to
make her understand that she could no longer afford to use her services in
the way that she had when Pitt was alive. Miss Stewart offered to work for
nothing and falling into a half-curtsey grabbed Hester's hand and kissed it.
Hester was moved and grateful, and before Miss Stewart left she made Hester a gift of 'a beautiful cobweb lace veil and a pair of sleeves to match'.[9] It was
but a brief moment in a life that Hester was beginning to find unbearable.
London was a city filled with memories. When one of her few remaining
confidantes, George Jackson, the brother of Francis, who had helped Mahon
escape, returned from Berlin, she anxiously sent notes to arrange to meet

him. He listened to her grievances. Aside from the financial constraints of her situation, there was her rift with Canning, her sense of betrayal and anger. She felt excluded from society by circumstance and conviction. The future she saw there, one of pity, sympathy and a superficial social circle discussing fabric and fashion, was not an attractive prospect. She was making plans to move out of England to the Welsh countryside.

3
First Love and Escaping

From the conviction that you were never sent upon earth to be regarded
with indifference, and never have been, prevents my feeling any sense of
shame in repeating what you know, that I loved you! yes to Idolatry.
Lady Hester to Granville Leveson Gower, 27 December 1804

Chevening Manor

Hester's preparations to go to Wales were reminiscent of an earlier escape from London society. Five years before, following the heartbreak of her first, and unrequited, love she left Pitt's houses in Downing Street and Putney for the calm of his old residence at Walmer Castle on the Kent coast. Finding solace in the huge grounds, she created a garden for her uncle. There, in a pattern that would recur throughout her life, she tried to subsume her pain in the meticulous arrangement of the tiniest details. Each plant, each shrub, occupied her mind constantly every minute that she was awake, and she rarely slept. Her resolve to heal was only fragmented by occasional but long letter-writing sessions to her absent, and otherwise preoccupied, beloved.

~

Hester's first serious romantic attachment was to a man as different from John Moore as it was possible to be. She was already twenty-eight years old when they first met, but in spite of her age and her unassailable confidence in her position as hostess of the Prime Minister of Great Britain, Hester behaved like an adolescent in love. The object of her affections, Granville Leveson Gower, was an effeminate dandy, adored by many women. When he met Hester he was recently returned from Europe, where he had wooed and bedded the already married Countess Harriet Bessborough, sister to the Duchess of Devonshire. It was an affair which would last for many years and produce two illegitimate children; in 1804, when Hester met Granville, their first daughter was just four years old. Granville was a libertine who routinely lost large sums of money at piquet and received amorous missals from numerous women, all of whom believed, probably with justification, that they had some place in his affections. But he was also an intelligent, conniving man who managed, through political acuity, to keep allies both among the Whigs, through Bessborough and her sister, and in the conservative camps, principally because of his close friendship with Canning and the concomitant, quickly developing relationship with Pitt.

Hester and Granville met in the middle of the first decade of the nineteenth century when Hester was living what she would later always refer to as the best, the greatest, years of her life. Pitt appeared to trust her implicitly, and with his faith came a unique and powerful position. She wrote to Jackson that when her uncle went to parliament, leaving her at Walmer, she was given 'orders how to act in case of real alarm in Mr Pitt's absence, and also a promise from him never to be further from the army than a two hours' ride'.[1]

Lady Grisel Stanhope had waged a determined campaign throughout Hester's childhood to curb the clumsiness she thought her granddaughter's unusually large size might induce, with the result that Hester's bearing and elegance were frequently praised both by her peers and in society newspapers. She was unconventionally attractive, guaranteed at least the semblance of popularity because of her political affiliations from a society eager to curry favour with her uncle. Her conversation was publicly described by contemporaries as witty and 'full of clever observation'. Acerbic and voluble, in an unfashionably open way, about those whom she despised, she was more often respected than liked. The marked absence of numerous former acquaintances in the Montagu Square years suggested that many people who aspired to be her friend were motivated by political expedience rather than affection. Hester was independent and strong-minded, traits which were not generally well liked in women but which guaranteed her the admiration of certain men, usually those who did not feel threatened by her, such as Pitt and Moore. Pitt was resigned to her stubbornness, declaring that: 'I let her do as she pleases for if she were resolved to cheat the devil she could do it.'[2] Her dress sense, as well as her posture, bore testimony to her grandmother Stanhope's careful schooling. She wore the finest, most elegantly cut clothes, refusing to adopt any risqué or extreme features of current fashion, such as transparent gowns or exposed breasts, and maliciously parodied the constantly changing whims of the Whig *bon ton* to anyone who would listen. But the mimicry did not detract from her air of aloofness, so remarkable that she later recalled a friend of her uncle's comment that he thought she would never marry till she found someone as clever as she was. To which Pitt purportedly replied, 'Then she will never marry at all.'[3]

Granville was equally physically striking, even taller than Hester, who generally towered above her male associates, and slim. He wore his medium-length chestnut hair swept over his eyes in a flick and was 'one of those men who, once seen, leave an impression on the memory'.[4] He responded to Hester's attentions, as he did to most women's, with enthusiasm. He may have been genuinely attracted to her or his interest may have been politically motivated, but he acted like an ardent suitor and Hester responded with a public and dramatic passion that became the talk of society. Hester was in love and it was all she could think about: 'from the first moment I discovered every thought was devoted to you'. It was a sudden passion developed 'but too early in our acquaintance' and she knew no shame.[5] Granville was the 'beau nom grave dans mon coeur'.[6] They were constantly seen together. Hasty hand-delivered messages, filled with short declarations of love, followed Granville across London. His visits to 10 Downing Street frequently involved an overnight stay. Harriet Bessborough watched and listened as the gossip spread. Granville was her lover and the father of her child, but she bided her time, playing a dual role in a careful game as Granville's confidante and Hester's acquaintance. Then, when Hester began to look wistful in company, she at last wrote a letter:

I have very good reason to believe Ly Hester has taken a strong fancy to you and imagin'd you return'd it, and had serious intentions . . . Think how many unpleasant things any thing like a scrape with her might entail.[7]

Granville had begun to feel uneasy about his latest conquest. Hester's 'strong passions' which she indulged 'with great latitude' meant that any hopes of discretion were lost.[8] Moreover, he had no intention of marrying her, the very end she seemed now to be pursuing. Bessborough had warned him, 'If Mr Pitt knew even what had passed already do you think he would like it?',[9] and Granville, suitably chastened, began to make his lack of interest clear. Hester persisted, and Pitt, anxious both to protect his niece and to retain Granville's services, acted diplomatically. He spoke to his niece and was shocked by the violent emotions he was forced to concede were out of her 'power to command'.[10] In the autumn of 1804

Granville was offered the post of ambassador to St Petersburg; he accepted with alacrity and by 11 October he was at Whitstable ready to leave. His last exchange with Hester was not a pleasant one. She wrote a passionate note that had two possible meanings: either Hester was so distraught at his departure that she was threatening to kill herself, or the sexual tension of the preceding months were too intense to bear and as a last attempt to win Granville she was offering him sex. This she did 'trusting in his honour for secrecy and to his absence for putting an end to what could not continue without danger'.[11] Hester also offered to give Granville a locket containing a lock of her hair, which he refused, feeling it might carry some promise he did not wish to fulfil. She found herself completely unable to conceal or control her 'affliction at your departure' and was left feeling 'too much shamed and humiliated'.[12] Granville retreated further, spending the eve of his departure in the solicitous and passionate company of Harriet Bessborough, from whom he took a 'heartrending' leave-taking, afterwards indiscreetly passing on the note that Hester had sent him, so Harriet could offer her interpretation. Guiltily, in his last hours, he bought a trinket to send to Hester, but on Canning's advice desisted, sending instead just a note to see how she was.

Hester was left distraught and ill. Various rumours circulated around London society: she had tried to commit suicide on Granville's departure; they had been lovers; she had every right to expect him to marry her; and later, months later, that she was pregnant. Hester withdrew from the circuit of parties and dinners but, ironically, still continued to see Harriet Bessborough, whose manipulations had helped to orchestrate her loss. Not until the Queen herself advised Hester that possibly Bessborough was not her best choice of companion did Hester realize her mistake. One afternoon, unannounced, Hester's carriage pulled up outside Bessborough's London home. In a scene that Harriet described in a letter to Granville, Hester broke down in hysterical tears and told her she was going to avoid her company. A few years later Bessborough's Machiavellian machinations in the relationship between Lord Byron and her daughter Caroline Lamb would earn her Byron's hatred; he dubbed her 'The hack whore of the last half century'.[13]

In December, Hester retreated from London society to Walmer Castle, seeking escape in the views of wintry grey water visible from the dining room, a room she had carefully furnished and designed for Pitt when Walmer was his main residence. From the exterior, Walmer had the air of a fort rather than a home, set on the busy coastline with its constant activity of naval preparation. But the Lord Warden in the early years of the eighteenth century, the Duke of Dorset, had extended and altered the living accommodation, so that the castle's prepossessing walls belied the graceful first-floor rooms. Hester had first taken up residence with her uncle in Walmer after her grandmother's death in a period that was filled with frenetic activity. Pitt entertained frequently and his predominantly male, military guests made Hester the centre of the evening's entertainment: 'There are generally three or four men staying in the house, and we dine eight or ten almost every other night,' reported Hester.[14] Now, with Pitt preoccupied with his duties in London, the castle was quieter. It was also close to the home of Mahon and the heavily pregnant Catherine. So, while still regarding her brother as someone who 'would never do for public life', Hester was grateful for his avoidance of London society, as it left him merely curious that she was 'not well or as gay as usual' and ignorant as to any scandal surrounding her.[15]

Hester waited for some word from Granville and, when nothing arrived, wrote with a touching humility to Russia, blaming her own behaviour for his silence as well as for much else that had occurred. It was a long letter of twenty closely written pages, a confession of how her love had been and a generous exculpation of his part in the whole affair. She confessed her own inability to deal with her distress in a socially acceptable way:

> I have often told you that by nature I was born a tyrant, it is therefore in vain for me to deceive myself, to affect to meet unhappiness with composure and resignation, which after all is but another sort of despair.[16]

As a consequence she would need to avoid his company, as well as the society of those who knew him:

> I am perhaps a force upon my feelings. I may be able to drown my sorrows in tumult but I cannot die by inches, which would be the risk if ever I run the risk of being thrown into your company.[17]

The thought that she might have to 'see what I have loved more than my own soul upon the footing of a common acquaintance' was abhorrent. It was better never to see Granville again. The letter may have acted as a purgative; Hester's involvement in her uncle's public life, which had ceased in the aftermath of her liaison, was renewed around the time of the letter in a dramatic way.

When Pitt was asked to be prime minister for the second time he displaced Addington. Addington, although a personal friend of many years, had only achieved the position in the first place by uniting with the opposition. Now, as Pitt remained in control by the slenderest of majorities, he offered Addington a place in his cabinet in an attempt to appease his detractors. Addington accepted. Pitt was grateful; Canning who had made no secret of his hatred for Addington throughout his ministry, lambasting it in malicious satires, was not. He felt unable to remain in Pitt's administration and on 1 January 1805 he wrote a letter to Hester, a woman he believed stood 'before pages of preface and apology' in matters relating to the Prime Minister.[18] While Canning did not dispute Addington's right to a peerage or a pension, he did not wish to be an active participant in a government in which Addington too was a member. He asked Hester to explain his position to her uncle, so that he might accept it as inevitable, rather than calling for his dismissal or accusing him of lack of duty. Appealing to her own sense of importance, he stressed that she was the only 'human being' with whom he had discussed his situation and that he was trusting in her to make his appeal understood. Hester intervened with her uncle and Canning was persuaded to remain in office, a move that Hester later came to regret.

After her diplomatic intervention and its successful resolution, Hester once again sank into brooding for her lost love. Pitt, knowing her enjoyment of organization, deviously set her the task of sorting out the castle and various buildings attached to it. Dissatisfied with the scope of the improvements he initially suggested, Hester devised a plan of her own. Designing the garden at Walmer completely obsessed her, as she subsumed her depression in the minutiae of its execution. It was a tonic to her soul; when she wrote to Francis Jackson in February she showed a sense of perspective on the whole romantic interlude that had been missing since it began. She was conscious that she had shown her taste 'more than her prudence in admiring an object which fills more hearts than one', and although her heart 'like the compass' pointed to her lover in the North, she was 'not idle, as I have the charge of improvements here'.[19]

With various shrubs and plants, a gift from Lord Guildford and his neighbouring estate, Hester set about transforming a barren area of land behind the castle, which was nothing but scrub with a chalk pit. On the recommendation of the Walmer gardener, Burfield, she planted evergreen oaks with a mixture of furze and yellow broom. Recovering her confidence with the initial success of her plans, she persuaded some regiments stationed at Dover to help her, using a combination of flattery and charm. The soldiers duly set about 'levelling, fetching turf, transplanting shrubs, flowers etc'.[20] Then, beyond the paddock, after the careful geometric patterns and sweet-smelling abundance of the walkways and kitchen plots, Hester made a glen. It was an almost wild garden, where steep woodland trails weaved through dark trees, romantic and brooding; a place that would be described by a local as 'a perfect marvel of beauty' and one that delighted her uncle, who loved its 'avenues and alleys', finding them like the ancient castle itself.[21] The creation of the garden brought Hester to the point where, although pale and still shaky, and suffering from uncharacteristic fainting fits, she was able to return to the society she had shunned. In June, just nine months after her parting from Granville, her return to society brought fresh gossip as to whether she had been pregnant or not. As Harriet wrote to Granville:

My sis. and all her family return'd home from a ball last night full of Hetty and the story of the accouchement which they insist upon she affiches – that is, she goes out without rouge, much fairer than she was.[22]

But with Pitt's support, Hester resumed her position at Downing Street and Putney until his death, spared from further public humiliation by the political power it afforded, secure in her inviolable role as first lady of the government.

Hester's garden at Walmer was not unique to her; there was a vogue for wilderness gardens. But the romantic relationship with nature endemic to the period and its inevitable influence on Hester led her to create a gar-

den of seemingly wild pathways and deep woods to heal her heart and her
pride. When the strictures and limitations of London society, coupled
with her grief, proved too much for her, Hester again acted on a
Rousseau-like desire to escape to a natural and idyllic state. Driven by her
unassailable conviction in the restorative powers of the countryside, Hester prepared to leave Montagu Square for Builth on the banks of the River
Wye in the spring of 1809.

It was not an immediate decision. Hester had relatives in Scotland, and it
was only after some deliberation that she decided to return to Wales, where
she had spent a pleasant short trip the previous year. She had travelled largely in the company of Reverend Price, and it was to him she now wrote of her
intended journey, enclosing simple, but very precise, instructions for a Mrs
Price, the proprietor of a farmhouse in Builth that she had admired. For herself she would take only three rooms: the main parlour and a small bedroom
with a dressing room above. The spare room above the kitchen she would
have for her maids. The parlour chairs were to be made of rush or wood and
the carpet should be green baize. The bedroom would also need two chairs,
a chest of drawers and a table but no bed as she would bring her own from
Montagu Square. As with many other houses where she later stayed, Hester
wanted the walls to be green: 'a beautiful green' that was 'pale and yet lively'.[23]
Mrs Price would supply crockery and china, but Hester would have beeswax
candles sent from Bath, as the one problem she encountered on her previous
visit was the difficulty in finding them locally. Once the decorating was
under way her concern was that no borders or ornament were added and
that the walls were left wholly green. So, to this end, she wrote again, just
before her arrival, with further instructions.

The villagers awaiting Hester were surprised by the arrival of a horse, a
beautiful dark stallion that she had arranged to be sent before her.
Accompanied by his groom, he was not Hester's horse but that of her
brother, James. He was no longer a riding horse and was worn out with
badly damaged feet, but he had carried James for two thousand miles, at
one point travelling nine hundred miles without resting, with only dried
peas to eat. Hester rewarded his endurance; in Wales he was put to pasture
in soft, low land close to her home so that he might rest. The workmen
were still decorating the cottage when Hester finally arrived, so, for those
first weeks, Hester took over the role of foreman, supervising and dictat-

ing each phase. From a local landowner she acquired two horses for riding, and from a nearby farm a cow she called Pretty Face, which, much to her new neighbour's surprise, she duly learned to milk.

When Hester had lived in Burton Pynsent with her grandmother, she had settled into rural life well, gaining a reputation for her ability to break unruly horses and for her generosity to those who were less fortunate. In Wales she quickly took up the same role, as a kind of benevolent aristocrat, much in the way both her grandmothers, Stanhope and Chatham, had been to retainers on their estates, even though her finances were considerably less. She gave medicine, money and reams of heavy dark striped cloth, perfect for the coming winter weather, to the poorest locals and organized excursions in the coach she had brought with her to outlying areas for others. She retained only a couple of servants from London, one of them, Elizabeth Williams, a woman who, with her sister, had been educated by Pitt and retained as his maid after the death of her parents, former servants of the Chatham family. Apart from a brief interlude when she hoped to be married, she would spend most of her life with Hester.

In late summer, James was released from duty and came to visit, bringing his friend Nassau Sutton. Nassau was a young officer who had been stationed on the Kent coast. He was ill and Hester immediately set about ministering to him. Now, with friends and family around her, Hester began to socialize again, inviting Reverend Price and his father to dine with her brother at the Royal Oak, a local inn renowned for its home-cooked food. It was not until the advent of autumn, when James was recalled to join his regiment in Spain, that Hester grew discontented with her rural retreat. In a final generous gesture she left two portraits for Mrs Price, one of her beloved uncle, the other of the Duke of York, as well as most of the furniture and fixtures, and then, reluctantly, returned to her house in Montagu Square.

In Wales she had avoided news from the city. On her return to London, Hester found all that she most feared. General Moore did not receive the honours she had fought for. Granville was back from Russia and the gossip about the humiliation of her obsession had been renewed with his return. Moreover, he was engaged to be married to Harriet Cavendish, the niece of the Countess of Bessborough, a pretty, popular girl of twenty-four, nine years younger than Hester.

James's departure was imminent, so the prospect for winter was one of long days confined to her town house, constrained both financially and by her wish to evade Granville and those who socialized with him. With no desirable alternative and buoyed up by her conviction that travel provided 'a constant change of ideas',[24] Hester prepared to go to Europe with James. In spite of what transpired, the trip was meant as no more than a break from the boredom of her London life and not as a permanent move. In a codicil she added to her will before her departure, she gave instructions to her executors in the event that she and her brother were both lost at sea, making clear that these were a safeguard, nothing else, and that they would probably return to England together.

Since it was inevitable that James would leave her to join his regiment, Hester needed to find a companion. In keeping with the fashion of the times, she contacted her uncle's physician, Walter Farquar, to see if he could find a suitable medical man to accompany her, both as escort and doctor. On Farquar's advice she wrote to Henry Cline, the famous surgeon. Cline, thinking a younger man more suited to the voyage, spoke to his son. And so, through Cline's son, Hester met Charles Lewis Meryon.

Meryon was only a young student at St Thomas's but by February 1810, when he set sail with his new employer, he, like Hester, had known terrible loss. Of Huguenot descent, Meryon had taken his BA and MA at Oxford before coming to study under the elder Cline in London. He was a mild-mannered, charming man of short stature, not particularly handsome, with a slight stutter. From a large but close-knit, comfortably middle-class family, Meryon was an industrious student whose family were proud of his academic achievements. During his studies he managed to combine good exam results with drinking and the enjoyment of female company, winning him an easy popularity with his fellow students. Then, towards the end of his student days, he fell in love. The girl's name was Elizabeth, and although just eighteen to his twenty-seven, she reciprocated his affection. Meryon married her and by March 1809 she was carrying his child.[25] In early December Elizabeth bore him a little girl, Lucy Elizabeth Meryon. Sadly, Elizabeth lived only a few days after the birth and Meryon, unwilling to care for a newborn baby girl, paid for someone to do so until his sister Sarah and her husband William agreed to take her into their home.

Meryon recovered from his loss by throwing himself into a wild social life, involving sleepless nights and alcohol. A heavy cold contracted on an overnight journey was neglected and consequently developed into an infection. Meryon found himself lying sick in bed, in London, with a cough so severe that he was afraid of consumption.[26] The son of his teacher was a good friend and came to visit. Shocked by Meryon's illness and similarly fearful of consumption, especially given the Meryon family tendency to the disease, his friend suggested going abroad, mentioning an opportunity his father had told him of: Pitt's niece, Lady Hester Stanhope, was looking for a physician to accompany her on some travels she was undertaking in the immediate future. Meryon was enthusiastic. Many physicians were forced to remain in London because so many of the wealthy patrons who could afford to procure their services were based there, but Meryon longed to travel. Reaction was almost immediate, and the elder Cline spoke to Hester and a meeting was arranged for four days later, in the hope that Meryon would have recovered sufficiently to dine with her. Cline had advised Meryon that the position would not be financially rewarding, but Meryon was impressed by rank, almost to the point of snobbishness, and relished the opportunity to work for someone with breeding and an 'air of nobility'.[27] The dinner was a success and Hester immediately secured him. It was a strange match, one that would endure far beyond what either Hester or Meryon could anticipate in those first days of tentative acquaintance. Making further provisions for his daughter, Meryon left to join Hester in Portsmouth even before Lucy Elizabeth was baptised.

4
Childhood

'Hester to be sure shows herself to great advantage on horse
back and peaks herself on her horsemanship and very
vain that her opinion is often asked. . .'
Grizel, Countess Stanhope to Lady Chatham, 19 Aug 1797

Malta

ARRANGING PASSAGE WAS NO EASY THING in 1810, especially if, as was Hester's case, you did not have the finances to travel privately. However, Hester was determined to leave England and wrote to her cousin General Richard Grenville, First Lord of the Admiralty. It was a letter that demanded rather than asked a favour: her uncle had increased the navy during his administration by six hundred ships; it was unthinkable that his niece would not find passage on one of them. Hester and her travelling companions – her brother James, Nassau Sutton, Elizabeth Williams and Meryon – were all given passage on board the frigate *Jason*, which was offering protection to a convoy of merchant ships heading for Gibraltar.

Hester leased out the house in Montagu Square and supervised the packing of her belongings, arranging for several trunks and deal boxes to be stored in England.

The inventory of what was to remain read like a catalogue of memories with items from each phase of her life: William Pitt's state gown of black silk and gold lace was folded into a leather trunk; books, jewellery and a set of old spurs were wrapped in another; several deal boxes were packed with household items – French porcelain decorated with butterflies, assorted candlesticks, cotton bed linen; and dresses from Hester's babyhood, including a pink one and a calico one, were packed and stored away.

∾

The dresses were from part of Hester's early life lived only minutes from Montagu Square, in St Anne Street, an attractive road with elegant town houses, many of which were just that, houses in town for people who had country estates but needed to be in London for parliament or other business. Hester Pitt, Lady Mahon, mother to Hester and sister to William, chose the house in preference to another, suggested by her father-in-law Lord Stanhope, in the more fashionable Grosvenor Square.[1] In the years following their wedding at the unassuming Parish Church in Hayes, Lord and Lady Mahon divided most of their time between Chevening in Kent and their Mayfair home. The birth of their first child, a large well-built baby, was heralded with much celebration and only a tinge of regret that it was a girl and not the hoped-for son. Hester Lucy Stanhope was born on 12 March 1776, and the very same day her grandmother, Lady Stanhope, travelled up to London from Kent to sit by her daughter-in-law's bedside. It was a relatively easy birth and within just two days Lady Stanhope was able to write to the Chatham grandmother that both mother and child were doing well:

> Last night our little one enjoyed herself thoroughly and this morn-ing I saw her take the breast at once with great pleasure, the nurse has two very fine breasts of very good milk.[2]

Lord Mahon watched his baby getting dressed and 'saw her in attitudes' that Lady Stanhope wished 'no other gentleman will ever see her in!'[3] In those first days the concern was for the health of the baby, but Hester was large, unusually so, and growing fast, and so what was a blessing of strength in the first year quickly turned to concern that a girl child should develop so rapidly. Her grandmother consoled herself that Hester's awk-ward 'overgrown limbs' would be 'more proportioned to her height' but despaired that her appearance was essentially 'male, puffy, flabby'.[4]

The year that had began so auspiciously with a healthy baby ended in sadness when Lady Mahon lost her second child, a much longed-for son. Both parents were distraught; the baby was born in apparent good health and even had 'motion in the limb for quarter of an hour'.[5] Lady Mahon consoled herself with her thriving daughter while Lord Mahon threw himself into scientific pursuits. It was a productive and busy time for Charles and within the year he developed a system of fireproofing and invented two different kinds of arithmetical machines. Hester found time away from motherhood to work alongside her husband as his secretary and adviser throughout 1777 and 1778 while he wrote his 'Principles of Electricity'.

Then, in 1778, a second baby was delivered successfully, the only disap-pointment being that this child too was a girl: Griselda. The following year Hester fell pregnant again, but in February 1780 hopes of a son came to nothing when a third daughter, Lucy, was born. Lady Stanhope named the baby girls her 'three Graces', but was concerned for the health of her daughter-in-law. Unlike after the earlier births Hester did not immediately recover; she was tired and pale, an invalid without the strength to get up for very long or leave the house. Too ill even to write to her mother, it was not until late April that she was able to reassure the anxious Lady Chatham that she was recovered. Lucy, like the other two girls, continued to be healthy and strong and was already deemed 'the Greatest Beauty of the three'.[6] The still ailing mother visited Chevening where she was able to 'take the air' with Lady Stanhope without any ill effects and, by mid-May, Lady Stanhope reported that Hester was 'so much mended in her looks, and in every respect seems so well'.[7] Her brother William visited her and was pleased at her improvement, hoping that it heralded the beginning of a complete recovery. It did not; by the middle of July, in a tragic and sudden reversal, Hester Pitt was dead. Charles was not only widowed from his wife, companion and workmate but also in charge of three motherless girls, the eldest of whom was just four years old. He was devastated. From her writing desk overlooking the gardens at Chevening, Lady Stanhope wrote sad letters to friends of the couple which were filled with concern for her son's great sorrow and worry about the effect of the shock on him, and in which she expressed her apprehension over the future of her three granddaughters. Charles and the children left the London house with all its memories and moved back to Chevening, where the two youngest girls thrived in the fresh air, enjoying the attentions of their grandmother. Only Hester, unusually subdued, seemed old enough to be aware of the enormity of their loss. Charles brooded and grieved, saddened still further by any sight of his daughters.

Lady Stanhope did her best to bring up the children. But she was struggling. Lucy was teething and her cries echoed through the house every night, while Griselda worshipped Hester and copied her in everything, good or bad. Without the easy sociability of his wife to support him, Charles withdrew further from the household and concentrated on political activities. Before his marriage Charles's public reputation for eccentricity had made him something of an outcast. On his first appearance at court he had refused to powder his hair in keeping with the fashion of the time and was mocked for his short, shocking coal-black curls. But Hester's charm and social grace had redeemed him. Now she was dead. Needing both a male heir and an anchor to ensure his social position, as well as a stepmother for his three daughters, Charles took his second wife. The match seemed to have none of the passion and gaiety of his first. At the behest of his family, Charles asked Louisa Grenville, his late wife's cousin, to be the new Lady Mahon. From a curly-haired young woman concerned about her pet dogs, Louisa Grenville became one half of a convenient marriage to an eccentric husband who was still grieving for, and in love with, his first wife.

From the beginning, Louisa compensated for the aloofness of her family life by enjoying the social whirl of London. Hester recalled her stepmother's life as being filled with London parties, dressmakers and beauty treatments. She rose early every day and, after a brief outing, returned home to have her hair dressed by a French servant. After this she would often go out to dinner, followed by the opera or a party, where she would stay until it was almost light again. The children grew up estranged from her, cared for by a system of governesses and their doting paternal grandmother.

The three girls continued to be healthy, although Hester showed a disturbing tendency towards eye inflammations. Rarely a month passed without her having at least one, sometimes two, sties on her eyes, which were not only painful but disfiguring. The sisters bickered over their toys but were mostly very affectionate towards each other, although a clear hierarchy was developing. Griselda followed Hester in all things and their relationship was a rollercoaster of passionate embraces, where they acted as if they had not seen each other for days instead of just an hour or two, and fights which left them scratched, bruised and crying. The governesses who replaced her mother's gentle care were the bane of Hester's childhood: strong-willed and disobedient, she was punished often and severely. The least conventionally attractive of the girls, Hester's appearance was of concern both to her carers and to Lady Stanhope. Moreover, Hester seemed unconcerned, a trait that both her stepmother and grandmother reassured each other she would outgrow.[8] One governess attempted to jam her heavy figure between two boards which were then pulled together to make her slender. The adult Hester's height and bearing, her changeable, intensely blue eyes and fashionably pale skin, which even Beau Brummel was reputed to admire, would be her most striking features. But as a child, in her 'small blue striped cotton gown', she was seen as awkward and ungainly, with a tendency to nasty, pus-filled sties and a habit of 'poking her head'.[9]

In spite of any familial concerns, visitors to Chevening usually admired the toddlers, including the rambunctious Hester. A funny child, she kept the rest of the family entertained with her pranks and jokes, and less amused with her mischief. But while her talent for mimicry and horsemanship gratified her grandmother, it could not compensate for her lack of ability and interest in traditional feminine pursuits such as needlework and music. In one attempt to deal with the issue Lady Stanhope arranged for music lessons. Hester enthusiastically took up instruction but her singing voice proved to be louder than it was tuneful and she soon gave it up, preferring to spend her time playing outside with her pony.[10]

Within nine months Louisa fulfilled Charles's hopes for the new marriage and produced the first of her three sons. Philip Mahon was quickly appropriated by his half-sisters. But Philip was just a tiny baby so Charles frequently found himself turning to his eldest daughter. She seemed able, through her hearty gaiety, to lift his spirits from the fits of depression which gripped him, in a way his other children could not.

Then, in March 1786, the death of Charles's father, the Earl of Stanhope, brought change to the house. His last hours were a touching leave taking of his wife: 'Happy if we could go together, but what would become of the poor little things without their grandmamma.'[11] Within days, the dowager Lady Stanhope moved out of the stately home and into the dower house at Ovenden across the park. Charles, now the new Earl, took his father's place as Lord Stanhope and his seat in the House of Lords; his eldest son, Philip, became Lord Mahon.

As master of the estate, Charles began to impose his Jacobin principles on the household. Any resistance from Louisa was met with furious rages. In one fit of temper, he had the family carriage and horses taken away. Louisa, accustomed to being driven to her various social engagements in the greatest of style, was more than a little upset, but Charles seemed oblivious. Then Hester got herself a pair of stilts and in front of her father played around in the mud, teetering along the dirty lane. Her father asked her about her particular game, and she cheekily replied that she didn't mind the mud but that her poor stepmama was suffering because she had always had a carriage and wasn't very well. As a result Charles bought new horses and a carriage from London but still, in the spirit of his original gesture, had all the armorial bearings removed. More and more eccentric in the ever rarer hours he spent with his family, he wore boots all day indoors, sitting with his feet cocked up on a fire grate, eating bread crumbled into milk 'like chicken feed' and only occasionally deviating from his sparse diet to binge on 'lots of chocolate'.[12] His eldest daughter, at first tolerant of her father's strange moods, found them ever more difficult. Fits of rage, reminiscent of those his daughter would suffer from in later years, would leave the household terrified and shaken. In her teens, alienated from a society she longed to be accepted by, Hester turned to Pitt, now prime minister, for support. Pitt, sorry for his niece, the daughter of his favourite sister, now began to take an active role in her life.

Pitt's government had organized a frantic recruitment drive to replenish the troops in the war with France. Each county called for men to defend the country, and Kent responded spectacularly. In the midst of the patriotic fervour that swept the country, six thousand volunteers offered to defend the English coastline. As an act of gratitude, a pageant of magnificent proportions was planned, the venue: Lord Romney's park. Moreover, the King himself would attend to review the prospective soldiers. It would be the most important social event of the Kent calendar of 1796.

Entertainments and festivities were organized around the moat; Kentish aristocracy donned its most fashionable clothes, and Queen Charlotte accompanied King George III on his journey from London to enjoy the display of military pomp and prowess. But Charles, whose anti-war stance was as well known in Europe as it was in England, could hardly subscribe to an event whose purpose was to celebrate and glorify a war he thought heinous and immoral. Lucy had already married and left Chevening but his five remaining offspring were forbidden to attend. Well aware of Hester's wilfulness and expecting rebellion, Charles monitored her movements in the days preceding the review. To his relief, just the day before, Hester excused herself from the house to visit the neighbouring Crump sisters, an elderly pair, who Charles was certain would not attend the ball. He had not reckoned on his daughter's charm. The sisters were sympathetic to the young woman with a strict father. On the morning of the review Hester was dressed in borrowed finery and driven, in the Crumps' carriage, although unaccompanied by them, to the review she so longed to see. In her enthusiasm she was too early, and when she arrived the tents were still being pitched. Disregarding the impropriety of doing so, she remained on the site, watching and waiting for the events to begin.[13] The spectacle dazzled her: the glorious red and gold uniforms and, at the centre of everything, fêted and admired, William Pitt. The gawky, elongated adolescent had grown up and Hester's elegance was noticed and admired. Initial insecurities were hidden in a haughty demeanour, then banished by the rapt attention of the soldiers, dandies and courtiers whom she amused and impressed. In later years Hester would reminisce that Lord Romney's review was where she came of age: previous balls had been tempered by familial presence and restraint; at the Kentish review Hester related to strangers, acquaintances and friends as an adult for the first time. Even the King could not ignore the arrogant, but impeccably mannered, young woman, asking his entourage why he hadn't seen her before. When he found out that she was from Chevening, he exclaimed she was far too pretty to be kept prisoner at 'Democracy Hall' and invited her to a place of honour by his side at table. By the end of the night Hester had gained another admirer, and the King exclaimed that he would like her to ride bodkin between himself and the Queen in their carriage. The Queen was less impressed; she declared that, as Hester had no maid to accompany her, the whole business would be far too inconvenient.[14]

While Hester's scheming recalcitrance enabled her to escape intermittently from the tempers and trials of her family life, Griselda was less fortunate. At nineteen she was unable to take the stifling atmosphere any longer; following Hester's suggestion she approached her uncle, and Pitt offered Griselda the use of his cottage at Walmer. She accepted and was able to offer an occasional refuge to the siblings who remained in Chevening. Lord Mahon visited her whenever he could, discovering in the grassy expanses and proximity to the sea a convenient escape from home. It was at the Walmer cottage that Griselda met and fell in love with an army officer, John Tickell. It was an uneasy match. The precise nature of the difficulty was unclear; either Tickell's financial and family circumstances were misunderstood by Griselda or they were misreported to her. Whatever the cause, the revelation of his true, and greatly reduced, circumstances meant that Griselda risked appearing to be the victim of deceit. Propriety demanded that she end the relationship, which she did, but was distraught to the point of madness afterwards. Seeing his niece's distress, Pitt intervened. He restored Tickell's fortunes with a new appointment and attended Griselda's small wedding on the Kent coast.

Hester alone remained in Chevening, still able to some extent to cope, by sheer defiance and will, with her father's mood swings but suffering herself from headaches and fits of agitation caused by the tension and misery at home. She filled her days with her horses and the incessant correspondence she would keep up for the rest of her life. Her maternal grandmother in Somerset was one frequent recipient of the long, rambling, gossipy letters that Hester wrote from the house, which she was more and more beginning to see as a prison. Eventually, unable to bear her father's tempers, she wrote that she would like to stay with Lady Chatham in the countryside. Hester, worried that her grandmother would say no, reassured her about her need to escape to the peace and quiet of Somerset. In a passage that was poignantly prophetic of her later years, Hester hoped that her nervousness would improve and expressed her fear that, if it did not, she would have to avoid the world for the rest of her life.[15] Lady Chatham responded with enthusiasm, happy to have the company of her slightly wayward granddaughter.[16]

5

Departures

I have always thought happiness chiefly rested in the mind and since
I left England I am more than ever convinced of this truth. I like
travelling of all things; it is a constant change of ideas.
Lady Hester to T. J. Jackson, 17 July 1803

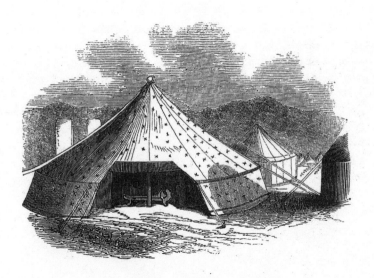

The tent that was used by the Princess of Wales
before Hester and Michael shared it

THE TENTH OF FEBRUARY 1810 WAS GREY AND WET. From a hotel in Plymouth, just prior to their departure, Meryon wrote to his sister that his health was much recovered. The voyage was not an easy one. After being delayed by inauspicious winds a tempest caught them in Trafalgar shoals. As the ship was tossed in a shallow, treacherous sea, washed by great floods of water, ripples of superstition ran through the ship, concerning this expanse where so many of Nelson's men had lost their lives.[1] Yet in spite of these difficulties they arrived in Gibraltar after just twenty-eight days. It was a lovely arrival, warm and balmy: weather that reminded Meryon of July in England. Flowers bloomed and the grandeur of the approach to the rock made the travellers gasp in awe. Settled in Gibraltar, Meryon immediately wrote to his family to assure them of his safety. The journey, he wrote, had been awful but his new situation more than compensated:

> I find my situation not merely such as satisfies, but one that gratifies me. . . . for there is in both [Hester and her brother] such an air of nobility, such a highly cultivated mind, which I am convinced nothing but high birth and the first society, and that, too, from one's infancy, could give.[2]

Meryon found that the intimacy of living in a ship, coupled with the drama of the weather, had created a bond between Hester, James and himself. Pleased with the attention, ever conscious of the difference in rank, Meryon wrote delightedly to his mother that his new employer seemed to put him 'rather on the footing of a friend than of a dependant'. Hester was 'the best lady who ever breathed'; he was filled with optimism for the coming days.[3]

Hester was less enthusiastic about her new temporary home. Gibraltar was one of the few destinations in the south still accessible during the war and its society was largely that of the English aristocracy – people likely to view Hester in exactly the same way as the people she had left England to avoid. The Governor of the island, General Campbell, personally settled Hester and her brother in his own residence, which was known as The Convent. The doctor was put in nearby rooms. Far from being restful, the constant circulation of wealthy travellers and small groups of Spanish refugees made Gibraltar a busy, cosmopolitan place. In deference to her background, Hester was invited to dine with 'the first society of the place' at the Governor's table, which she did, although rather through a sense of obligation than because of any desire to mingle.[4]

Unaccustomed to the sweltering heat and consequently suffering, Hester habitually lay in bed till midday, eating breakfast at one or two, before walking with the doctor to discuss how she was feeling. Only in the afternoons could she escape the petty conversations and endless gossip of England to go riding on 'beautiful Spanish horses' costing fifty dollars apiece, a small sum and a price even Meryon could afford.[5] But only a week into the trip, the company livened up with the arrival of a group of young aristocratic British men, friends of James, who were also enjoying General Campbell's hospitality. Howe Peter Browne, the second Marquess of Sligo, was travelling around the Mediterranean in a yacht; he was accompanied by Mr Hume, a man who amassed a fortune in the East Indies, and had recently been joined by Michael Bruce, the son of a wealthy Scots banker, who was making his 'Grand Tour'. They were all attractive, in their early twenties and very wealthy. Their entourage of servants included two Albanian guards dressed extravagantly in national costume and a man employed as Sligo's 'en suite painter', who made sketches of any memorable views. Unconventional in dress and behaviour – Hume's mistress dressed as a man – the group diverted Hester for a while with their slightly scandalous aura and apparent indifference to society opinion. Michael endeared himself by his admiration for Sir John Moore, whom he, although not a soldier, had followed to Salamanca in 1808. Michael found Moore 'very civil and kind' and joined his troops on the tragic retreat to Corunna.[6]

The yacht was called *Piraeus* and would be the cause of Sligo's prosecution and eventual imprisonment in Newgate. Unable to find sufficient crew to man his boat for the duration of the trip, Sligo enticed Elden, a seaman in the King's service, to desert and help navigate his voyage. At a time when all able-bodied men were needed for the war effort it was a heinous offence with a grave penalty, and Sligo was aware that he had been caught and would face serious consequences when he returned to Britain. However, for the immediate future, the impending trouble only seemed to add to the interest and popularity he had with fellow travellers. Although fully aware of events, Hester found him charming and mischievous, rather than malicious. Lord Byron, a fellow university student of Sligo who would later meet up with Hester's group, described Sligo as a rascal who had 'done a number of young things', while retaining the conviction that he was 'a good man'.[7]

Meryon, gaining in social confidence from his relationship with Hester and James, immediately started to befriend Michael, 'a most pleasing, clever young man'.[8] But Bruce had no interest in Meryon, who reported to his family, 'though I court his acquaintance a great deal he won't fancy me'. Hester's party diminished when Nassau Sutton left them to go to Minorca, having first made plans for the whole group to be reunited in Sicily. Hester, bored with the constant socializing, was considering where to go next when her brother received orders: he was to rejoin his regiment in Cadiz. Hester was distraught. James's imminent leave-taking and the danger of his new destination brought back all the misery of the past year. Afterwards, Hester withdrew as far as she could, spending a considerable amount of time alone, worrying over James's safety and waiting anxiously for news.[9] Hester bade farewell to Sligo's party when they too left, intending to follow Sutton to Sicily.

However, political events intervened. Napoleon had married Marie Louise in early March, so that he was now related to the Queen of Sicily; the French, commanded by Murat, who had since been named King of Sicily by Napoleon, were amassing an army in Calabria ready to attack. The plans that Hester had already begun to make for her party's onward journey to Sicily were abandoned and an alternative destination sought. A practical alternative was Malta. Open to the English, and easy to plan, Elizabeth Williams had a sister there. Elizabeth's sister had also been in Pitt's service but married well with her employer's blessing. She lived with her husband, Mr Fernandez, the Commissary-General, in a very comfortable home in Valletta. Although their home was grand they were not part of the aristocratic social scene, and Hester, worn out by the social obligations of Gibraltar, eagerly agreed to stay with them. Arrangements were made easily: Captain Whitby offered her passage on the *Cerberus*, which she gratefully accepted, and by early April their voyage was under way. Unlike their first voyage, it was a lovely trip with calm waters and blue skies, and Hester was greeted on arrival by the island's governor, General Oakes, who urged her to reconsider her accommodation and be his guest. But Hester was determined to minimize her exposure to the expatriate community and politely but firmly refused, saying she had promised to stay elsewhere.

The Fernandez home was a former hostel of the Knights of St John. A grand, but slightly jaded, building, Hester found the quiet homeliness of the Fernandezes' a welcome return to the family life she had lost with her bereavements. Meryon, eager for adventure and longing for a return to the gaiety of Gibraltar, was bored. Much to his relief, however, it seemed that General Oakes was not to be ignored. He was even more adamant in his insistence that Hester and her group join him for dinner than Hester was in her determination to avoid society. Eventually, she gracefully acquiesced, finding, as she had expected, that the company of the society women was shallow and inane. Despairing of their limited exchanges, Meryon wrote to his family:

> She has the most thorough contempt for her sex, at least that part of it who converse on nothing but visits, capes and bonnets and such frivolous subjects.[10]

Meryon had no such misgivings. Oakes entertained Neapolitan and English aristocracy at his banquets, and Meryon, unlike Hester, was dazzled by the 'string of Lords and Ladies and Counts and Countesses' he sat with at dinner. While Meryon flirted with well-born women and basked in the conversation of titled gentlemen, he worried over Hester, who was given to public outbursts in which she refused to 'hide her contempt with any ladies'.[11]

When they had been there less than a month, a familiar yacht was seen docking at the harbour. It was Lord Sligo and his group, who had been similarly thwarted in their plans to stay in Sicily. They landed in Malta and rejoined Hester. Unlike in Gibraltar, Hester was now without a male chaperone of rank, as both her brother and Sutton had left the group. So it may have been the freedom from the possibility of family censure that made the proceeding events possible – or perhaps she just fell in love.

Michael Bruce was twenty-two years old, twelve years younger than Hester. He was well educated, having been to Eton and Cambridge, and well born. Even Meryon, still smarting from the way Michael had snubbed him in Gibraltar, conceded that he was 'handsome enough to move any lady's heart'.[12] And Michael was very taken with Hester, from the beginning of this, their second meeting, finding her a woman of 'very extraordinary talent' who had inherited 'all the great and splendid qualities of her illustrious grandfather'.[13] At first Meryon thought Hester disinterested, more concerned with her generally poor health than with socializing. Either he was mistaken or Hester's feelings burgeoned in a matter of days. Within a short time of their meeting, Michael left his own travelling party to join Hester's, claiming she was 'much more agreeable, much cleverer and better informed' than his companions and offering to act as her '*compagnon do voyage*' now that her brother could no longer accompany her.[14] What was worse, from Meryon's perspective, was that Michael continued to show a contemptuous disregard for him, regarding the doctor as his social inferior and doing nothing to hide it. Meryon, all too aware of his own position in society and eager to meet people 'above him', could no longer relax in Hester's easy acceptance. At first seeing Michael's attitude as a challenge, he persisted in his attempts to interest, even charm, him. But the result was that Michael became more openly antagonistic, irritated by the doctor's persistent ingratiation. As Michael quickly became Hester's 'intimate friend', the doctor found that her new companion's treatment of him had the added detrimental effect of excluding him from society where he had previously been welcomed.[15] Thwarted in his attempt to mingle with expatriate aristocracy, Meryon began to explore native Maltese society instead. Unhappy that the local women were jealously guarded by their male relatives, he decided to explore the less salubrious areas of town. Here, he found the information that he was after and wrote to his brother-in-law that, although he did not yet know about 'the naughty part of the sex', he had discovered where the brothels were located and would send more details with his next letter.[16]

It was a sweltering summer, even by Maltese standards, keenly felt by the English group, who suffered and sweated in temperatures frequently as high as 90F. In an attempt to escape the stifling heat, Michael and Hester agreed to leave the bustle of Valletta for General Oakes's country residence in San Antonio, just five miles away. Its position had the added advantage of being removed from the prying eyes and gossiping tongues of Valletta's expatriates, allowing the couple to spend considerable time with each other without fear of public censure.

The house had a rather ugly exterior that gave no hint of the beauties lying behind the massive blocks of soft grey local stone. The only noticeable architectural feature was a single square bell tower, like that of an English country church, rising above the flat roof. Vines wandered and weaved chaotically over every visible surface. Yet inside, immaculate, luxuriously furnished, high, stone-floored rooms gave respite from the sun and, most wondrous of all, led out to the walled garden, a magical, magnificent place. There, a single long terrace was crowned with a double arcade, bordered with a mass of orange, lemon and pomegranate trees, and the air was heavy with the smell of myrtle and fruit blossoms. Michael and Hester walked there, in the first tentative days of their relationship, eager to spend time alone together. But Meryon doggedly accompanied them, disgruntled and disapproving that Hester had chosen to 'fix in a large chateau, herself, a single lady, with two single men'.[17] He had begun to enjoy the social life in Valletta's underside and was dismayed by this retreat to the countryside, especially given Hester's increased reluctance to see him. However, he did not blame Hester but her lover, and busied himself with his regular correspondents, complaining:

> I don't like Mr Bruce, he seems desirous of excluding me from the great nobilities with which he is intimate, and of inducing Hester not to bring me forward so much as her accustomed goodness prompts her to do.[18]

Michael showed a dispassionate interest in Meryon's professional abilities but adamantly continued to exclude him from social events. Writing constantly, Meryon continued to complain about a situation he thought 'enough to make the tongues of scandal wag against any other woman' but grudgingly conceded that Hester's health seemed to have improved as a result of her involvement and that she was beginning to look 'rather fetching'.[19]

From the palace of San Antonio, now firm in their intent to remain together, Hester and Michael planned the next stage of their trip. It was decided that the best plan would be to head for Constantinople, by way of the Greek islands, both destinations that were open to British travellers. Hester, buoyed up by her affair, had recovered her confidence in her own political abilities; she was planning an intrigue. It was a romantic and improbable escapade, but Hester decided that they would go to Constantinople, where she would make friends with the French Ambassador. Then, having used the friendship to obtain a French passport, she would head for Paris, get to know Bonaparte well, and return with her information to England, where she could enlist help to subvert his plans.

Yet even as the couple made their plans and delighted in daily visits from their host General Oakes, the tension between Michael and Meryon grew. By the end of June they were quarrelling openly. Meryon had moved from being a curmudgeonly letter-writer to open confrontation, and Michael retaliated. Meryon had no illusions about Hester's feelings for Michael, finding that 'when either he or I must be sacrificed it is easy to see who will suffer'.[20] He blamed Michael's low opinion of him for Hester's changed manner, which had made him 'injured in her estimation'. It was an intolerable situation. Worn out by the incessant bickering, Meryon finally capitulated and asked if he could eat alone in future. All too happy to prevent the frequent altercations, Hester fixed another table, leaving Meryon to inform his family that 'until the unpleasant fellow quits us, I shall take my meals by myself. When that will be, I know not: for he accompanies us on our voyage to Constantinople . . . '[21]

The voyage proved difficult to organize. Few ships were heading in the direction of Constantinople, and those that were could not offer passage. Having made the decision to continue on their travels together, Michael and Hester faced a dilemma. Unconcerned about her own reputation, Hester worried that Michael's behaviour might ruin his chances of preferment on his return to London. Secrecy was out of the question. The numerous aristocratic travellers in Malta might already be writing letters back to England with salacious gossip about the romantic liaison of Pitt's niece and the young Bruce. Michael's family would know what was happening; it was only a matter of when and how they would find out. If they were displeased then Michael could be cut off, which, given his financial dependence on them, would mean an end to their travels. It seemed to Hester that the only honourable thing to do was to tell Michael's father herself. Taking fate into her own hands, some time in June she wrote an impassioned letter to Michael's father, Crauford Bruce, a man she had never met. A eulogy to her lover, it spoke of Michael's virtues – 'his elevated and statesmanlike mind', 'his brilliant talents' – and, with shocking frankness, the beauty of his body. To know Michael was to love and admire him, and she did. Having first appealed to a father's pride in his son, she went on to reassure. She had no plans to ruin him, to get him under her power or to destroy his life. She loved him to distraction and wished only for his future happiness. Humbled by her love, and by the realization of the social impossibility of a permanent relationship, Hester acknowledged that one day she would have to let him marry another woman, someone more worthy of the position he could and would aspire to. She promised to do so gracefully when the time arose and gave her word that she would make no trouble. She hoped her openness did not displease him and explained that her sole motivation was love. Gossip and scandal 'as far as relates to *myself*' did not concern her, but the favourable opinion of the father of someone she so tenderly adored was her only driving force.[22]

The heat was starting to upset Michael but, despite suffering from a fever, he too wrote to his father to tell him about the affair. His letter was filled with praise and admiration for Hester's ancestry and connections. Michael was proud to love her; he felt no shame in having a relationship with someone who had such 'an exalted mind'. Hester's conduct was blameless and honourable; if his father was displeased then it should be with him: 'If there is any fault I am the guilty person and upon me you must wreak your vengeance.'[23] Michael was brought up in an atmosphere of openness and liberality and he appealed to those very qualities of his upbringing with confidence and honesty. With trepidation and in the knowledge that the wait for a reply would in all probability be a long one, the couple consigned their letters to the vagaries of the transcontinental mail.

Early nineteenth-century post was part chance, part careful method that had been slowly improved over the past few centuries. Hester made free, and improper, use of the system of 'Free Franks'. Since 1660 the postage on letters relating to government business was free. Although all members of the House of Lords and House of Commons were entitled to the privilege, it was only supposed to be used for mail that related to government affairs. Living in Downing Street as the Prime Minister's niece, Hester had often marked letters as being exempt from postage. Now travelling, and likely to incur substantial mail costs, she included her travelling companions in the system she continued to take advantage of, inviting Meryon, early in their travels, to tell his sister to direct her letters to him via Downing Street, marked with Hester's name.[24] But the question of cost was not the only one; reliability and speed were real issues, with mail generally carried on any available boat with no guarantee that a letter would ever reach its destination, whether the vessel carrying it did so or not.

Hester did not catch Michael's feverish malady, but the strain was showing on her in a different way and, aggravated by the humid climate, a large pus-filled boil began to grow close to her ear. Her face swelled up and, determined that her lover should not see her affliction, Hester kept to her own chamber for ten days, admitting only Meryon to treat her. The success of his ministrations restored him to Hester's favour and, fully recovered, the first thing she did was speak to Michael about his treatment of the doctor. The tension between the two of them diffused a little and polite conversation superseded the rows. Meryon made allowance for Michael's arrogance on the grounds of his wealth and upbringing, conceding that it was understandable that he would not choose someone like his humble self as 'his intimate friend'.[25] It was a reconciliation of sorts and Hester further limited the opportunities for conflict by suggesting that they each eat breakfast in their own apartment, only meeting up as a group for dinner. After dinner, when Hester and Michael had company, Meryon was welcome to join them. However, when the couple were spending the evening alone, the doctor had to amuse himself. Meryon was mollified but, understandably apprehensive of the journeys ahead, wrote to his sister: 'must Mr Bruce and I who are probably to spend months together, live like cat and dog, always bickering?'[26]

Meryon was also trying to find some company of his own. He enjoyed some solitary excursions to Valletta and, around the time the group began to search for an onward ship, he befriended a local girl. She was just eighteen, the same age as his wife had been, and attractive in the buxom way he found most pleasing. A young mother, separated from a cruel husband, Meryon was originally asked to tend her through a sickness. Moved by her plight and aroused by her beauty, Meryon found himself wanting 'as much comfort as he had been called in to give'.[27] But the girl was not legally separated. She was the first of several dalliances that Meryon would enjoy and not a serious prospect for the future. He prepared to leave with Michael and Hester as soon as passage was finally found.

Meanwhile, Napoleon's armies were successfully sweeping across mainland Europe; Malta no longer seemed as remote from the possibility of danger as it had when the group arrived, so it was with a sense of relief that the party accepted passage on the frigate *Belle Poule*. Captain Brisbane would carry them to the Ionian islands, and they would spend a little time sightseeing in Greece before finding further passage on to Turkey. A number of the Ionian islands were popular British destinations, having been taken from the French the year before, when the British fleet disrupted communication between the islands and their controller. Corfu alone remained a French outpost and would do so until 1813.

The party that embarked on 2 August was smaller than the group that had arrived. Hester's maid, Elizabeth Williams, was courting, having fallen in love with a friend of her sister. She would remain in Malta until she was married. Hester, wishing her every happiness, gave her a generous marriage gift of £100 and employed another English maid, an elderly woman called Anne Fry.[28] Elizabeth was Hester's last link with the life she had left so recently and the parting was a sad one. Hester was now travelling with two men, one she had known barely eight months, the other for only five.

The projected trip to Constantinople would be a long one, necessitating hard riding overland. Once again, Hester packed up many of her belongings, instructing Meryon and Michael to do the same. Boxes and trunks were sent back to England, and Hester sent a gift and note of fond farewell to General Oakes, their host. The gift was a little box, plainly made, and Hester apologized for its humbleness in a note that heralded a correspondence that would continue between them for years.

6

Anticipation and Arrival

I believe it has never yet been expected that a man sd. be a saint, at least
till he is married, and if I most solemnly declare that I never had or ever
will have further claims upon your son, than any women he might have
picked up in the streets, how can he shock the world?
Lady Hester, 12 December 1810

Constantinople

WHEN MICHAEL AND HESTER set off on the *Belle Poule* they were still fretting over the outcome of their letters, but Captain Brisbane was an excellent host and pleasure in the voyage helped to alleviate some of their anxiety. Warm weather and good winds – Meryon described the water as 'scarcely rougher than the bosom of a lake' – brought them to the coast of Zante in only seven days.[1] It was, and still is, a beautiful sight. As they rounded the north-eastern tip they saw tiny, luminously white houses clustered at the foot of hills covered with gracefully narrow cypresses and the pewter-coloured foliage of knotted olive trees. The travellers alighted to spend a few days sightseeing, while the *Belle Poule*, with Captain Brisbane, continued on its way. Hester and Michael were left under the care of the Commander-in-Chief of the Ionian islands, Major General Oswald, who agreed to arrange onward passage for the group when they chose to continue. With its sandy beaches and fertile landscape, Zante was known as the 'Golden Island', and when the group left for the next leg of their journey they did so with a feeling of regret and with the shared hope that their travels might bring them back again.

Their letters arrived in London with surprising alacrity, after less than two months, in the middle of August. Crauford Bruce's replies, which he wrote without delay, were a lot slower in getting back to them. When they arrived, they could have made Hester and Michael very happy but unfortunately for them their letters were not the only ones that Crauford received. Shortly after he had posted his encouraging responses, a folded letter, marked on the back with a Dover postmark, came. It was anonymous and began:

> Your son is gone to Constantinople with an artful woman as his *mistress* Hester Stanhope. She means to make him marry her, he knew her first criminally in Malta. For God's Sake do not neglect this caution but send for him without a moment's delay or it will be too late.[2]

This was the prompt for Crauford to write and post another two letters, markedly different from the last ones, but which would reach Michael and Hester together with the others, causing confusion and misunderstanding.

When the party reached Patras, Sligo rejoined them, although without his yacht, which had been remanded back to Malta in line with the enquiries relating to the charges that would later be brought. After an idyllic communal meal at Lepanto, in a bower of myrtle and laurel, they landed at Corinth. Michael and Meryon were starting to enjoy the journey a lot more. Meryon's relationship with Sligo was much better than the one he had with Michael; Sligo even told him personally about the affair with the *Piraeus,* and it may be that the presence of a third man eased the tension. However, Hester was beginning to be ill from the constant motion. It was still a long way to Constantinople and another rest was agreed upon, this time for just three days. Their initial impressions of Corinth were disappointing. Humid, with overgrown marshes and rife with malaria and plague, every year the city's population was drastically reduced by outbreaks of disease.

Meryon paid a courtesy call on the son of the Governor, or Bey, of Corinth, and was received very graciously with coffee and a large pipe more than a foot long. In return, the Bey himself, too old for visiting, sent his harem to call on Hester. This included his wife and a dozen beautiful young girls, her slaves, all completely covered in black cloths known as *ferigees*,[3] so that only their eyes were visible through narrow slits. When they arrived unexpectedly, Michael, Lord Sligo and Meryon were chatting with Hester. They fell silent as an interpreter was shown into the room. After the initial platitudes the interpreter declared that the Bey's women had arrived but could not go in until the men had left. The three gentlemen decided, then and there, that this was an opportunity not to be missed and, hoping for a glimpse of the faces of the women, hid themselves in a cupboard as soon as the interpreter left to fetch the harem. From their carefully concealed spot they had a good, but hidden, view of all that went on. Hester went along with the joke and the women were ushered in to her. After a few minutes they relaxed, unveiled their faces and made themselves comfortable on the two or three sofas scattered around the room. They were graceful and beautiful with long black hair and olive skin, and the three men were enthralled. After a time, however, through a series of gestures and signs it became clear that they wanted to compare their bodies to Hester's, so gradually they began to expose parts of their bodies. Veil upon veil was removed to expose beautiful jewelled wrists and ankles. Long legs and naked feet were displayed to the rapt, secret audience. One woman, dismayed that Hester's eyes were not circled by kohl in the Turkish fashion, brought out a stick and proceeded to make her up. Some more clothes were removed until finally a breast was laid bare, at which point Hester's face showed a look of such horror that the men could not suppress their amusement. At the sound of a muffled laugh the atmosphere changed immediately. Quickly, fumbling in their haste, the women pulled on their veils and made panicked gestures enquiring after the noise. Hester did her best to calm them but the ladies left soon after, terrified that the Bey find out and in his jealousy have them killed.[4]

Early the next day they left for Athens, their next major resting place en route for the Ottoman capital. Thieves and bandits were always a threat to foreign travellers in these parts, especially to ostentatiously wealthy ones, so the caravan that set off the following day was not only magnificent but armed up to the hilt. Sligo's Albanian servants carried their customary daggers and guns, but everyone else, twenty-five people in total, was armed with sabres and pistols.

Land journeys were complicated and often fraught in this part of Europe in the early nineteenth century. The first stage was to find a horse, hired as much in advance as possible, usually from the nearest town's local postmaster, at a cost of a shilling each for the day.[5] When the travellers came to an agreed meeting place to take up their mounts, the horses and guides would be ready. If for any reason they were not, the Greeks who tended the animals were savagely beaten and whipped by their Tartar overseers. For Hester and her companions, the next part of their trip was made even worse because only packhorses, slower, stolid animals, were available to carry both people and luggage. By the time they reached the slightly forlorn harbour at Kenkri, a small port on the isthmus of Corinth, they only wished to rest until the next day's voyage.

A short and pleasant sail brought them to the narrow entrance of Piraeus by noon. Just as they arrived, a cry from one of the crew alerted them to a young man perched on top of the pier head beneath the rocks of Colonna as if about to dive in. Sligo immediately recognized the dark tousled hair of his friend Byron, who, seeing that all heads on the boat were now pointing towards him, demonstrated his diving prowess by performing an elaborate dive into the sea beside them. Sligo greeted him from the deck and invited him to join them as soon as he was suitably dressed and they were properly landed.

Lord George Gordon Byron had begun his Mediterranean tour in 1809, spending time in Athens, a stay which saw the early dawning of his love of all things Greek and his support for the cause of Greek independence from their Turkish conquerors. This was a return visit. Living at a Capuchin monastery that housed a friar and six boy pupils, Byron was living a life that was 'nothing but riot from Noon till night', amusing himself with the youths and noting with pleasure that young Greeks, unlike Turks, did not retain their lower garments when bathing.[6]

Athens was just six miles' ride from the harbour, but there was no postmaster in the vicinity so Sligo galloped ahead on a horse, borrowed from Byron, and arranged for riding horses to be sent back from the city to collect Hester, Michael, Meryon and their retinue. For two hours, they relaxed in the sun until Sligo returned with their mounts, and they rode together, quickly and easily over the gentle rolling countryside, enjoying the occasional sight of an ancient monument. Hester and Michael were, at last, able to take a house alone together after Sligo offered to share his apartments with Meryon. While Meryon was all too happy to share with Sligo whom he thought, unlike Michael, possessed all the attributes of a 'true gentleman', he was less content with the state of the rooms, which he thought rather poor.[7] Sligo, he grumbled, seemed to enjoy living in a simplicity that was in marked contrast to his means, something he could not begin to understand. However, it is also likely that, in spite of his protestations of pleasure at staying with Sligo, he was again resenting Michael's proximity to Hester in view of his own exile. Hester and Michael's house was not particularly grand either: it was old and white with beautiful high ceilings, a shady courtyard and, much to Hester's pleasure as she was beginning to enjoy the Eastern habit of frequent bathing, its own bath.

Perhaps being alone in their own house gave Hester and Michael more time to discuss their worries, but the strain of waiting for Crauford's response was beginning to blight their relationship. Hester loved Michael but, and this is a fact that has often been overlooked, she did so unselfishly. She made it clear to Michael that she did not wish their relationship to jeopardize the relationship he had with his family, and that if it did, they should separate. Crauford was financially responsible for Michael's freedom to travel and his disapproval would have brought about the withdrawal of that support. But if Hester ended the relationship as a consequence she hardly stood to gain, so her concern was not motivated by material concerns, pressing as they were. Michael, who was convinced that his own liberal upbringing and his father's views would lead him to accept their liaison, urged Hester to be patient and to wait.

It had been a long hot season, with no rain for more than six months. During the heat of the afternoon Michael, Hester and Sligo found it best to rest, riding or exploring in the morning and socializing late at night and into the small hours. During the day Meryon found himself busy with a steady stream of patients, eager to consult the physician of a titled English lady. In the evening, much to his delight, Hester regularly invited him to her late-night parties, where Byron was also a frequent guest. Byron was still enjoying the company of the six boys, in particular that of a young boy called Nicolo. Born in Greece of French parents, the liaison between Nicolo and Byron was a subject of speculation and scandal among expatriates in Athens. When Nicolo suffered from a mysterious ailment, rumoured to be an anal rupture, Meryon was consulted and duly remarked that Byron 'seemed much interested' in his patient.[8]

Meryon was in awe of the poet's rank, reputation and wealth, but not to the extent that he did not derive some amusement from the idiosyncratic habits which, he noted, were solely a consequence of vanity. In particular, he observed the way that Byron contrived to move from chair to chair when crossing a room, rather than walk for any distance where his limp might be more obvious.[9] In fact, the interaction of each member of Hester's group with Byron was complex and contradictory, the balance of their relationships subtly shifted by the charismatic presence of the newcomer. Meryon, wrongly as it turned out, thought Hester and Byron were both very taken with each other. He wrote to his sister that Hester was 'much pleased' with him, which was 'saying not a little in his praise', while Byron he suspected of being 'a little keen'.[10] Nothing could have been farther from the truth. When Byron wrote to his friend Hobhouse, his depictions of Hester's Athenian soirées were not pleasant reminiscences of evenings with a charming hostess, but rather long evenings of constant argument 'with that dangerous thing – a female wit!' He claimed that in spite of constant incitement he refused to argue because he despised women 'too much to squabble with them' and found her 'no different from other she-things' except in her disregard for convention, presumably because she was carrying on a flagrant affair, a trait he did not find endearing.[11] Hester was used to being treated as an equal by people of far more political consequence than Byron, so his patronizing moralizing did not endear him to her. She dismissed him as behaving like a moody adolescent: 'one time he was mopish, and nobody was to speak to him; another he was for being jocular with everybody'.[12] Finding him much less physically attractive than he believed himself to be, Hester dismissed his much acclaimed looks as having 'a great deal of vice' in them. It may be that Hester's opinion was further aggravated by some jealousy, as Michael, who until this time had been slavishly devoted to her, developed a crush on the new visitor. When the opportunity for them to get passage on the final leg of their journey to Constantinople arose, Michael entreated Byron to join them. He refused.

The passage they arranged to carry them onwards was not ideal. A Greek cargo ship was sailing from Piraeus to Constantinople and, for a sum, the travellers were offered passage. It was a filthy vessel, riddled with lice and vermin, with no accommodation for passengers of rank. The only cabin stank of effluent and had to be whitewashed with lime before Hester would agree to the journey, while Sligo, Michael and Meryon planned to sleep on deck in spite of the cool October weather.

On the evening before their departure Michael dined with Byron for the last time. They did not drink heavily, so later events could not be blamed on alcohol-inspired sentiment. After eating, they took a stroll together to the edge of Piraeus overlooking the sea. Looking out across the fading light of the evening seascape, Michael was overcome by emotion and made a profession of friendship and affection for Byron. Byron later interpreted it in a letter to Hobhouse, perhaps correctly, as a homosexual overture, saying that Michael was 'smitten with unimaginable fantasies ever since his connection with Lady H Stanhope'.[13] It was an opinion not lost on Hobhouse, who had, after a meeting in Malta, suspected Michael of being a 'very handsome' bisexual.[14] Byron rejected Michael's tentative advances, saying he was too old for a new friend, and saw Hester's party off the following day.

In spite of the precautions they had taken, the voyage was not a pleasant one. Not only disgusted by the crew's total lack of personal hygiene – sailors frequently urinated where they stood – the group, along with everyone else on board, suffered from an itching rash caused by flea bites after only a day at sea. A few days later the servants quarrelled with the sailors and the whole of Hester's party took to sleeping with pistols at hand. One week into the journey, a sudden severe storm struck the boat and Meryon woke suddenly as his cot was flung sideways across the deck. Anxious to help the crew do whatever was necessary to secure the vessel, he roused himself quickly, scrambling to his feet, only to find that far from fighting the elements to steady the ship, the crew were running round in panic, collecting money from the passengers to make an offering to St George so that he could safely deliver them. Heartily sick of the tribulations of the voyage, they eventually managed to dock safely in Heraklion, where they unanimously agreed to proceed to Constantinople by land. Hester was again seasick and tired. While Meryon tended her, Michael and Sligo set off on post horses for Constantinople to see if they could find a way of easing the remainder of the journey for the rest of the group. When they returned five days later, they were accompanied by a Turkish official; he was pleased that Hester was honouring his city with a visit and would do everything he could to see that she arrived in comfort. In spite of her hopes, he advised strongly against travelling by land, and so the sea voyage was resumed, but this time in two immaculate, exquisitely gilded galleys, sent from Constantinople expressly to carry them there.

Just after midnight, following many weeks of travelling, the travellers finally entered the city of Constantinople. There were no street lights and a lone servant was dispatched into the pitch-black strangeness of the winding streets to find and hire a sedan chair for Hester. And so, in a chair carried high above the harbour steps and narrow alleyways, surrounded by the rest of her travelling companions on foot, Hester arrived in the heart of the Ottoman Empire. A porter walked before them carrying a huge lantern to lead the way, and all of the travellers huddled close to the comfort of the light. Then, as they approached a steeply ascending narrow path, first one, then another, began to hear, at first in the distance but drawing ever closer, the noise of howling animals. In minutes, they were aware not only of their noise but of their smell and presence as hundreds of stray dogs lined the shadowed edges of the streets, barking and snarling, but too wary to approach. The dogs followed them until they got to the district of Pera, where a house had been prepared for Hester and rooms found in a lodging house for the others. It was a terrible arrival and an inauspicious introduction to the East. Hester's house was tiny and the rooms were as filthy as the streets had been. Tired out, it was not until the small hours of the morning that the travellers were able to bed down for the night in what little comfort they had.

Pera was primarily a kind of Christian ghetto. New European arrivals were encouraged to stay there and many Westerners were already settled in the district, but it was truly awful. Rubbish was piled high on the sides of the roads, tumbling over onto the main thoroughfare, while the atmosphere was thick with the stench of rotting fruit and meat, mixed with human excrement, which oozed into the open air from the outdoor pits that served as privies. Hester, understandably, hated it and channelled all her energy, and everyone else's, into finding her somewhere else to live.

She eventually found a small but very beautiful house ten miles from the town, in an area called Therapia, on the banks of the Bosphorus. Three storeys high, it had an interior of riotous colour where every wall and ceiling was painted with frescos. Each floor had its own grand salon with a series of four smaller rooms opening from it, but the most wonderful feature of the house was the view, which Meryon described as 'decisively the noblest in the world'.[15] From her room Hester could see over to the Asian coast and to the mouth of the Black Sea; the splendour of the view and the intricacy of the decoration enchanted her. Constantinople was redeemed; together with Michael, she took the house for six months.

As the couple waited amidst the foulness of Pera for the house to be ready for their move, the long awaited mail from England caught up with them. It was a package of four letters and a packet of contradictions. The first two letters were everything the lovers had hoped for. In Crauford's first reply to Hester he praised not only his own son's merits but Hester's breeding, confiding his hope that she might be able to help him realize his plan for Michael to have a political future. He entrusted Michael's 'future character and achievements in life' into her hands.[16] The letter showed all the liberal-mindedness that his son had been brought up to expect, as did the one that Michael received in the same packet:

> In Hester's letter to me there is such frankness and candour, that it gives me the greatest confidence in her assurances as to her determination.[17]

Crauford's main concern was that the couple keep in regular contact with him and that Michael avoid any actions that might jeopardize his future on his return home. The couple assumed, probably wrongly as events transpired, that Crauford understood they were having a physical relationship, accepted it and, concerned with any repercussions that public awareness of it might have, was simply urging discretion. However, any assumptions they made were challenged by the other letters in the post, namely the letters written after Crauford had received the spiteful anonymous letter with the Dover postmark on 3 September.

Crauford was concerned and, while he did not outlaw the relationship, his letter to Hester was filled with anxiety that his son's character 'through life . . . should appear without stain or reproach'. He ended by trusting in Hester 'to do what is proper', even if that was against her inclinations.[18]

His letter to Michael was similarly wary. As a father, Crauford wanted to appear liberal and lenient and, above all, show that he trusted his son, but as a man of society he was not immune to the scandal that could ensue from the liaison. He was concerned that Michael was risking a move so far from respectability that it might hinder him in his later career and fill him with regret and remorse. He worried about his son's return to fashionable society and, above all, he was anxious that there must be 'something fallacious in the mind when a woman can depart from the circumspect proprieties of her sex and yield her reputation in society for the temporary gratification of any passion'.[19]

The happiness that followed the reading of Michael's father's first letter quickly dissipated with the concern that was brought by the second. The censorious letter spoiled the idyll of their Turkish hideaway; Hester's

worst fears consumed her and within days her physical health, always so
dependent on her emotional well-being, had deteriorated. When she and
Michael moved to their new home, Hester immediately became so ill she
had to stay in bed, tended to by Meryon. Both she and Michael wrote a
reply to the letters while they arranged the move from Pera, then another
from their new home.

Hester's reply to Crauford was just as difficult to write as her first, con-
fessional letter had been. She stated her intentions: had Michael been cut
off from his parents because of the affair, she would have left him, but as
it was, she did not have to. The position for men and women was clearly
different. Michael did no harm in having sex before marriage – after all,
no one expected a bachelor to be a saint, and once he was married, she
would make no further claims whatsoever on him. Hester, whose pride
and lineage had been discussed in every fashionable circle in England,
wrote that she would make no further claim on him than she would if she
had been a prostitute he had picked up on the street: 'I most solemnly
declare that I never had or ever will have further claims upon your son
than any woman he might have picked up in the streets.'[20] She admitted
that her conduct in the eyes of society would be perceived as shocking
and as a result pledged to avoid 'ever setting eyes upon a modest woman'.
English society women who married for the sake of a title, house and fine
diamonds, but who had every intention of sleeping around after their
wedding, would never get the chance to sneer at her. Moreover, she
despised their hypocrisy and did not wish to spend time in their company.
The letter was passionate, reminiscent of earlier messages to Granville,
but with much more strength. Hester was confident in Michael's love, but
equally determined to show her own, when the time came, as if she was
resigned to the fact that having the affair necessitated a sacrifice, one that
she had measured and was prepared to pay.

Michael's letter to his father was as enthusiastic in its praise of Hester
as hers was of him. He was fully aware of the unselfishness of her love and
knew that she cared about his happiness and future welfare; she was
immensely talented and charming, as well as beautiful: all things that his
father would find out for himself when he met her, just as Michael wished
him to. Crauford's letter had not so much criticized Hester as shown concerns over their conduct and the scandal that could result. Michael's reac-

tion shocked everyone, including Hester. Far from heralding a cooling of the affair, Michael asked her to do the only thing that could legitimize their union: he asked her to marry him. But Hester refused. Intent on keeping her promise to Crauford to make no lasting claim on his son, Hester told Michael that the disparity in their ages made any sanctified union impossible.[21] Her refusal and its unselfish motive signified a new period in their relationship; the affair continued, but both were now unflinchingly aware that it would be, by its very nature, finite.

The difficulties with the external world seemed to banish any remnants of bad feeling Michael had for the doctor. In the mild early winter months of November and December they spent their afternoons together, sometimes also with Sligo, riding and shooting and, very occasionally, when a local obliged them, sailing on the Bosphorus.

Meryon was the one member of the party who was unaffected by Crauford's letter; he was thoroughly enjoying himself. Game was plentiful and he had acquired a fine Persian stallion, which was proving an excellent ride. Every evening he dined with Hester and her guests, only retiring after coffee had been served, with the result that he wished for nothing more than to spend the rest of his days in the same way, with a lady who was 'a hundred times more liberal to me than I believe other noble personages are to their family physician'.[22] Meryon's only grievance was that, unlike in Malta, he was finding it difficult to get to know the local women, who were all covered from head to toe and very reluctant to speak to a young European gentleman such as himself.

Crauford's letters of disapproval were only the beginning. Before the end of the year, more mail caught up with them, this time from Hester's brother, James. He was furious. His letter was a tirade warning against the disastrous consequences that could arise from their affair, especially if any children were conceived. He made a list of 'feeling observations on the misery attending those who are not born in wedlock' and finally closed by challenging Michael to a duel.[23]

Michael's reply was as calm and reasoned as James's had been histrionic. His main reaction was one of surprise and he questioned the reason behind James's attitude: had he heard of his proposal and Hester's refusal? Moreover, Michael was worried that once again other people seemed to have been minding his and Hester's business. James seemed to be saying that he only realized how appalling his sister's situation was when he 'received a letter since from a friend', yet Michael had written an explicit and honest account to him. He was indignant that James was more affected by gossip than by his own frank account. Finally, he replied to James's challenge with the kind of bravery that Hester loved in men, as well as with a good deal of gallantry:

> I am ready to stand the responsibility of my own conduct and give you the satisfaction you require and in the hour of trial you will find me a man of honour, courage and spirit.[24]

In order to diffuse the tension, later in December, Michael and Hester agreed to spend some time apart. Michael would go on a tour of Asia with Sligo to look into the possibility of a future journey with Hester to Persia; Sligo hoped to buy seven or eight mares to take home with him. Michael would be away for three or four weeks at most, but Sligo would go on to Malta where he would, at Hester's request, meet with General Oakes. Hester's departure from Malta had seen the beginning of a regular friendly correspondence between her and the General. She was now starting to worry that he too would hear malicious gossip about her relationship and wished to pre-empt any stories by telling him the truth of their situation. So far her letters had hinted at the intimacy between her and Michael but no more; rather than write explicit details, she asked Sligo to carry the story on her behalf.

While Michael was gone, Hester tried to get to know more of the local people and join them in their entertainments, one of the most popular of which was public executions. These were well-attended regular events, which for both Meryon and Hester, used to London hangings, were not particularly remarkable in themselves, the main difference being in the Eastern method of capital punishment: beheading rather than hanging. As a mark of respect for her attendance at one execution Hester was presented with the recently removed head of a minor Pasha on a silver plate. It was almost perfect, with the fleshy parts having been removed and replaced with perfumed cotton. Hester's only misgiving about the gift was that she thought it a shame that the 'poor head' be handed around 'like a pineapple'.[25] Meryon showed a similar fascination with the local displays of killing, even consulting the local Pasha as to when there might be one that he could attend. The Pasha was amused by the European interest in beheading and asked how many people were put to death in London each year. Meryon replied forty or fifty, and the Pasha exclaimed in amusement that, in that case, they weren't any less bloody than the English.

While Hester was alone in Constantinople she also found that the British community were eager to have her join their social circle. Stratford Canning was a young diplomat who had not been stationed there long and was eager to widen his circle with the inclusion of Pitt's niece. Hester tentatively accepted his first invitations but, finding that British etiquette prevailed so that she was forced to spend most of her time with women whose conversation she regarded as frivolous and boring, she soon began to decline them and concentrate on her ever-increasing circle of Turkish acquaintances. In this regard she was shocked to find that Canning was no use whatsoever, doing everything he could to avoid fraternizing with local people while recreating an English upper-class society in miniature. Much to her surprise she found that by far her greatest source of introductions was her physician. Once established in lodgings in Trianda, Meryon quickly established himself as a medic for the wealthier families. The successful recovery of a Danish baron who was visiting a minor Pasha secured his reputation and his Turkish patient list grew rapidly. Meryon secured Hester's invitation into the homes of several prominent men, and she discovered that, as a westerner, she was in no way bound by the strict codes of dress and segregation to which local women were forced to adhere. Freed both from the restrictions of eastern society as well as from the proprieties of her own, Hester was able to enjoy the company of men and women equally.

Buoyed by her brief but successful forays into Constantinople society, Hester invited the Captain Pacha, Hafiz Ali, along with several other influential neigbours, to dine at her home, donning, in what was her first gesture at adopting local dress, a sash and sword in their honour. They responded enthusiastically, attempting to eat with a knife and fork – the Eastern custom was to eat with the right hand – and drinking wine, usually forbidden by the Islamic religion, with their meal. In a reciprocal gesture the Captain Pacha invited Hester and Meryon on a tour of one of the ships of the Turkish fleet. There was a condition attached: Hester could not appear in female dress before the crew and would need to wear male military clothing. For the first time, Hester dressed as a man. With a great deal of enthusiasm and excitement she put on a big pair of overalls, a military greatcoat and a dashing cocked hat; the Turks loved her. While Canning, scandalized by what he saw as a huge breach of convention, muttered his disapproval to anyone who would listen, Hester revelled in the attention, declaring the ship wonderful and the Pasha to be 'a very handsome, agreeable man'.

The mild weather of early winter finally gave way to a terrible, bitterly cold March. Snow fell heavily and incessantly, and the house at Therapia, which had been so perfect in the warm days, proved to be draughty and impossible to heat. Hester developed a nasty, hacking cough, spending most of her time in bed while Meryon ministered to her. She was still recovering when Michael and Sligo, the latter en route to Malta, briefly, returned. In Britain, Hester had frequently visited the spa at Bath whenever her health failed and was as great a believer in water cures as her uncle had been. On his return journey Michael had visited Brusa, a nearby town renowned for the medical benefits of its sulphurous springs. When he saw, and more importantly heard, Hester's racking cough, he immediately decided that the group should relocate there to see if it would benefit her.

Meryon, equally solicitous of Hester, immediately set about making local enquiries and discovered that, while the waters were indeed excellent for the constitution, Brusa was likely to be very short on accommodation suitable for someone of Hester's rank. The only sensible idea seemed to be for Meryon to travel ahead and check out what was available and, if successful, make suitable arrangements. The severity of winter was followed by an intensely hot spring, necessitating night travel to avoid the high temperatures of the day, so late in the evening of 1 May Meryon set off by barge for Mudania, where there were post horses to continue on to Brusa. One of Meryon's patients had given him an introduction to a French silk merchant, M. Arles, and Meryon lodged with him and his family while he scoured the area for suitable rooms. On the sloping sides of Mt Olympus he found exactly what he was looking for: three small cottages, simple but immaculate, with lovely views of the Vale of Brusa and the baths. Hester was as delighted with them as Meryon and found the situation of Brusa perfectly idyllic, surrounded as it was by walnut, chestnut, fig and cherry trees, with fresh water springs running from the mountain in tiny waterfalls, fed by the early spring melting of the summit snow. The streets of the city itself were less perfect, suffering from the filth they had found in Constantinople and the putrid stink caused by the lack of gutters, which caused the roads to ooze with thick foul mud.

Life in Brusa proved to be a return to the halcyon days Hester and Michael enjoyed before Crauford's letters. Time apart had benefited the relationship and the couple settled quickly and happily. For once Hester found some female company that she enjoyed, that of Mlle Arles, the daughter of the silk merchant, who spoke perfect Turkish and was happy to act as an interpreter so that Hester could meet illustrious local families. The question of Hester's gender became a topic of much speculation and debate amongst the townspeople. Her height was unusual for a woman and her European dress looked much like a longer version of the skirts worn by Turkish pageboys. Strangest of all to the Turks she rode side saddle, as did all female Europeans, and not astride as eastern women did. The curiosity of the Turks was finally satisfied when Hester, finding an initial experience much to her liking, became a daily visitor to the hamam. The hamam was, and still is, an eastern ritual. Now, as then, most hamam have separate days for women and men to bathe. Usually housed in ornate domed marble buildings, visits to the hamam were the social highlight of the week. The process involved taking several baths and entering various rooms of different temperatures – hot sulphur tubs were followed by cool marble rooms and steamy enclosures. Hester would leave Michael early in the afternoon and go off on horseback, joining a group of around fifty local women. The women were like gaudy, sparkling butterflies, wearing layer upon layer of bright diaphanous clothes and heavy jewels and ornaments beneath their *ferigees*. When they bathed the clothing came off, although, much to Hester's amusement, the rings, bangles and beads of gold and silver remained. She admired the natural grace with which the women seemed to move, finding it in complete contrast to the rigid elegance she had grown up with and found so difficult. Delighted by the way they braided each other's hair with fresh flowers and ate and chatted, she wrote to General Oakes, 'How beautiful are these Asiatic women!'[26]

However, Hester was less enthusiastic about eastern harems. Intrigued by Mary Wortley Montagu's description of a typical Turkish harem, she managed to secure an invitation through one of the women she bathed with. Unlike Lady Montagu, she did not admire the cloistered, opulent lives of the occupants. While she did think highly of their good natures and generosity, she was disgusted by the way they entertained each other with erotic dances in scanty clothes. But in her correspondence she was explicit that her disapproval was not of their blatant sexuality but of what she felt was the inherent lesbianism. For Hester, sexual arousal between two women was an aberration and passions should only be excited 'by that which God created for the purpose, *a man*'.[27]

Meryon was enjoying Brusa too. Hester was pleased with the houses he had found and on one occasion even admired his skill as a horseman. On the outskirts of the town twenty beautiful horses grazed. They were the property of a deposed Pasha who lived in the city and were hobbled together tightly by the forelocks in a manner common in the East but which Hester openly condemned as ridiculous and cruel. Tired of the poor quality of local riding horses, Hester decided to buy one for a mount. The stallion she chose was high and skittish and, when he was unfettered at her request, he immediately reared so that his Egyptian groom refused to try to mount him. Hester's only companion on the shopping expedition was Meryon and turning to him she asked if he would mind 'venturing his neck'. With his heart in his mouth, Meryon dutifully tried to mount the horse, which immediately became nettled and tried to throw him. But he persisted, earning Hester's respect, and in quarter of an hour the horse settled and proved itself to be an excellent mount with 'the temerity of a lamb'.[28]

Not long after this, Meryon left the group to return to Therapia. The lease on the house there had expired and an alternative had to be found for their return to Constantinople. Finding new accommodation was not easy; while they had been staying in Brusa a terrible fire had burned most of Pera, including their first residence, to the ground; the victims of the blaze had taken up all the available lodgings. Making enquiries of his former patients, Meryon learned of a village, just three miles south of the city centre, called Bebec. With an almost exclusively Turkish population, Meryon knew it had a good chance of meeting with Hester's approval, so when he found a roomy house with its own marble bath he immediately procured it for the group. Bebec was less oppressively hot than Therapia and, just as Meryon had thought, Hester was delighted to be away from Canning's English social circle.

They were still settling into their Bebec home when Michael received a letter from Sligo. It said that he was trying to find enough time to have 'a long conversation with the General on the subject of Lady Hester and you' but kept being 'interrupted in the middle of it'.[29] Only three days later, a letter from General Oakes confirmed that Sligo had finally discussed the situation with him. Hester's judgement of the General's friendship was not misplaced; he did not moralize and was deeply worried about the 'trouble and distress' that the 'Prejudices of the World' might bring upon the couple.[30] He offered to be of any service that he could. Furthermore, he vowed that it would give him pleasure to promote their 'comfort and happiness'. He asked Hester to reconsider Michael's offer of marriage, feeling that although it might limit his progression within some English society, her reputation would be saved. Hester was grateful for his support but adamant about her decision. She replied:

> I know how to make the best of my situation, and have sense and feeling enough never to wish to force myself forward as to make it at all awkward to him; all the society I want is that which, if I had been nobody, I could equally have enjoyed – a few of his men friends and those of my own, who this nor any other imprudence would not have deprived me of.[31]

General Oakes warned her that he knew that James was resolute in his disapproval of the match; Hester, furious at her brother's lack of understanding, and seeing the same ingratitude she so despised in Mahon, wrote that she would not allow him to harass her further:

> If he chooses to act as a brother towards me in private, it is all very well; if not, I shall never cease to pray for his welfare, but I can never see him again, nor will I allow him to torment me by letter.[32]

Given the situation, returning to England was impossible for Hester and Michael if they were to continue their affair. Remaining in Constantinople for another winter, when Hester's health had suffered so badly the previous one, was also out of the question, so plans for the next journey took up most of the summer. Hester and Michael reconsidered their plan to try to acquire French passports with the aim of travelling overland and spending time at Napoleon's court. Employing a combination of charm and outright arrogance, Hester asked the French chargé d'affaires, M. Mauburg, to help them to procure passports. As it was forbidden by French law for citizens from countries at war with each other to converse at all, her request was the beginning of a clandestine intrigue. Late at night, sometimes even in the small hours of the morning, Hester, usually accompanied by Meryon or Michael, took a boat across to the Asiatic side of the Bosphorus, where she held illicit meetings with the young and inexperienced Frenchman. Unfortunately for their plans, Stratford Canning heard a rumour about the night-time encounters and sent his spies to watch Hester's movements. Catching them deep in discussion, the spy was able to report back to Canning that Hester hoped soon to have her passport for the South of France.

Uninvited and unannounced, Canning arrived at Bebec, only to leave in an abject rage just half an hour later and immediately issue orders that the British Embassy was to be shut against Hester and her companions. Hester's first and only real concern after he had gone, sure that her antecedents would guarantee her own patriotism, was for her dependants. She summoned Meryon to her main reception room and invited him to sit down. She knew that he was willing, and indeed keen, to accompany her to France, but by doing so he might be prohibited from returning to England. Her own position was clear to her: she no longer had any motivation or desire to return, no friends or family whom she was afraid to be indefinitely separated from. However, Meryon had family, friends and a career to develop, so exile was unthinkable; she wanted him to reconsider and perhaps go home. It was only with a good deal of reluctance that Meryon agreed to think it over and, when he wrote to his parents that he might return sooner than he expected, his letter was tinged with regret and disappointment. Meryon was in a quandary. Hester had not bargained on one thing: his attachment to France, the country of his ancestors, was almost as great as his love of England; when coupled with his wish to remain in Hester's service, there was no real choice to make. Over the ensuing days, Meryon persuaded Hester of his true wish to accompany her, no matter what the consequences, and finally she acqui-esced. But Hester did not forgive Canning for his interference, livid at what she saw as the presumptuous behaviour of someone who was not an aristocrat and therefore had no right to challenge her. She wrote to Arthur Wellesley to complain. With characteristic forthrightness she also sent a copy of the letter to Canning himself. His response was exactly what she expected; he was mortified, particularly by her final quip where she suggested his ideal role might be as 'Commander-in-Chief at Home and Ambassador Extraordinary to the various societies for the suppres-sion of vice and cultivation of patriotism'.[33]

While Hester and Michael had some minor worries about any reper-cussions there might be in England, Wellesley dismissed the whole matter as trivial bickering between bored expatriates, endorsing Hester's letter of complaint: 'Answer: none required.' A greater hindrance to their plans than Canning, but possibly not unrelated, was the lack of response from France. A mild upset stomach of Michael's became acute and he suffered from persistent diarrhoea, which Hester attributed to Constantinople's general lack of sanitation. Winter was once again drawing closer, and Hester decided that they could wait for the French no longer; they would go to Egypt instead. With the abandonment of the plan, cordial if not amicable relations with Canning were restored, a recovery from which Hester would benefit twice in the coming years. Both Meryon and Hester advised the Pasha that they were soon to depart, prompting him to arrange a private meeting with Meryon. Much to the doctor's surprise, the Pasha asked him if he might ask for Hester's hand in marriage. Hester, while admitting that she was pleased, graciously refused the offer.

7

Change and Beginnings

I can assure you that if I ever looked well in anything
it is in the Asiatic dress.
Lady Hester

A Druse Holy Man

By the morning of 27 October 1811, Hester completed the arrangements necessary for them to leave Constantinople. Accompanied by Michael, Meryon and a small retinue of servants, she boarded a boat and set course for Alexandria. She had hired a small boat called a caique, a vessel built for lightness and speed. Caiques sit shallow on the water but sink farther in with the weight of the cargo they are designed to carry; their decks are wide and galleys consequently spacious, but the lack of depth brings a propensity to roll in rough seas (all facts which would be of serious import in the coming days).[1]

Hester conducted the preparations for the trip with her usual precision. In the days before the voyage she was a familiar and formidable figure on the quay, striding purposefully around neighbouring vessels, dressed as for a Georgian dinner party, giving orders and highly detailed instructions. The boat was again dirty and uncomfortable, and Hester set about engineering its refit. She ordered that the interior be whitewashed and arranged for partitions to be made to create separate, and appropriate, living spaces for the people on board; she also ensured that all the trunks were bound with tight cords and all their keys labelled. Copious amounts of food and fresh water were loaded and a flask of fine wine placed in Hester's cabin for her enjoyment at dinner. Each detail was personally dealt with and meticulously carried out in a way that reminded Meryon of his father.[2]

In spite of all the careful preparations, the journey did not begin well; contrary winds saw the caique beached both at Prince's Island and at Chios. The brief landing at Chios brought surprising pleasure, the travellers delighted by the beauty of the countryside and what Meryon described as 'the vivacity of the inhabitants'.[3] The group spent ten days on the island. Hester enjoyed the silver cliffs and improbable medieval villages that seemed to tumble down the craggy hillsides. Meryon, as usual, enjoyed the friendliness of the local women. After the weather had picked up, Hester was reluctant to leave and tried to persuade the others to stay a little longer, but the captain was anxious to reach his destination and his urgency, reinforced by gentle winds and blue skies, prevailed.

It was a pleasantly uneventful leg of the voyage, although Hester's seasickness flared up. Winds were southerly and the climate was dry and mild, so that, by Saturday 23 November, they were able to stop in Rhodes for a few hours to take in water and fresh bread. Hester vacillated between her wish to spend a few days on Rhodes and her longing to have her seasickness over and done with once and for all. So, urged on by the captain and his confidence in the weather, they set sail. Rhodes is the last point of land between the Aegean Sea and Egypt. The distance to Egypt is only three hundred miles, and the party had the expectation, given the favourable conditions, of arriving in less than a couple of weeks. However, the clement weather saw them only halfway through their journey. The wind changed first from south to north, 'which was against them', and then 'became very violent with a tremendous sea'.[4] Rather than fight nature, the captain changed course and attempted to go back to Rhodes. The return journey was easy, with the same wind they had struggled against now assisting them. Within five days their fortune reversed again as the caique was tossed by heavy seas and violent winds. Even more alarmingly, the boat sprung a leak and the hold began to fill with water. The captain found that despite all best efforts water could not be pumped off the boat. Meryon later recalled, 'It is seldom that Levantine ships have pumps, or, when they have, they are so little use as to be found unserviceable when wanted; and such was the case with ours.'[5] All of the sailors and the men on board, Michael and Meryon included, began bailing with buckets at every hatch. Thrown about by the sea, praying for a change in weather, for four and a half hours the men struggled with the rising water.[6]

Hester behaved heroically. Despite her dubious health she dressed herself while asking her maid to make up a small box of her most precious belongings. From her cabin, she produced a small cask of wine, which she proceeded to serve personally to the men during their labours. Michael, with a renewal of his intense passion and admiration for her, told his father how it would be impossible for him to do justice to 'the coolness and intrepidity displayed by her' at this time. Hester braved the elements raging across the deck while passing her best crystal glasses filled with Turkish wine to sailors and companions in the midst of their battle against the sea.

Exhausted and lost, the crew of the caique did not sight land until after midnight. By this time the fight against the flood was all but over and the ship was swamped. Rather than run the risk of being swept past the coast or sinking before they could reach it, the captain gave the order to abandon the caique for the longboat. In the pitch-black and angry water, with the deafening noise of the incessant rain, it seemed they were about to die. Of the twenty-five people on board most panicked: hysterical servants screamed and cried out, and even hardened sailors fell to their knees praying for deliverance, invoking the Virgin Mary with cries of 'Panagia mon, Panagia mon'. This was a dangerous group for a small lifeboat, but even in the chaos Hester acted with a good deal of spirit and dignity. She urged the group to abandon all luggage; she herself retained only a tiny box in which she kept some mementoes of her Uncle William, her dead brother, Charles's hair and the glove, carried to Montagu Square from the battlefields of Corunna, stained with the blood of John Moore. All of the jewellery and clothes that she had brought from London when she first left more than a year ago, and all that she had since acquired, went down with the boat. She showed no sign of fear or sadness at her loss when she was carried onto the lifeboat. Only the drowning of a small dog, whom she subsequently referred to as 'her treasure', far too distressed to jump from one boat to another, caused her to lose her composure and she cried out when it refused to come on board and was abandoned to its fate.

Yet land was half a mile away. Still fighting the swell, the sailors managed to row to it and scramble ashore. Hester and Michael hoped this was Rhodes, but it was just a rocky outpost completely surrounded by water. Hester and her maid were carried to a cave well above the waterline in the cleft of a rock, while the rest of the group remained together below, barely managing to secure the boat. Fatigue was their most 'urgent sensation' and they composed themselves 'in our wet clothes to sleep'. The company woke gradually from their exhausted oblivion at first light to find the storm somewhat abated and frantically argued as to how to proceed. The situation was dire. In their haste they had brought neither food nor water and the rocky island was without both. Hester's ailing constitution was sorely weakened by this time (Michael would write to his father that her health had been so afflicted by the disaster that he was scared he might lose her) so she readily agreed to a party of sailors and the captain sailing out in the longboat to get help. The remaining survivors waited on the rock, increasingly sceptical as to whether their would-be rescuers would return. Michael later recalled:

> We were exposed to all the horrors of famine – for we were landed upon a barren and desolate rock without a morsel of bread or a drop of water, and in this situation we remained nearly thirty hours.[7]

The English people regretted not sending one of their number with the longboat and peered out over the horizon anxiously throughout the day until sunset when, at last, they saw the returning boat. The arriving rescue party no longer had the captain with them, for he had refused to make a return trip, and it was apparent that they had celebrated their own escape with a little too much arak. Fortunately, they still had the foresight to bring some much needed food and water. Hester was now very ill, and Michael urged that they stay on the rock for at least another night both so that her health might improve a little and for the crew's drunkenness to pass. But the crew was adamant; they must all leave immediately. The party was faced with the prospect of remaining abandoned on the rock and dying from thirst or being rowed by a handful of drunken Greek sailors for several hours in the darkness. They unanimously agreed they would go in the longboat, although it must have seemed barely the lesser of the two evils. It was more than four hours before they reached Rhodes, but just as the boat pulled into shore a large wave swept over and they were swamped and staved. The travellers were stranded once again. They found themselves on a bare and stony shore; the only visible shelter was a deserted windmill. The men took some shelter among some rocks, while Hester settled down in the mill with Mrs Fry, her English maid, on a bed of straw. The large rats, which completely overran the dilapidated building, proved too terrifying for the old woman and she left the mill to join the men outdoors, whilst Hester, refusing to be outdone by some vermin, remained 'huddled in a corner' alone.[8]

This was to be the end of the drama, and the next morning they proceeded to a village further up the coast where everyone was able to rest and recuperate. A local chief gave £30 to help them out, while Meryon was dispatched to Smyrna with drafts for £500 from Hester to her London bank so that they could acquire medicines and other essentials. Stratford Canning, in spite of the tension that had previously existed between them, also gave considerable financial help. Sixteen years later Hester would still recall his 'kindness after the shipwreck' when she once again asked him for help.[9]

Having lost all their belongings the party had to find a way to clothe themselves, and it was at a somewhat recovered Hester's insistence that the party were urged to adorn themselves with Turkish dress, which she acquired from a local outfitter. Wearing Turkish women's dress was out of the question as far as Hester was concerned because it meant she would have to be veiled, so a male costume was ordered.

Michael and Hester adopted the new outfits, but the servants rebelled and many of them left the entourage as soon as they were able. Hester donned pantaloons richly embroidered in gold, a silk and cotton shirt with a striped silk and cotton waistcoat, Turkish boots and a colourful sash into which went a pair of pistols and a sabre. This dashing ensemble was completed with a turban worn at a jaunty angle with a large bunch of fresh flowers at the side. Enchanted by her new appearance she wrote to General Oakes: 'I can assure you that if I ever looked well in anything it is in the Asiatic dress.'[10]

Obviously she enjoyed the freedom of movement, the loose comfort of the flowing fabrics and the ease with which she could now ride and move. Hester, whose figure had been so punished by her governess in the interests of fashion, was never to wear the whale rib corsetry, the long, heavy silks and brocades of her sex and culture again. More than a little proud of her demeanour during the whole shipwreck adventure, Hester wrote:

> Could the fashionables I once associated with believe that I could have sufficient composure of mind to have given my orders as distinctly and as positively as if I had been sitting in the midst of them.[11]

Hester established herself at Trianda, three miles outside Rhodes town. The town was a busy and wealthy port, a regular stop on journeys to and from Egypt. Hester did not like it, but she loved the surrounding countryside and the idyllic nature she found in the gentle, fertile hillsides beside the blue-green of the Aegean. Meryon, for his part, found the island amongst the most picturesque he had seen and spent considerable time wandering around the medieval city, with its ancient street of the Knights of St John of Jerusalem and the huge stone balls that were a silent testament to the din and violence of the Turkish siege, making notes for a journal he had started keeping.

In the months after the shipwreck, Hester began to travel the tourist trail in earnest from the Egyptian pyramids to the sites of the Holy Land. Restless and exiled from many of the other English aristocrats by the blatancy of their affair and the scandal that could consequently dog Michael on his return home, they led their group from place to place. Hester's promise to Crauford that she would keep away from 'respectable' women was ever present in her mind. The shipwreck had brought them close to death and Hester, while honouring her lover's father, was now going to live all she could. What little there was in Hester of nicety and propriety died in the water with the wreck. The change of costume, which began as a temporary convenience, was to herald the beginning of a new identity. Hester discovered that her outfit's liberty of movement was matched by the freedom of passage and the acceptance that its very conspicuousness afforded her. The great eastern men she met had no preconceptions as to how to react to something as exotic as a western woman in man's clothes; the result was they accepted her on her own terms.

The sheer charm of the onward sail from Rhodes went some way towards dispelling the horror of the shipwreck. The *Salsette* was under the agreeable command of Commander Hope, who, hearing of Hester's predicament, had chivalrously offered the whole party passage on his frigate. Hester was delighted by the excellence of the vessel and, enchanted by her rescuer, nicknamed him 'Chivalry Hope'. But Hester was discontented with her new destination; she hated Alexandria, describing it as hideous, although not as bad as their next stop, Rosetta, which was plagued by an 'inconceivable number of fleas' that infested every building and tormented the travellers incessantly, day and night, biting them and leaping over their clothes and skin.[12] So, weary, scratching and sore, they left precipitously for Cairo in Nile barques, beautiful carved and gilded boats, some with a single lateen sail, some with two or three, billowing above tiny, intricately decorated cabins. For three days they languished in these dragonfly vessels, at last enjoying the sensation of travel for its own sake again.

They entered Cairo on donkeys, packed up and tacked with local saddles made not of leather but of a webbed material with dashing bronze stirrups and reins of tasselled silk. The whole party were still dressed in their post-storm extravagance of striped silks and jewel-like colours. Yet the splendour of their caravan was easily outshone by the first cavalcade they passed, which Hester declared to be the grandest, most extravagantly dressed she had ever seen. It was the Pasha of Egypt with his colourful retinue; he was returning to his palace from a ride. The native ass-drivers begged the English party to dismount as a mark of respect, but Hester, not happy about being given orders by her servants, refused. The Pasha, Mehmet Ali, said nothing and passed by, and the travellers continued towards their lodgings, their servants muttering about possible repercussions. Michael and Hester installed themselves in a town house, while Meryon found rooms in an Italian merchant's home, where he stayed with the merchant and his mistress, a black slave.

The Pasha was one of the most powerful figures in the East and it was clear to Hester that she needed to present herself to him. Mehmet Ali was neither Egyptian nor Arab but had been born in the now Greek town of Kavala to a family of Albanian shopkeepers. His education was basic, but practical. Married at eighteen, his first wife not only mothered the first five of his ninety-five children but also provided the fortune that enabled him to trade on his own.[13] He did not join the Turkish army until he was thirty, yet in a short time he had reached the rank of officer. In 1801 he successfully drove out the French soldiers left by Napoleon after his defeat by Nelson in the Battle of the Nile; within a few years he was appointed as the Sultan's viceroy, the Pasha of all Egypt. Egypt had long been part of the Ottoman Empire but power was largely controlled by the Mamelukes, a people descended from the Turkish slaves of Egypt's Ayubid sultan in early medieval times. In order to realize the potential of the power afforded by his position, the Pasha knew that he would have to destroy them. He invited all the leading men of the faction to a banquet in honour of his new position, surrounded the city walls with his troops and, as soon as the visitors had gathered, massacred every single one of them.

Hester was unperturbed by the Pasha's bloodthirsty reputation and her first concern was to put together a costume that she could wear to visit him. There was no restriction on the kind of dress available in Cairo and Hester could have ordered a European gown had she so wished. Instead she chose spectacular Tunisian dress: purple velvet pantaloons, richly embroidered with gold, a matching waistcoat and pelisse, and two cashmere shawls, one to wear as a turban and one as a girdle. The turban necessitated yet another, even more dramatic, change in Hester's appearance, as long hair made it impossible to wear properly. Hester not only cut her hair, which hung around her shoulders in keeping with contemporary western fashion, but shaved her head, so she became totally bald in emulation of eastern men. Michael's outfit was equally dramatic and, happy they would make the desired impact, they sent word to the Pasha of their intent to visit. The Pasha, impressed by this woman of obvious rank and intrigued by the combination of decidedly feminine, if foreign, features with masculine dress, responded by sending five fantastically caparisoned horses to bring her to a pavilion of the harem garden, a sumptuous room where the Pasha reclined on a scarlet and gold divan. Eastern traditions of hospitality were observed and Hester and Michael were offered pale green sherbet and coffee, which they accepted, and a narghileh, which Hester refused as she didn't yet know how to smoke.

Mehmet Ali was a small, middle-aged man whose own dress belied his importance and was overshadowed by his guests, but he was taken with Hester and made her a present of one of his own horses.[14] During her short stay Hester continued to keep company with Ali, riding with him and talking to him for hours at a time. It was a relationship that would last far beyond their weeks in Cairo.

A tour of the pyramids was essential for any English travellers in Egypt. Michael, Hester and Meryon joined up with her cousin, Henry Wynn,[15] who had arrived in Cairo with only two companions, a servant and a dragoman, having crossed the desert from Gaza so he and Hester could make the trip together. Leaving Cairo with laden camels, they reached the east bank of the Nile and the old ruined city by dusk. Hester was exhausted and retired with Michael as soon as they had eaten, but the remaining young men of the party, eager for an evening of entertainment, ordered some dancing girls. When they arrived, the girls seemed reluctant to entertain the eager Englishmen, and Meryon suggested plying them with alcohol. It had the desired effect; the semi-naked women danced with a lot more verve than grace, as Meryon later commented, but still to the men's enjoyment. While ogling the girls, who were barely covered by their scanty veils, the men discussed the lack of corsetry and stays in female eastern dress; how, contrary to common opinion in England, the eastern girls' figures were none the worse for it. It was a subdued group of hungover Englishmen that met with Michael the following day, ready to explore the ancient monuments while Hester remained indoors.

The party's travel difficulties had not ended with the shipwreck. During their return to Cairo, Hester, Michael, Meryon and Wynn took a small, decidedly shabby-looking boat, rowed by a single man, to make the necessary Nile crossing. They only made it halfway across. A plank from the bottom of the boat gave way and, in a miniature parody of their earlier disaster, water – thick, muddy, Nile water – rushed in. Only Wynn's servant, George, had the presence of mind to act quickly. Grabbing his turban from his head, he hurriedly stuffed it into the leak; then, pushing his fist in the face of the very frightened boatman, told him that, if he didn't row with all his might, he would kill him with his bare hands. It was just the encouragement the man needed and he began to row frantically. On arriving at the shore, George pulled out his turban, and in a second the boat sank. Wynn was shaken by the whole experience, sufficiently so that he left Cairo soon afterwards to return to England.

It was another bad incident in a stage of the trip that Hester was finding less and less enjoyable. She was not impressed by the pyramids and Egypt was a disappointment; her friendship with Mehmet Ali was the only good thing that had come from their visit. It was time to travel on. The next leg of the trip was motivated by discontentment but also by a youthful memory of a prophecy, at this point something she took no more seriously than a joke, which would ultimately change the course of her life just as drastically as the shipwreck had done.

∽

Seventeen years earlier, in 1795, London society gossip was filled with stories of Richard Brothers, the prophet. Brothers had been a lieutenant in the

King's navy for many years. On returning to London he claimed to be visited by visions and voices convincing him that he was a messenger of God. However, he was not consigned to the lunatic asylum; his charisma along with the occasional germs of truth in his predictions made his small house in Paddington Street one of the most popular haunts of society men and women. He held an almost daily morning salon where even members of parliament, drawn by a mixture of curiosity and belief, visited him.[16] As well as aristocratic consultees, Brothers had a staunch band of followers, each of whom testified to the divinity and veracity of his proclamations. Most of these devotees were active republicans, many of whom admired Earl Stanhope, Hester's father, for his views. One young, fair-haired woman follower called Sarah Flaxmer even stalked Stanhope, listening to his speeches in the Commons and trying to gain admittance to his Mansfield Street home.

By March, Brothers was too fashionable, and too militant, to be allowed his freedom any longer; he was arrested under warranty from the state 'on suspicion of treasonable practices' and following proceedings at the Kings Arms Tavern, in Palace Yard, was put in custody.[17] Pitt was among the people who examined him, and at some point Brothers asked to see his niece, saying he had important information for her. Pitt probably told Hester about the request, although it was not until later that Brothers and Hester actually met. Meanwhile, Brothers' disciple Flaxmer published a pamphlet called 'Satan Revealed' which used Brothers' visions as a means of interpreting the twelfth book of Revelations. Central to Flaxmer's prophecy was a powerful woman, 'a woman clothed with the sun'; she would be the 'Female leader of the twelve tribes of Jerusalem'.[18]

In early May the government chose not to detain Brothers for treason but, instead, to proclaim him insane and have him committed to Bedlam.[19] And it was amidst the cacophony of Bedlam that Hester met the man who had a prophecy for her. Echoing the words of Flaxmer, but relating the prophecy to Hester herself, Brothers told her she would one day go to Jerusalem and lead the chosen people. Lady Hester Stanhope would spend seven years in the desert: she was the Queen of the Jews.

What began as a joke, a prophecy made by a madman heard in the house of the insane, would in later years become all important to Hester as she tried to fulfil the role that Brothers had defined for her.

But, in 1812, Hester's concern was more that she looked like a queen. In her horseback trek across the East, over Syria and the Holy Land, she would command a procession magnificent and unforgettable to all who saw it. Accompanied by Meryon, Michael and two Mameluke servants, given to her by the Pasha as a parting gift, as well as her small train of servants, she made yet another fundamental change in her habits: she began to ride astride in the oriental style. It was a shocking decision, something that she later and quite correctly imagined would be gossiped about in fashionable houses, where her scandalous behaviour was a favourite topic.[20] Meryon, on his return to England, wrote a book about this style of riding, mentioning Hester as the first woman he had known to deviate from the convention of a side saddle. In Cairo she bought a bridle and saddle of crimson velvet, decorated with gold thread, perfectly suited to her new style of riding, and a Turkish riding habit to match: a satin vest with long sleeves, slashed from wrist to elbow, and a red jacket and trousers ornate with gold patterns and pictures, with a turban made from a cashmere shawl. She would be the epitome of eastern style.

May was a busy time in Jaffa. It was not a big town but the new governor had done as much as he could to gentrify it. In late spring the streets were crowded with merchants trading in luxurious cloths and religious trinkets to the remaining Easter pilgrims. These pilgrims, on the whole, were poor and came into town, weary and disillusioned, on laden donkeys and mules. The British agent, Signor Damiani, greeted them on their arrival and urged them to take up his offer of hospitality. Neither Hester nor Michael was anxious to spend any longer than was necessary in the smelly, hot, busy streets. They stayed only as long as it took them to rest and re-provision, before they set off for Jerusalem, where Hester would meet the second of the powerful eastern men who would influence her life.

On the way they camped for a night, under the stars, by a small village on the outskirts of the town. Hester and Michael shared a grand marquee, said to have once been used by the Princess of Wales, while the rest of the party settled in various tents around them. The marquees were six in total, green and embroidered with flowers. The night was lovely and Meryon was enchanted; the weather was perfect, the scenery picturesque and he was living in a society that was everything he aspired to. Hester revelled in the freedom and respect she was finding in the East. Only Michael was unsettled enough to be in correspondence with his father about plans for his return to England.[21] The idylls of camping did not please them for long; the following morning they were plagued with mosquitoes, flies and fleas, engendered by neighbouring rice marshes, and quickly moved on.

The next trek was more difficult with steep and rugged mountain paths, so they did not arrive at a village until the evening. Prettily situated in a clearing amidst fig and olive trees, the only entry to Jerusalem was by way of a path that meandered through it. Consequently, the local sheikh made it his business to extract a toll from passing pilgrims. Abu Ghosh had a fiercesome reputation but, curious at the eccentric European who rode in such finery and no doubt associating her with greater opportunity for extortion, he greeted the travellers warmly and slaughtered a sheep in their honour. Ghosh was pleasantly surprised by the education and rank of his guests, and his wives cooked a feast of dolmades – vine leaves wrapped around minced lamb – marrow stuffed with rice and a dish of rice with chicken and spices.

In spite of the hospitality the Mameluke servants were wary; they had heard many stories of Ghosh and their experience of the Turks was rife with treachery and dishonesty. Selim, one of the Mamelukes, said that it wasn't sensible to rest without guards when it was clear that Ghosh's men were obsessed with the vast wealth they thought was in their trunks. Hester, while accepting that Selim might be right, decided that the best way to circumvent the risk was to ask Abu Ghosh himself for guards, so that he would be honour-bound to ensure their safety. It was a ploy that she would use again, buoyed by its success on this first occasion; Ghosh himself sat up with his men around a fire while Hester's party slept. In the morning they paid his men and gave him a gift, parting the best of friends and with Ghosh's brother as guide and protector to accompany them on the final stretch to Jerusalem.

It was an amusing trip. Hester jokingly recalled Brothers' prophecy and was hailed as Queen of the Jews by her companions. She laughed out loud and said that she now had so much faith in the prophecy that she expected the rest of it to come true. As they approached the city their amusement gave way to silent awe. For miles there had been nothing but bare, craggy mountains and desolate views, and now, before them, was the walled city, standing as if completely isolated from the world around it. Entering by Bethlehem Gate they arrived at the Franciscan monastery, where the men stayed while Hester was settled in an adjoining house. Both places were far from comfortable, being flea-ridden and dirty, but there was no alternative to be found, so they resigned themselves to spend the whole of the first day trying to make them as habitable as possible.

The promise of the approach was disappointed soon after their arrival when they found that Jerusalem, far from being a place of holiness and reflection, seemed little more than a market filled with peddlers constantly trying to push their wares, vying with each other to get the most custom. But somewhere amidst the merchants and their rivalry was a man Hester wanted to meet: the Bey of Mamelukes, Ishmael.

Ishmael Bey was the only survivor of the Mameluke massacre that her new friend from Cairo, the Pasha of Egypt, had perpetrated. On seeing the city walls surrounded by the Pasha's men he had galloped on his horse to a platform surrounded by a wall. This platform looked down on open space, a good distance below at the foot of the castle mound. He charged his stallion at the citadel wall, the horse took the jump and miraculously landed safely. In disguise, he flew across the desert, was robbed and left for dead, but nevertheless found his way to Jerusalem, where he threw himself on the mercy of the Pasha of Acre, Suleyman Pasha, the sworn enemy of Mehmet Ali and another man who would come to have an important role in Hester's life. The Pasha of Acre gave him sanctuary but little else. He was destitute, still suffering from the wounds of a beating in a hovel in the city, but Hester gave him money and offered Meryon's services. He was grateful and Hester formed an alliance with him, as strong as the one she had made in Cairo with his arch enemy.

By the end of their stay, the party were weary of the heat and of each other's company. The truce that had existed between Meryon and Michael since their time in Malta came to an end and they began to bicker again. Michael was given to fits of temper at the servants which, at times, Meryon thought were unprovoked and needless; yet Hester, much to his dismay, seemed completely oblivious to her beloved's faults. Meryon was wrong about Hester, and her letters to Crauford in the preceding months

show that she was all too well aware of Michael's temper and 'unconcili-
ating manners'.[22]

The cacophony of the streetsellers, the fairground of sites where they
were given the chance to see an impression of the virgin's foot or an
impression left by the sleeping Elijah, and the crowds of beggars that followed wherever they went left them disgusted and disappointed. Relations in the party deteriorated still further; Hester's increasing unease
with Michael was not helped by fact that the proprieties of the town
forced them to sleep apart, and Michael's warring relationship with
Meryon worsened as they were compelled to lodge together. Moving
seemed the only way to escape and by the end of May they were packed
up once again, travelling to Acre. The journey was long, hot and uneventful. En route Hester received an invitation from an Acre gentleman called
Catafagio to be a guest in his beautiful house on a quadrangular courtyard shaded by matting, one of the best in Acre.

Encouraged by her success with Mehmet Ali, and curious to meet the
man her new friend so despised, Hester visited the Pasha of Acre, who,
perhaps in competition with his enemy, promptly made her a gift of a
beautiful, grey stallion.[23] The Pasha's minister, a horribly mutilated man
missing part of his nose, an ear and his left eye, also befriended Hester
and presented her with a cashmere shawl. But he was not the only person
in Acre with hideous and painful injuries; the previous Pasha, Djezzar,
was renowned for his cruelty. Suleyman's minister had also been Djezzar's
minister until, in a fit of cruelty, Djezzar had ordered that he be mutilated.
Djezzar then put the poor, pleading man into an oven where he half
baked him; horribly burned and choking, he was led out to a scaffold and
had a halter fastened round his neck. The minister begged and pleaded
for his life, saying that he would gain many, many thousands of pounds
for Djezzar if he would spare him. Djezzar's cruelty was matched by his
greed; he imprisoned the man, releasing him on a daily basis to arrange
his monetary affairs under strict guard. When Djezzar died, the new
Pasha retained the minister, restoring his liberty and the rewards that his
office carried.[24]

Catafagio, their landlord, had a country house in Nazareth and he
extended his hospitality to include it should the party wish to make the
extra trip. They did, travelling overnight to avoid the intense heat of the

day. Nazareth was arid and dusty in the early summer months; a few fig and olive trees did little to relieve the dreariness of the land. The religious sites were less commercial than those at Jerusalem and some of the surrounding villages where Catafagio took them were surprisingly green and lush. Sultry afternoons, too hot for riding, were spent indoors writing and reading. Eager to escape Hester's continued criticisms and the doctor's bickering, Michael made an independent trip to Galilee accompanied by his Mameluke servant, Joseph, but finding the heat too oppressive, passed the white-hot noon in the house of a local priest. Hearing a row outside the door and recognizing Joseph's voice, Michael stormed outside, ready to join in. He found a shabbily dressed local with a long beard insisting on speaking with 'the visiting Englishman'. Michael prepared to help Joseph get rid of the visitor but was surprised when the peasant addressed him in perfect English, introducing himself as Sheikh Ibrahim. When Michael returned to Nazareth, the Sheikh, who was really the Swiss traveller Johann Burckhardt, accompanied him. A broad-set man of medium height, his outfit of rough cotton with a woollen abbaya made him indistinguishable from the locals but, on closer inspection, the thick facial hair did not conceal Burckhardt's blue eyes and Germanic features. Hester took an immediate dislike to him, largely because he lectured her for most of the two days he stayed with them on how she should acquire various antiques, which he felt she was better able to afford than he.[25] In contrast, Burckhardt's first instinct was to respect her, and he wrote in his journal:

> The manly spirit and enlightened curiosity of this lady ought to make many modern travellers ashamed of the indolent indifference with which they hurry over foreign countries.[26]

Sadly, in spite of his travels and education, like other European expatriates he was concerned that she might like the Turks too much; he hoped that the excellent manner in which she was received would 'not impress her with too favourable an opinion of the Turks in general'. With all the limitations of his society he declared her to have 'more foibles than a lady in man's clothes should be guilty of', seemingly oblivious to the fact that Hester wasn't the only one who was dressing up.[27] Hester always admired honesty and forthrightness; many of the influential figures she had met in the months just passed, such as the Pashas of Egypt and Acre, had given her respect, even admiration. Hence Burckhardt's game of pretence, in spite of the advantage and benefits it undoubtedly gave him, just wasn't her style. Some years later she admitted that, while respecting his abilities as a traveller, she thought him 'full of envy, malice and very insincere'.[28] The encounter was brief and polite; it was only much later that a state of warfare by correspondence would exist, briefly, between the two.

The tension between Meryon and Michael continued, with Meryon increasingly finding himself to be the subject of Michael's disapproval and tantrums. He retaliated with hatred; Michael was spoiled, selfish, petty and childish, and the doctor started to wonder if he could continue on a journey of which Michael was such an integral part. But Michael's discontent was not solely for the doctor; he argued with Hester and found continual fault with the two Mameluke servants, sacking both of them in a fit of temper. In the midst of this dissension and disagreement, Hester had a riding accident. She did not fall badly but her horse bucked and came down on top of her leg. In agonizing pain and unable to move, she lay in bed, suffering from bad headaches and soaking in sweat, obsessed with leaving the oppressive heat of the Nazarene summer for cooler climes. The plan she entertained was to return to Acre and, from there, head to the mountains of the Syrian province of Sidon, travelling along the coast in order to escape the stifling Nazarene temperatures.

The region around Mount Lebanon had two attractions for Hester: it was the home of the Druse, a mysterious mountain sect in whom both she and Meryon were interested, and it was cooler, greener and better watered than the surrounding countryside. Only Michael showed any reluctance to the plan. Ultimately persuaded by the idea of a cooler climate, he capitulated, and as soon as Hester was able to ride they returned to Acre so they could make preparations to leave. Travelling by night to avoid the sun was essential, but Hester was still weakened from her accident and a single night's riding was insufficient, so it was not until twilight on the second day, greeted by crowds who had heard of the arrival of an English princess, that the splendidly caparisoned group rode into Sidon. It was absolutely beautiful. While the coast was arid, the land around was thick with banana and blackberry trees and the town gardens were green and lush, irrigated by the River Awali, which was channelled into the centre of the town. Twin castles rose in front of the mountainous landscape, one of them, the Sea Castle, detached from the main body of the land, almost appearing to float beside it, while the ruins of the ancient civilization straggled out far beyond the modern city boundaries.

The party settled themselves at the home of the French Consul, who had offered his hospitality, in the Khan Il Frange, the House of Foreigners. A calm place with gently repeating arches on two levels and a wide courtyard, it offered tranquil respite from the noise and smell of the traders and the workings of the port. Within hours Hester received an invitation that was more than even she had hoped for: she was to ride to Dayr-El-Kamar, 'The House of the Moon', on Mount Lebanon; the Emir of the Druse had invited her to be his guest.

8

Triumph and Belonging

Now upon Syria's land of roses
Softly the light of Eve reposes
And, like a glory, the broad sun
Hangs over sainted Lebanon
Whose head in wintry grandeur towers
And whitens with eternal sleet
While summer in a vale of flowers
Is sleeping rosy at his feet.
Thomas Moore, 'Lalla Rookh', 1817

Mar Elias

THE DRUSE SECT, with which Hester's life would become so implicated, has inhabited Mount Lebanon since the eleventh century. Today, there are around one million Druse, living mainly in the Lebanon and Syria, but with smaller communities in Israel and Jordan. Easily distinguished by the traditional costume some Druse choose to wear, they are welcoming and generous to visitors to their regions. Yet it is still an extremely closed religion which forbids conversion, either to or away, and intermarriage with any other faith. Originally developed from Muslim Ismaili teaching, the fundamental tenet of the religion is belief in Al Hakim, an eleventh-century caliph, as a manifestation of God. Much of the religion is secret, hidden not only historically from the Turks, who were seen as persecutors, but also from the majority of their own followers: the *juhhal*, or 'the ignorant'. Only the *uqqal*, or 'the knowing', participate fully in services and have an understanding of the teachings of the *hikma*, the Druse religious doctrine. One of the main dogmas of the faith is metempsychoses: transmigration of the soul exclusively from human body to human body – not animals as in many other religions – of either sex; it is the work of the soul 'to react properly to any temptation its current body is subjected to'.[1] A consequence of this was that in the early nineteenth century the status of women in their community was completely unique in the East. Druse women were able to own and inherit property, to become *uqqal*, as well as to hold positions of secular importance. A contemporary of Hester's, Hubus Arslan, dominated her clan 'to the exclusion of several Arslan emirs qualified to occupy the position'.[2] Writing not long after Hester's death, an English soldier, who had lived in the region for ten years, would declare:

Indeed there are some Druse ladies now in Mount Lebanon, whose wisdom, tact and discrimination are so highly prized by their immediate relations amongst the sheiks, and they too, some of the most influential leaders of the Druses, that no project would be considered complete, unless it had been submitted to their judgement and approval.[3]

The region of Mount Lebanon was not wholly Druse; it was divided into a number of feudal cantons, or *muqata'at*, managed by emirs of sheikhs of prominent families who were mainly Druse, but also Maronite, a Syrian Christian group with close ties to Rome. These village leaders had the power to settle most internal disputes and to mete out even the most severe forms of punishment; only if arguments were irresolvable were they taken to the Emir Bashir Shihab.

The Shihabs were the most important and powerful of the élite families who controlled the various factions of the region. Born into a noble Turkish family, Bashir II had gone to Dar-el-Kamar to seek his fortune at the court of his father's cousin, Emir Yusuf. Yusuf was not a popular man; he taxed highly and meted out cruel punishments to defaulters. Another prominent family, the Druse Jumblats, represented a threat to Yusuf's rule. With the Jumblats' support Bashir II crushed Yusuf and was elected to the Emirate. While the Christians regarded him as a benevolent despot, the Druse saw him as evil, merely tolerating his reign. Bashir's own religion was a question of conjecture and mystery. Circumspection about his own faith was obviously essential to ruling a multi-faith region, for in addition to the Maronites and Druse there was also a very small Shiite minority, so the Emir had both a mosque and a church in his palace. The French poet Lamartine said of the Emir that he could seem a Druse to the Druse, a Christian to the Christian and a Muslim to the Muslims. Only after his death would the surviving text of his will show that, in spite of the fact he had made no obvious demonstration of his faith, Bashir II was born, and died, a Maronite.[4]

Hester awaited the arrival of Bashir's cavalcade, which would accompany them up the mountain, and in the meantime wrote to Michael's father. She queried his long silence – neither Michael nor she realized that his letters were all being held up by the plague which was raging in Constantinople – and explained their monetary position. Hester's meagre allowance was sufficient for her to live in comfort in the East but not enough to enjoy the lavish itinerant lifestyle into which she had thrown herself. Crauford was supplying Michael with the money that was paying for their journey, and the shipwreck had meant Michael had drawn on Crauford considerably more than usual. Hester's letter was intended to circumnavigate any misgivings Crauford had about the sudden increase, as well as to stress the benefits that the influence and favour of eminent locals, often secured with presents and hospitality, might have on his son's future.

The grandeur of Bashir's travelling party stunned even Hester. Twelve camels, twenty-five mules, four horses and a private guard of seven ostentatiously uniformed soldiers were sent to accompany them on the short trip. After only a mile or so they were already at the foot of Mount Lebanon, with its crumbling, sandy soil and hot temperatures, which cooled as they climbed. Wherever possible the land was terraced for the cultivation of figs, mulberry and tobacco plants, the means by which the Druse subsisted. Where crops could not grow, goats and sheep were at pasture. It was not a difficult or remarkable journey to Dar-el-Kamar but during it Hester passed through a mountain village, one where she would spend many years of her life: Joun.

Dar-el-Kamar was not a rural backwater but the major artisanal centre for the region; shawl weaving, silk and cotton textile production were common Maronite trades, while blacksmiths, tailors and soapmakers all ran busy and lucrative businesses. It seemed a harmonious multidenominational community, with only the distinctive dress of the Druse marking them out. This was a markedly different costume from other groups in the East; the men wore a short tunic of dark green wool, patterned with stripes, often white, which met at the top in a kind of cone shape, and beneath this was a longer tunic and white cotton pants. The women commonly wore blue gowns, open in front to expose the neck and bosom, a fact which Meryon took some delight in, and carried a strange conical headdress known as the tantur, which echoed the decoration of the tunic in its shape. A kind of pointed helmet of silver or copper, covered by a veil of black or white muslin which floated behind, the tantur was also worn by Maronites. Many women never removed the tantur, not even to wash their hair, and if a Druse woman was found to be unchaste on her wedding night, the return of the headdress to her father signified that her husband had murdered her for being unsuitable and for bringing disgrace on her family.[5]

The Emir's palace was across the valley from the village itself, in Beitte-dine, and Hester's visit had been anticipated with many preparations for her comfort. To modern eyes the beautifully restored palace at Beittedine is the perfect realization of an eastern fantasy: a mirage of cool courtyards and elegant walkways through intricately decorated archways that lead to the improbably green garden with its flagrant red roses. But Meryon hated it, claiming that 'the palace is destitute of beauty', and criticized its newness and irregularity, 'built by additions made as fancy or conve-nience suggested, and money and leisure permitted'.

The Emir was a prepossessing figure, with thick eyebrows bushing out above his small piercing eyes and a massive beard, reeking of tobacco, reaching to his waist. However, Hester's initial impression, one she would come to revise drastically, was that he was 'a mild, amiable man'.[6] A devi-ous and callous politician, the Emir would later boast of how he con-trolled his subjects: 'every three or four years [the inhabitants] would rebel, although they never succeeded. I would kill, hang, imprison and beat without opposition to make them submit.'[7]

The head of the Jumblat family, the man who had helped the Emir gain his power, was also called Bashir. Together the two men had shared the expense of bringing many persecuted Druse from Aleppo to settle in the villages of the mountain in 1811. Sheikh Bashir Jumblat was the governor of the region and there was no ambiguity about his religious beliefs; a Druse by birth, he was devout in his faith and much championed by co-religionists as a result. Their support gave him a localized power equal to that of the Emir, so that both Bashir II and Jumblat treated each other with a wary respect, even addressing each other as 'brother'. With the encouragement of the Emir, Jumblat invited Hester to spend two nights at his palace in Moukhtara, just three hours from Beittedine. Smaller than Beittedine, Moukhtara's most noticeable feature was the elegantly spi-ralling twin staircases, curling up to a first-floor entrance. Even Hester was intimidated by the Sheikh, referring to him as 'a Lucifer', but she rev-elled in visiting a palace 'which has been the scene of several massacres'. His reputation was such that fears for Hester's safety controlled her visit and every morsel of food or drink she touched was first tasted by a ser-vant to see if it was poisoned.

Hester and Meryon were fascinated by the Druse. On hearing, incredulously, that they ate raw meat, Hester ordered a huge sheep and took it to a village, inviting locals to share her feast and watching, shocked, as it was killed, skinned and brought in as raw slices upon a plate. Men and women greedily grabbed pieces with their hands, devouring not only the bleeding mutton but the huge chunks of fat and gristle around it.

The Thursday night meeting of the *uqqal* was a particular topic of conjecture because the latter part of it was closed even to ordinary Druse. Maronite and Muslim villagers suspected that because the *uqqal* were of both sexes and the closed meetings therefore involved fraternization between men and women, they might be a forum for 'peculiar and dissolute practices', including 'communal sexual rituals'. Michael, although less intrigued by the sect than his companions, was interested in finding out about the meetings. The *holowe* were holy buildings, simply constructed often on the top of the highest peaks with glorious views, which hosted the meetings and provided a place to study the two main holy books of the Druse: *Copy of the Secret* and *Essence of the First*. The *holowe* were carefully guarded, and when Michael rode up, as quietly as possible, one Thursday night when it was almost dark with the intention of spying on the religious rites, he was driven away by furious Druse.

Michael, now unwelcome among the Druse, resolved to move on to Aleppo and invited Hester to accompany him. But Hester had other ideas. Aleppo was rife with a disease known as the Aleppo button, characterized by a single scabby ulcer that could appear anywhere on the body. Ugly and disfiguring, the blister itself remained for a year but left a permanent scar like a large pox mark. Still proud of her pale complexion, which she had successfully guarded from the severity of the sun, Hester lived in dread of any condition that could blemish it. Moreover, her success with the Druse had given her another idea. The Bedouin Arabs were a people swathed in a mist of similar rumour and romanticism to the Druse; she would go to Damascus and find them.

Separate trips to Damascus and Aleppo also provided a temporary solution to the situation between Michael and Meryon, which was now intolerable. Increasingly exasperated by their incessant bickering, Hester took Meryon aside after Michael's departure; she was sympathetic but firm. Conceding that Meryon was frequently provoked by Michael, she nevertheless reasoned that as Michael was her lover and his family were her friends, she would not and could not take Meryon's side. The only solution was for them to part. As Michael was in Aleppo, there was a short-term hiatus from the tension, but ultimately, inevitably, Meryon would have to leave, and with her help, recommendations and good wishes accompany another aristocratic traveller.[8] Meryon, considering his options, thought of returning to his family and resuming his medical studies. However, within less than two weeks, Hester was hesitating. Michael was still in Aleppo, so Meryon could escort her to Damascus. At this stage, anxious to retain some kind of companion, Hester urged him not to do anything in haste, to wait 'until we have seen what may turn up in the winter'.[9] The plan to go to Damascus had developed ambitiously. Perhaps with the aid of the Bedouin, or perhaps without, Hester wished to go to Palmyra, the ancient kingdom of the Syrian desert. She would be the first European woman ever to do so, but the undertaking would be neither easy nor cheap.

With the latter difficulty in mind, she once again wrote to Michael's father, tentatively mentioning her idea, carefully broaching the possibility of the 'great expense' it might entail and deviously justifying it as necessary to secure both the security of his son and her own.[10] Ever anxious to secure support from the highest source possible, Hester wrote to the Pasha of Damascus to announce her imminent visit. His reply was the expected warm invitation, but it came with a warning: to enter Damascus, she would need to be veiled. The city was devout and fanatical; native Christians were confined to their own quarter of the town and forbidden, by law, to wear any brightly coloured clothes; women wore muslin even over their eyes. If any of the crowd took offence at an uncovered female face, no one would be able to protect her from the ensuing riot.

When Hester arrived in Damascus, accompanied by more than a dozen horsemen and as many loaded mules, it was the middle of the afternoon. She sat astride a bay stallion, wearing a Turkish man's riding costume with a Baghdad mantle. She did not wear a veil. Crowds gathered to stare but instead of reacting with the customary outrage, possibly because they were unsure if the mounted figure was male or female, they began to cheer, even saluting her with the greatest mark of respect, the scattering of coffee grounds in her wake. Such delighted enthusiasm from crowds was a new feature in Hester's life, and not an unwelcome one; it continued through her stay and every time she left her house large crowds of women would encircle her, aware now that she was a woman, believing her to be a queen and hoping for a glimpse of her white face.

Damascus was a city of fountains. Dancing, bubbling water played on almost every street and in every square. The house which had been prepared for Hester's arrival was in a Christian quarter, but again she refused to live in a Frankish ghetto and was moved to a Muslim quarter close to the palace. Her new home was a beautiful one with six spacious rooms, a private courtyard with its own fountain, shaded by large lemon trees. Damascus was observing Ramadan when the group arrived and for the first time in their journeying Hester and Meryon found a city illuminated at night. In the evening, when fasting was over until daybreak, all the streets were lit with lanterns and burning torches balanced in convenient nooks. Night-time streets in the East were customarily pitch-black and deserted, and sleeping rhythms were governed by the cycles of natural light, but during Damascene Ramadan the darkness came alive. On evenings, which Meryon would describe in letters home as 'magical', they found wrinkled, cross-legged storytellers regaling crowds with tales of Arabian Nights, belly dancers undulating to pipe players, coffee houses packed to overflowing with city folk breaking their fast. Hester slept during the day, but Meryon found his services much in demand as the applications to him for medical advice were numerous beyond measure. While he admitted that some only consulted with him in the hope of catching a glimpse of Hester, many others suffered from incurable diseases which he could do nothing about. The combination of late nights, rich food and a heavy work load took its toll. While Hester and her dragoman interpreter, M. Bertrand, rode to the palace to meet the Pasha of Damascus for the first time, Meryon lay at home with diarrhoea.

The silence felt almost palpable in the series of long narrow rooms, dimly lit by flickering candles, through which Hester and Bertrand were led. Heavily armoured soldiers stood in a seemingly endless and shadowy line, motionless as empty suits of armour, against each wall. At last they came to a gilded salon where, at the very farthest end, the Pasha sat, completely alone on a sofa of crimson velvet. A small, extremely dignified man, he did not stand to receive her, but gestured to her to sit. Their exchange was brief and amiable. Hester remained completely at ease but her dragoman stuttered and stammered through the exchanged platitudes, his usually fluent English faltering. By the end of the encounter, Hester had made yet another powerful ally; she presented the Pasha with a delicate snuff box, and in return a fine grey thoroughbred awaited her on her return home. An alliance with the Pasha was a first, crucial step towards Hester's planned desert journey. Various English travellers, all with the cultural advantages of being male, had tried and failed to do this in the past, while others, such as Burckhardt, had suffered greatly in the attempt. One man had been successful by travelling in the wet season, disguised as a peasant and drinking rainwater to survive. The Pasha, while admiring her courage, tried to dissuade her. But Hester was adamant, so that, probably in deference to her stubbornness, he finally relented on condition she could only go if accompanied by a huge and formidable escort, which he would, at a cost, help to provide. In this way the Pasha could, firstly, ensure her safety, avoiding any unpleasant international repercussions to himself, and, secondly, almost certainly make a tidy profit from the whole enterprise.

For Hester it was not an ideal solution. A letter that Crauford Bruce had written four months earlier in May, expressing concerns over Michael and Hester's expenditure, had just caught up with her. Hester replied quickly, although with an uncharacteristic lack of honesty and in the full knowledge that the trip would be completed before he would even receive the letter, much less reply to it; she hoped he wasn't too displeased with the amount they were spending and that if she heard word that he was they would curtail it, but, most importantly, the trip to Palmyra was so well under way that it could not be stopped.[11]

Muhana Al Fadil, chief of the Hasanah tribe, arrived in Damascus with his Bedouin to see the Pasha. On hearing of the powerful European woman who was visiting the area, he invited her to dine with him and his family. Hester, in her correspondence, described Muhana as being the chief of all the Anazah tribes. It was not true. The Anazah were indeed the most powerful Bedouin tribe in Syria; the Hasanah branch was strong enough to have forced the rival Mawali to allow them to use the pasture between Palmyra and Homs. But other family groups within the Anazah were a serious threat to them, principally the Fid'an and Sba'ah. Muhana's meeting with the Pasha, initially to negotiate grazing, was the prelude to their alliance in 1814, when the Pasha would support the Hasanah in a hopeless battle against other Anazi tribes for the right to move in the area around Palmyra.[12] Muhana was a young man, only in his mid-twenties, his shabby, ragged clothes giving no indication as to the huge number of men who followed him. He discussed the trip to Palmyra at length, speaking eloquently and persuasively; Hester would see Palmyra under his protection. On receiving word of this recent development in the progression of Hester's plans, Michael, accompanied by the Consul General Mr Barker, immediately set off from Aleppo to join her, motivated by a combination of concern for Hester and fear of missing out on any excitement. If Hester was travelling to Palmyra she would do so accompanied by him and with a caravan. Hester was horrified at the prospect and wrote to tell him so. When Michael and Barker arrived in Damascus, they brought an alternative proposition: a 'tartaravan', a wire cage-like structure carried by teams of men. The idea filled Hester with horror. Envisioning an enclosed machine, carried by men who would run away at the first sign of attack leaving her helpless, she emphasized to Michael that 'the swiftest horse' was the only way to travel; the Arabs ensured their own safety by keeping the fastest animals they could find, and she intended to follow their example.

Meryon was making his own contacts in the area and had struck up a friendship with M. Lascaris, a former Knight of St John and a great champion of emancipation for all people. Lascaris lived in a village on the outskirts of Damascus with his wife, a woman who was a living testament to his beliefs, as she had spent the early part of her life as a slave. They were not a wealthy couple and they lived modestly but they were well educated, spoke Arabic, Turkish, English and French, and Meryon found them excellent company. When he introduced them to Hester she was equally taken with them and wrote to England suggesting that it might be sensible for the British government to give them a small pension and retain them to provide intelligence of the region: 'The French are sending agents in all directions (at an immense expense) into the desert, and why do we not do the same?'[13]

The journey from Aleppo was more than Barker's constitution could cope with and by the time Michael brought him to Damascus he was ill. Reluctantly, Hester agreed to postpone her travel plans. Unhappy with

Michael's interference, she complained by letter to General Oakes:

> It seems very cross to be angry at people being anxious about you,
> but had Bruce [Michael] and Mr Barker made less fuss about my
> safety, and let me had perfectly my own way, I should have been
> returned by this time from Palmyra.[14]

Hester summoned Meryon from the Lascarises' home, where he had
been spending a few days, to tend Barker.[15] But she was restless. Frustrated
by the apparent failure of her travel plans, but not at all discouraged, she
decided to arrange another journey. Knowing that Michael's concerned
caution would only lead to further setbacks and delays, she kept her true
intention secret. So, while Michael and Meryon remained with the ailing
Barker, content in the belief that Hester was travelling to the neighbouring city of Hamah for a few days, Hester met with the Lascaris alone. She
told them of her plan and asked if they would accompany her as inter-
preters. They agreed. They only took the road to Hamah as far as Hems, a
small hamlet, where a single Bedouin awaited them. From Hems they
veered off, led by the Arab, into the desert. After several hours of riding
they reached their destination, Muhana's camp. As the weary three with
their Arab guide straggled into the gathering of makeshift tents and livestock, Muhana came out to meet them. Impressed by Hester's intrepidity
and, more importantly, honoured by her trust, he welcomed her to the
place that would be her home for the forthcoming days.

It was the beginning of a difficult and strange existence. Later travellers
and gossips who criticized Hester for the large entourage she kept and for
the money she spent would have been surprised, perhaps grudgingly
impressed. Muhana was not poor in terms of his people: he commanded
upwards of forty thousand men, tribes who moved in waves across the
wasteland, constantly breaking and joining camp. Everything the
Bedouin owned they carried, and home was a series of makeshift tents
made of black or brown sheepskins, goat or camel hair, often jumping
with fleas. It was a domicile, as English missionaries observed, that even
the Arabs would come to abandon in the coming fifty years when they
grew dissatisfied with the 'black tents of the Kedar' and started building
cottages. Vast numbers of livestock, almost their only subsistence, travelled with the tribe wherever they went: sheep, goats, camels and horses,

following and living in the camp. But Hester found the people beautiful. All of the children were naked, the women unveiled but covered in delicate indigo tattoos of mysterious designs, their lips dyed blue, their nails red with henna and their hands covered with myriad drawings of flowers, ferns and scrolls. It looked as attractive to her as it did strange. Another English traveller would note how the custom of staining the edge of the eyelid black, creating the same effect as modern eyeliner, gave the eye 'a large glistening appearance'.[16] Whatever jewellery the women owned they wore, so they were weighed down with bead bracelets and ring anklets, necklaces and pendants. Almost all wore huge silver hoop earrings. Yet the colour and ornament did not hide the fact that food was short and that many of the tribe were starving. Emaciated, wizened old men amazed Hester with their horsemanship; all of them impressed her with their loyalty to the chief, an obeisance that made the hierarchy of the *ancien régime* seem insignificant in comparison.

It was a society that Hester, bereaved of her mother at just four years old and largely brought up by her grandmother Stanhope in the pre-revolutionary conviction of aristocracy, related to. The admiration was mutual. Hester's horsemanship and courage earned her Bedouin respect while any doubts were dispelled by the financial rewards they believed she could bestow. They named her 'queen of them all'.[17] By the end of a week, when Muhana personally escorted Hester and the Lascarises to Hamah, Hester had made a decision: the Bedouin would accompany her to Palmyra in the spring.

Michael and Hester settled in Hamah during the winter and found a new cottage for the Lascarises nearby, which had a spare room for Hester's physician. Meryon joined them in December, finding that even the short trip from Damascus was rendered terrible by the severity of the season and the bitterly cold strong winds whipping him as he rode. While Meryon struggled against the weather, Muhana sent word to Hester asking if he might beg the services of her physician. Hester readily agreed, thus solving the problem of having Michael and Meryon in renewed proximity, while also pleasing the chief. So, in spite of the weather conditions, Meryon had only a few days to rest before resuming his travels; this journey would be more difficult as the Arabs were now camped in Palmyra and he would have to go through the desert in winter. He remained with Hester and Michael just long enough to celebrate New Year's Day and then, accompanied only by Lascaris again acting as inter- preter, Meryon set off on 2 January. The pair, dressed simply to avoid attracting potential thieves or bandits – simple cotton shirts, long trousers, and most essentially, heavy sheepskins, red boots and caps – departed on well-broken horses whose speed might mean their safety.[18]

Lascaris and Meryon's trip, through a winter that locals declared to be the worst in fifty years, provided an opportunity for Meryon to have yet another infatuation. As an old man he would say that he had never for- gotten Raby's smile. Raby was a Bedouin girl, 'full of life and activity', just fourteen when Meryon noticed her, worth a large dowry to her father and well beyond the reaches of the doctor, who nevertheless indulged in a lit- tle oriental fantasy of his own.[19]

Meanwhile, Hester and Michael faced more domestic difficulties: the house in Hamah was not built for such weather. Freezing cold gave way to damp, then pouring rain, and the mud and straw roof of the house gave no shelter, so that Hester and Michael were flooded more than once. As if to compound the misery two letters arrived from England; they had taken more than eleven months to reach Michael and Hester and did not con- tain good news. The letters were sealed together in a packet addressed to Hester Stanhope. One letter was specifically for her, the other was to be read by her and then, if she wished, passed on to Michael. They were from Crauford, in a similar, but more emphatic, vein to the second letter he had written following their declaration. Lord Sligo, following his successful disclosure to General Oakes, had arrived in England and given Crauford a full account of what was going on, including the fact that Michael had proposed to Hester and been turned down. Crauford wrote:

> Had I been on the spot, I should have joined my admonitions and recommended an indissoluble union; now my friends the period is gone bye, the world is in possession of your misconduct, and it never would do for your wife to be received in Female Society by suffer- ance.[20]

Crauford elaborated by listing the people who knew of their affair and stressing the fact that Michael would bear some of the brunt of Hester's family's reaction. While Hester was 'not like the common race of women, and does not submit her conduct to the common rules of life', Crauford felt that certain standards needed to be assumed. Hester had effectively cut herself off from all female society but, according to Crauford, this needed to be a permanent withdrawal so there could be no risk of corruption by association. When Lord Sligo explained she was not particularly fond of female company, Crauford insisted it would be something she missed and needed in time. The letter smacked of hypocrisy. It is doubtful that Crauford would have embraced any future marriage plans, even grudgingly. While he hoped that he might be 'admitted to the enjoyment of intercourse and communication with her', he resolutely forbade her to have any contact whatsoever with his wife and daughters. If Hester returned to England and lived openly as his son's mistress, her existence would greatly narrow his choice of wife because Michael would only be able to marry someone who accepted the situation. It was untenable. He urged Michael to travel, but to Germany, Russia, Italy, anywhere that was not at war and not in the vicinity of Hester, so that his passions would abate and, by the time he returned home, the scandal would have died down.

As if in a reflection of the personal drama of the pain of the letters, the River Orontes flooded its banks. Water rose up out of overflowing wells, pouring down the streets and pathways of Hamah and, for a while, the few cottages, huddled together on the outskirts of the main village, were completely cut off. It seemed to bring a lull in the drama and Hester and Michael drew close in adversity, poignantly aware of the finiteness of their relationship. By the end of January they had completed their replies. Hester had no doubts about her situation and said so; at the same time, she did not need to be reminded of it and warned 'from this moment all reference to it may end, or you will see soon the cloven foot in my character'.[21] For the rest, Hester wrote of money, the cost of the trip to Palmyra, the necessity of each expense and a justification for the extravagant plans that were under way. Postal times decreed that this letter too was little more than a gesture; by the time it reached England the Palmyra trip should have been completed.

Michael was less restrained. He was disappointed in his father and said so. He believed his father more tolerant than he was showing himself to be and had accepted the tone of the first reply to the news, disregarding his father's follow-up letter. Michael thought that Hester had done a truly noble thing in refusing marriage to him, the one thing that would have restored her to the favour of society. He chose to disregard Hester's scorn for polite society, clinging to the romance of Hester's gesture. That someone could love him so much that they might sacrifice their own reputation to save him social embarrassment overwhelmed him, and his resolve to remain with her strengthened for a time. Once more their letters were consigned to the haphazard chain of ships and horses.

Meryon's successful return from his Palmyra trip led to intense planning for Hester's own journey in the spring. Time not taken up with this or in reacting to the invasive weather was very social. Having established a relationship with the Bedouin, and in anticipation of travelling under their protection, Hester made them frequent visitors to her home. Up to fifteen nomads came to dine at a time and, presenting the starving groups with as much food as she could at a sitting, Hester delighted in watching them eat. They responded in kind. Hester's brightly coloured, embroidered Turkish costume was exchanged for that of an Arab chief, a simpler, but highly functional robe made of white cotton and red silk, with a long sheepskin waistcoat and boots. Hester enthused to Meryon and Michael about its warmth and comfort until they too adopted a similar style.

Palmyra featured largely in western consciousness for several decades from 1751 when Robert Wood published his book of drawings of the ancient city. In spite of its inaccessibility, Wood and James Dawkins had reached Palmyra and, while there, made detailed drawings of all of the most important monuments. But Hester had concerns beyond that of ruins and was disparaging of Michael's interest in historical buildings. Palmyra was the realm of an ancient queen, Zenobia; Hester's obsession with Zenobia was such that Meryon remarked of the trip to Palmyra: 'She sought the remains of Zenobia's greatness, as well as the remains of Palmyra.'

Zenobia came to the zenith of her power in the third century AD. After the assassination of her husband she used her position as regent to her eldest son to achieve the reputation and power of a queen. Her rise made Rome uneasy and an army was sent against her, but she defeated them. In 269 AD, to the amazement of the world, she invaded Egypt and conquered it within the year. When the Romans finally did take Palmyra,

Zenobia was spared, probably because of their admiration for her courage or legendary beauty, and taken back to Rome as a prisoner. The Queen of Palmyra was characterized not only by her courage but by her supreme riding skills, love of hunting and enthusiasm. Chaucer's Monk, in 'The Monk's Tale', speaks of her medieval reputation, one that survived through subsequent centuries:

Of Kynges blood of Perce is she descended
I seye nat that she hadde moost fairnesse,
But of his shap she myghte nat been amended . . .

Hir riche array ne myghte nat be told
As wel in vessel as in hire clothing.
She was al clad in perree and in gold,
And eek she lafte noght, for none hunting,
To have of sundry tonges ful knowing,
When that she leyser hadde; and for to entende
To lerne books was al hire liking,
How she in virtue myghte hir lyf dispende.

Palmyra needed a new queen, and Hester, already acclaimed *meleki*, the Queen, by the Bedouin, imagined it could be her.

By 20 March, the party that would travel through the desert was ready; seventy Bedouins, with long, ringleted hair carrying long lances plumed with ostrich feathers, were followed by camels loaded with provisions and presents to act as bribes along the way. At the very front, astride an Arab horse, was Hester, with Muhana's eldest son and twenty-five heavily armed horsemen. Meryon and Michael were left to bring up the rear. Before their departure, Michael joked in a letter to General Oakes that Hester might marry the chief of the Wahabees, another powerful Arab tribe, 'to bring about a great revolution in religion and politics', while Hester was content to be 'queen with them all'.[22]

The desert journey was not what any of them had anticipated; the land undulated gently under a carpet of thick grass and wild flowers, a brief manifestation of early spring, which would soon revert to scrubland and scorched earth. The first night was hard. In a scene reminiscent of the night following the shipwreck, Hester and her maid spent the night in a cottage overrun with large desert rats; but subsequent nights were less fraught. It was not until three days into their trip that they saw any other people. When they began to descend into a valley, they caught sight of what seemed like a thousand camels, appearing from over the summit of the facing hill and weaving their way down its side. As they grew closer, they saw the men, women, children and heavily laden animals of the Sba'ah, also an Anazah tribe, currently, and temporarily, affiliated with that of Muhana. There were similarities with the Anazah: the men wore their hair in the same long back ringlets, and the women's faces were covered with similar intricate tattoos, but the women's saddles were shaped like the skull of a horned ram.[23] Hester asked Muhana to stop their party, and a tent was set up. For a moment all was still as Hester, under the shade of her camel-hair tent, stared at the beautiful Sba'ah women, while they gazed back in wonder and curiosity at her.

The next day Meryon rode ahead with a small escort to ensure that Hester's accommodation was prepared. Under his supervision three cottages, one with a beautiful view of the ruins for Hester and Michael, were cleaned and swept. Meanwhile, the travellers were being greeted with yet another fantastic spectacle. As Hester approached Palmyra, she saw what she later described to be the most wondrous sight of all. From a cloud of dust, fifty or so men, naked to the waist ran towards their mounts, beating kettle drums and waving coloured streamers. The only materials covering their bodies were short white lace petticoats and belts made of leather studded with cowry shells and hung with boxes, flasks and various small tools. Feigning an attack on Hester's caravan, they reacted noisily as the Bedouin made a mock defence. The din and fury ended only when they entered the Valley of the Tombs and guides appeared as if from nowhere to lead the front of the train. They rode towards a long colonnade of pillars and consoles, although the statues that had once decorated them were long since gone. The colonnade ended in a crumbling stone arch and as they approached it they saw that, in lieu of the statues, beautiful adolescent girls were posed on the pillars. Each one carried a garland and was scantily dressed in a loose, transparent robe and white crêpe veil. By the arch there was another crowd of young women, similarly attired, and, as Hester passed them, they leaped from their stands and danced around her horse, scattering petals from the garlands. Crying 'El Sitt', they placed a circle of flowers on her head. For the first time, Hester was over-come by emotion. It was the first time a European woman had ever seen Palmyra and it was the first time the Palmyrenes had seen a female Euro-pean. As the procession advanced towards the cottages it 'was increased by the addition of every man, woman and child, in the village'.[24] And, in what she believed was a triumphant fulfilment of Brothers' prophecy years before, Hester was crowned 'Queen of the East'.

9

Sadness and Sickness

Come with me from Lebanon, my bride;
Come with me from Lebanon.

I adjure you, O daughters of Jerusalem,
If you find my beloved,
That you tell him
I am sick with love.
Song of Solomon

Eastern Jewels

THE ELATION OF THE ARRIVAL quickly gave way to fatigue and Hester spent the first day at Palmyra recovering in the cottage, while Michael explored the ruins using the Wood and Dawkins volume of pictures as a guide. Hester made her own investigations the following day, accompanied at her own instigation by a local sheikh, in order to allay any doubts that she had come to steal antiquities. The appropriation of foreign works of art and ancient treasures was big business in the early nineteenth century; Lord Elgin had been widely criticized for removing the Parthenon sculptures at the turn of the century. But shrewd Europeans, such as Bernardino Drovetti in Alexandria, made their fortune stealing Egyptian antiquities, in Drovetti's case with Mehmet Ali's support, and selling them to the highest European bidder. Understandably, many Arabs did not acquiesce in this theft of their heritage and European travellers were often accordingly viewed with suspicion, even aggression. However, several prominent British travellers were as opposed to the practice as the Arabs themselves. In spite of their mutual dislike, Lord Byron, for one, shared Hester's scorn for what he regarded as theft and stated:

I opposed, and ever will oppose, the robbery of ruins from Athens, to instruct the English in sculpture (who are as capable of sculpture as the Egyptians are of skating).[1]

While Hester's own strong views against the trade were made clear, her physician offered payment to any locals who brought him ancient engravings or stones. But their stay in Palmyra was not long, just over a week, and Meryon had failed to buy any ancient souvenirs when the group's departure was precipitated by the proximity of a tribe of Anazah Bedouin, the Fid'an, hostile to that of Muhana and soon to be allies of the Sba'ah.

A feast awaited them in Hamah, a celebration of their success. Meryon settled into his work – a fever accompanied by vomiting was spreading throughout the area – while Michael and Hester, who had only been in Hamah in order to reach Palmyra, planned where to go next.

The arrival of bubonic plague forced a decision: while a return to Sidon was possible, it was decided that Latakia, which was on a greener and more fertile coast, would be a better base for the summer. By late May they were settled in Latakia in a house which both Michael and Hester found delightful. Meryon, anxious to keep his distance from Michael and to set up his own practice, found a house of his own and employed two servants. Relief at escaping from the plague was short-lived; within less than a fortnight a neighbour, a merchant from Damietta, caught it and died. As the mood among Hester's staff became one of fear, the group once again became anxious to move. Before the end of June, ten more people in Hester's neighbourhood were dead of plague. But then a lull in the deaths saw Hester and Michael fixed on remaining. The epidemic was not confined to Syria; Malta was similarly infected, and Hester wrote to General Oakes, concerned both for his health and for that of her former servant, Elizabeth Williams, and her family.

The relatively low occurrence of disease from July onwards brought Mr Barker, the English Consul who had spent time with Hester and Michael at Hamah, to Latakia with his wife and children. Word of Hester's spectacular success at Palmyra had reached other expatriates in the Middle East and Hester dispensed letters of advice in response to queries for help. One Englishwoman wrote with her concerns as to what to take on an imminent desert journey. Hester strongly recommended she carry a chamber pot:

> Imagine madam a plain which seems never to end, and consider what you are to do when you travel eight or nine hours together? It will be in vain to see a bush or tree for any *little purpose* besides you will not be allowed to stray from the party.[2]

While Michael and Hester enjoyed the company of the Barkers, Meryon was kept busier than he wanted to be by a new sickness, an 'epidemical fever' that 'attacks everybody but kills nobody'.[3] In the apparent safety of their town, word reached them from Damascus that their friend Madame Lascaris was dead; her husband would follow three years later of a similar sickness in Cairo.[4] As seemed to happen so many times in Hester's life, one piece of bad news was followed by another. In the early autumn a packet of three letters arrived for her; they were from Crauford and they urged his son to return. Given Michael's previous defiance of his father's demands and the affection which still existed between him and Hester, the three letters would probably have had no effect were it not for a fourth letter which came shortly after. From a friend of Crauford, it stated baldly that Crauford was very ill and that his son should go to him.[5] Hester had not forgotten her promise to Crauford. Still believing that Michael should be free to perform 'his public or private duty', she insisted that Michael go at once. The plague in Malta and elsewhere meant that a different route would need to be taken, so Michael arranged to travel by land as far as Constantinople then, if the continent was open, head through Germany. He wrote to his father that he was coming, urging him to look after Hester's finances in the meantime, as he would sort them out himself on his arrival home. Money was continuing to be a problem. Hester had lost almost £4,000 in jewels and clothing in the shipwreck and her allowance of £1,200 per annum had been depleted early in the year. Over the summer Crauford had covered a bill of £1,000 that she had insufficient funds to meet; Michael was anxious that he would continue to do so until he got to England.

Michael left and Hester wrote to Crauford. The letter was almost maternal in its concerns that Michael should 'lose all his bad habits' and learn table etiquette, lost after so many Eastern meals 'dining on the ground and eating with his fingers'.[6] But it also contained a crucial piece of reassurance for Crauford, namely that she would not move from Syria until she heard from both of them that she could do so. It was not an easy separation for either of them. Although Michael's devotion would prove to be fickle, he acknowledged 'the violence I did to my own feelings when I separated myself from you'.[7] For Hester, Michael's return to England without her as a wife marked the beginning of a self-imposed exile from polite European society. Michael referred to his trip home as 'temporary separation' while Hester pledged, 'I shall take all the care I can of myself and hope to embrace you once more.'[8, 9]

On 7 October, Michael set off. Two days later, Hester sent the first of the many frantic letters she would write in the coming months:

soaked by frequent downpours. Sheltering beneath this makeshift canopy, her face now ravaged by the illness, pockmarked and dotted with suppurating blisters, and kept awake by a hacking cough, Hester could only think of hearing news of Michael and of leaving Latakia.[16] Any pleasure she found in the setting of the town was obscured by memories of sickness and Michael's departure. Sidon was six days' voyage away, but on 6 January 1814 Hester would wait no longer. In spite of the fact that she had to be lifted up onto an ass, Hester and her companions rode to the shore and sailed.

Once they had landed, Meryon travelled ahead to inspect their new home. The built-up suburbs that now stretch from Sidon to Mar Elias, their busy roads filled with the incessant honking of impatient traffic, give little idea of how it was in the eighteenth century. It was a lonely and wild spot, about an hour's ride from Sidon, and the ascent up the slope of Mount Lebanon was a difficult one, across a landscape that was barren and stony, relieved only by the silvery green of an occasional olive tree. The building was flat-roofed and made of stone, with several white-washed rooms and a small chapel dedicated to St Elias. The chapel stank with a heavy, putrid smell, which Meryon attributed to the decomposing body of a former patriarch who lay there, ostensibly embalmed, but evidently not well enough to prevent the odour of his rotten flesh permeating the whole building. Looking out from the hilltop the view was, and still is, of a hillside dotted with Phoenician caves, ancient hiding places that were both places of rest for the dead and of escape and sanctuary for the living. The path weaves up and over the countryside towards Sidon. Servants who travelled in the night made their way through thick undergrowth, constantly wary of the thick black snakes that frequent the area, stumbling over protuberant rocks. But even if the view was incredible, it did not compensate for practical deficiencies: the roof leaked, and consequently, during the rains of the previous month, some of the baggage had been damaged.

Hester remained in Sayda while the various repairs were done and the doctor went off to find himself a cottage in the village itself, which was called Abra, after Hester's insistence that the convent was too small for them to share. He would later say that at the time he could not begin to guess that he was 'destined to spend there nearly three years' of his life. By

1. Hester in full Arabic dress, cutting a characteristically dramatic figure complete with pistol and turban

2. Hester's brother: the fourth Earl Stanhope 'charming, charming, incomparable Mahon'
3. Hester's father: his Republican convictions earned him the nickname 'Citizen Stanhope'
4. Hester's lover, Sir John Moore, the heroic Scotsman, whose last words were 'Stanhope, remember me to your sister'

5. A locket belonging to Hester, now displayed in Chevening, which contains a lock of her uncle, William Pitt's hair. She was described as 'the preface and apology in all matters relating to Pitt'

6. A beautiful necklace, worn by Hester during her years in England, perhaps at Chevening or Downing Street, before the financial difficulties of her time in Montagu Square

7. Pitt's curative stay in Bath, 1805. One of a very limited series of caricatures drawn by Mary Cruikshank, it depicts the Prime Minister as he hears the news of Napoleon's victory at Austerlitz. Less than two months later, Pitt was dead.

8. Charles Lewis Meryon, Hester's doctor and devoted travel companion
9. Michael Bruce, Hester's younger lover: 'a most pleasing, clever young man'
10. Lord Byron, who encountered Hester in Athens: He dismissed her as 'That dangerous thing, a female wit'
11. Hester frequently made drawings of the people she met on her travels, here her sketch of two Turkish women

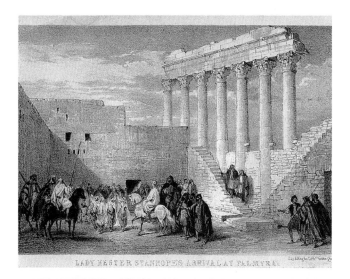

LADY HESTER STANHOPE'S ARRIVAL AT PALMYRA

SHIPWRECK NEAR THE ISLAND OF RHODES

12. Hester, Queen of the Desert, arrives in Palmyra, the first European woman ever to do so

13. In a shipwreck off the coast of Rhodes, Hester lost almost all of her personal belongings

14. Hester in Eastern dress astride one of her beloved horses
15. Emir Bashir Shihab: beginning as a friend of Hester he would become her greatest and most powerful enemy
16. The Emir's Palace at Beittedine

17. The ruins of Hester's palatial estate at Joun: the remains are a forlorn testament to its former grandeur. (The Datura flower, evidence of Hester's drug-fuelled later years, still grows nearby)

18. The Sea Castle at Sidon, still an incredible sight today

19. A portrait of Hester as a mature woman, probably painted in the period immediately following her death, which beautifully captures the piercing blue eyes and Pitt nose, often described by contemporaries

20. A photograph of Meryon, still looking dapper, even after his family tragedies

20 February, the masons and carpenters were finished and Hester moved in with a retinue that was considerably smaller than she had so far travelled with. The difficulties of transport meant that she had given away her horses, keeping only a donkey and retaining just a few of the servants who had been with her in Hamah. Feeling excluded from the convent unnecessarily, Meryon lamented his new isolation: 'I do not look forward to the time we shall spend here with much satisfaction. Solitude is agreeable when with a good library. . .Conversation soon wears out between two people.'[17] Any plans to return to England were now impossible; Michael's departure had left Hester a lone female, whom Meryon thought 'under my protection, and I answerable to her brother and friends for her protection in these distant countries'.[18] Hester thought differently; she had found the doctor far too easily panicked by the plague in Latakia and wrote to Michael, secretly confirming Meryon's suspicions, that although the convent was large enough for the doctor, she didn't want him to stay with her.[19]

Michael had finally arrived in Constantinople, only to learn that Hester had been dangerously ill. He wrote to her immediately, offering to rejoin her if her health was still in doubt or if she should suffer a relapse; he also wrote to his father that he would stay in Constantinople until he was sure she was recovered, so he could return to her if she needed him.[20] Later in the same month he wrote again, promising Hester a pension of £1,000 per annum. This was to be in addition to the government money of £1,200 that she already received. From Michael's and society's point of view, the liaison with him had ruined Hester's prospects of finding a husband; he was, therefore, in honour, now obliged at least partially to support her. With customary romanticism Michael vowed to remain in Constantinople until he received word 'of the perfect reestablishment' of Hester's health. But it was not the only reason for delaying his journey, and his other motive was far from altruistic. He had met a woman in Pera called Theophanie: Michael was already having an affair. It was brief and Theophanie would suffer Hester's fate of waiting in vain for Michael's letters:

> When you were near me the time that passed without your telling me 'I loved you' seemed to me endless, and now it is almost eight months that I have not received a line from you . . . [21]

In his correspondence with his new lover Michael admitted he did not see a future with Hester:

I told you that I admired a woman whom I regarded as a superior being, as my guardian angel, that perhaps heaven would never allow me to devote my life to her but that whatever providence decreed I should never cease to adore her.[22]

Hester's original words to his father had been chillingly prophetic: behaviour that was shocking in a woman did no harm to a man; Michael's notoriety was rendering him more exotic, and more attractive, to the opposite sex.[23]

The French Consul General, M. Boutin, was a young man, only recently appointed to his post. When Hester met him in Sidon she was very taken with him and offered to give him one of her servants as a companion for a forthcoming trip. Boutin's journey would not be a light undertaking; he aimed to travel through the mountains from Mount Lebanon to Antioch, dangerous territory, fiercely patrolled by the Ansary tribe. He did not have long to live, but his alliance with Hester would have far-reaching consequences in the near future. He gratefully accepted Hester's offer and, accompanied by her man, set off.

Hester's escape from the epidemic was short-lived. An outbreak at Abra caused chaos and Bashir II issued an edict giving Hester the power to take any measures she thought necessary to contain the disease. Hester quarantined those already sick to the valley, where they had a good water supply. But death surrounded them. Hester struggled to maintain the front of control and dignity warranted by the power Bashir had bestowed, emotionally distraught by the events around her:

I am so anxious about this subject I never felt the least afraid when I visited these people, I tell you quite the truth, but when I found the poor mother had made holes in the earth to bury her children, I could not stand that, yet I still behaved well till I came home, and then I threw myself down in the corner.[24]

The last epidemic had left its mark on Hester's physician. Meryon was petrified. Unable to eat or sleep, he fretted constantly at Hester, who found his behaviour 'unmanly' and 'like a fool'.[25] As the plague continued to spread all along the coast and into the mountain villages, despite every precaution, Hester was forced to keep within the wall of her convent. Almost defying the quarantine to last more than a few months, she made plans to travel to Baalbek, in the autumn. But the death toll mounted and, as upwards of ten people each day fell to the plague, finding anyone prepared to bury the dead became impossible, so that corpses lay in the streets and houses. The advent of summer meant that the glaring white of the walls and woodwork was dazzling. In an attempt to create a normal, if contained, environment, Hester ordered her servants to paint the shutters and door green, hanging pale green calico curtains on the windows. Flocks of sheep and stray dogs, which were believed to carry plague, wandered into the convent, putting everyone at risk. Still fighting the encroachment, Hester walled up the building and spent her time in correspondence. Most of her writing was to Michael: voluminous, detailed letters filled with the minutiae of daily quarantine and the irritation born of confinement. One May letter alone ran to forty-two double-sided pages. Among the details of redecoration and servant misdemeanours were worried queries as to why he was not replying to her mail:

> I have no letter yet from you what can have become of them? I am lost in conjectures about the cause of this long silence . . .[26]

The twenty-eighth of May was Michael's birthday and with the impending event Hester sank ever further into sadness. Wanting to mark the occasion, she presented Meryon with a nosegay, and he, wishing to reciprocate, wrote her a poem, comparing her to a poppy bowing its flower under the weight of the rain the night before:

So droopest thou; but when returns
Thy youth, for whom they bosom burns,
Thy faded cheek will bloom anew,
And thou shake off they sorrow too.[27]

But a month later Michael still hadn't written, and Hester began to suspect that he had met someone else:

Dear Love, what a time! It is now nearly 8 months since you left me and I am still in being. That you will fall in love is but to [*sic*] natural, or that someone will fall in love with you. I must not repine at it, for why sd I be the Dog in the Manger?[28]

Michael's absence brought one consolation: reconciliation with her brother James, who even considered travelling to Cairo. Genuine distress at Hester's illness had prompted James to make contact with Crauford, so that they could share any news of her condition, thus greatly improving communication between England and Syria.

The abating of the plague brought scant relief, as the heat in Mar Elias started to affect Hester's health. Prickly heat rash spread all over her fair skin, so that it became dark pink and incessantly itchy. Hester turned to Bashir II. He had a summer house at Meshmushy, high in the mountains where the air was cooler. Unable to cope with mid-summer temperatures at the convent, Hester asked if she might be his guest. To Hester's disappointment, Bashir's initial reaction was one of reluctance; some distant relatives of his were already settled there and he was loath to move them. Hester, feeling let down, replied by the same messenger: whether she could have the house or not she would go up the mountain, living in a tent if necessary. Bashir II acquiesced and his house was made available, through his agent Jamil Jabr, until the highest temperatures passed.

Hester was not an easy person to live with in the summer of 1814. The intensity of the heat made her irritable and short-tempered, the plague may have disturbed her mind and, as Meryon believed, the inflammation of the brain left invisible scars. Missing Michael, she constantly fretted over the lack of letters from him. Her unhappiness was taken out on her servants and Meryon; nothing was right; her servants were all idiots and Meryon irritated her into passionate rages. Hester, who had always eaten heartily and unfussily, now developed fads over what she would and wouldn't eat, and the cook was bullied and insulted. It was a trying time for Hester; she had survived the plague but she no longer had her lover, nor was there any possibility she might one day reunite with him. The affair itself had altered her future. No matter how often she protested that she didn't care about the opinion of polite society, it was only in 1814, with the realization that Michael had gone for good, that her exclusion was

made final and irrevocable. Late June brought another flurry of correspondence between Crauford and Hester, none of it pleasant. Hester
received a packet of three letters from London, one of which was expressly intended for Michael; she opened and read all of them. Crauford's letter to Michael detailed the harm that he felt had been caused by his son's
relationship. Hester was understandably livid, as she felt she had done her
utmost to protect Michael, even to her own detriment. From Crauford's
other letter it was clear that Michael had written to his father about the
difficulties of her situation. Hester, with her usual hatred of pity and her
fierce pride, wrote to Crauford that she had accepted the situation and
determined to put it behind her: 'I was born to be contented and make up
my mind to my situation, let it be what it may.'[29] She reiterated her
promise that she would not in any way jeopardize Michael's future or reputation and stated 'we shall not live under the same roof'.[30] It was the last
letter Hester ever wrote to Crauford; her postscript hinted at her anger:

> I might as well add that the unpleasant report spread in England that
> you have talked of protesting yr. sons draft to force him to obey you,
> has reached me.[31]

Michael was now in Vienna, and Hester, ever more anxious to have
word from him, enlisted the help of John Barker, who offered to send a
carrier to Hester immediately, should anything arrive.

The trip to Meshmushy was not a pleasant one. Hester's vacillation
between tempers and tears created an atmosphere fraught with tension as
her entourage waited for the next explosion. In a fit of pique, Meryon
stormed off when she commanded him to make lemonade. It was not his
job. He was her physician and demanded to be respected as such.
Overnight in Abra the doctor composed himself; he worried that Hester
was showing signs of madness, a lasting effect of her illness. He sent a
note to her, and she replied asking him if he would go ahead to Meshmushy and get her some medicine. Meryon arrived to hear that local
people were also questioning her sanity. She had badly beaten two of her
staff, ranting and screaming at all around her. Yet when Meryon met her
she was calm again. After her rages, she was always contrite and kind to
whomever had borne the brunt of them; Meryon was no exception.

Meshmushy was a mountain retreat, with beautiful, clear, sweet water at the bottom of the hill and a welcome cooling breeze. It was inhabited by only a dozen or so families. In the late twentieth century it was a diffi- cult place to reach, occupied by Israel and inaccessible to all but the most determined traveller. But after the withdrawal, it became reachable again via a single road, the only way of safety winding through a mine-littered landscape. The families who live there now are, for the most part, the same as those who did in Hester's time, proud of their mention in Mery- on's *Memoirs* and proud that they once produced excellent wine. It is much cooler, and less arid, than Mar Elias, shaded as it is by gnarled wal- nut trees and surrounded by tobacco plants. And, like the house in Mar Elias and her later home in Joun, Hester's building was perched at the top of the hill (where it still stands, although now heavily restored and mod- ernized), with an uninterrupted view across the landscape.

Hester loved the village and, in the refreshing climate, seemed happier and better tempered than she had been since her sickness. But in a short time more bad news came: her sister, Lucy, was dead. Hester worried over the fate of her seven children and wrote letters of concern, hoping that her other sister, Griselda, would look after her nieces. Grief for her sister and anger at Crauford consumed Hester. When Michael's long-awaited letters arrived, her reply laid bare all her fury at the treatment she had received from his father. In her mountain retreat, Hester brooded, hating the way her affair had been 'made the subject of public conversation'. She planned to go to France and meet her brother. She would see Michael only if their paths crossed by accident and only as a friend. England was out of the question as Crauford had made her a laughing stock. She declared him to be her enemy, 'his want of sense and feeling, and I may add candour, (for he has strangely deceived both you and me) has quite spoiled all never to be redeemed'.[32]

Hester was restless again; she was lonely and, having been cooped up all summer, resumed plans for the trip to Baalbek. But the prevalence of the plague in Damascus and in the villages of the Bekaa meant that delay fol- lowed delay, so it was not until October that they were ready to leave. Even then it was essential to take many precautions. The whole group travelled with tents rather than risk sleeping in an infected home, carrying provisions in the form of a kind of dumpling, made with minced meat, intended to last for the week, as well as utensils and fuel to allow Hester a fire in the evening.

No one would have to go to a village for shelter or sustenance. In total, fifteen mules were loaded for a party of sixteen, all mounted on donkeys.[33]

The villages in the Bekaa were very different from those of the mountain, with huts made of dried mud rather than stone, although fear of the plague prevented either Meryon or Hester going inside any buildings. When it was necessary to pass through a village, they did so as quickly as possible. After six days of meagre and, by that time, rotting food they arrived in Baalbek. As a precaution against tempests, which were common in the autumn, the servants set up Hester's tent in the ruins of an old mosque, where it would be sheltered. An idyllic place where weeping willows tossed branches over a shady path that led to town, it was surrounded by densely growing cypresses and plane trees, with their vivid autumn colours of gold and russet. After the trials of travelling Hester wanted for nothing more than a bath, and so, after a day or two's rest, Meryon set out to arrange for the local hamam to be cleaned for her visit. He arrived in the afternoon when, as he was well aware, local women bathed. The bath master, eager to encourage wealthy Europeans to use his facility, offered to clear the bath temporarily for the doctor's inspection. The naked women huddled in a side chamber while Meryon explored and appraised but, curious themselves, they peeped out at the European, and by doing so allowed the doctor to enjoy a few salacious glimpses of bodies normally completely covered from view.

Early in November, the storm they had anticipated arrived. Thunder and torrential rain confined the party to their tents, and it was only during the rare dry spells that they were able to ride out to see the ruins. As the weather deteriorated over the week that followed, fear that it might prevent them returning to Mar Elias precipitated their departure for Tripoli. The Maronite Convent of St Anthony was a well-known site on the way to Tripoli. Situated on a ledge of rock halfway down a deep, precipitous ravine leading to a heavily wooded river, St Antonius was a wild and prepossessing place. Its fame came from the general belief that numerous miracles had been performed there: lunatics and epileptics had ostensibly been cured; corpses, buried within its grounds, were said never to rot. St Anthony, however, who blessed the place in this way, was said also to have a hatred of anything female. Consequently, both the grounds and the building were completely prohibited to women and to the females of any animal species.

While cockerels wandered freely in the grounds, crowing and fighting, hens were cooped up in a separate building away from the convent.

On arrival, Meryon and the other men of the party were warmly received by the monks, while Hester was shown to a guest house fifty yards from the main enclosure. Hester did not like to be told where she could and could not go, and within hours of settling in her room sent a message saying that she intended to dine the following evening in the convent itself, in honour of St Anthony. The locals in her party, afraid that the monks might seek revenge, carefully checked the room she would use as well as ensuring that the short ride along the narrow, rocky precipice to the convent was uneventful. Hester was true to her word. At dinner time, she mounted a she-ass and rode it right into the great hall of the convent. The men looked on aghast, waiting for a furious St Anthony to take his revenge at any minute. The monks argued; some thought Hester was important enough to be allowed to visit; others thought it sacrilegious; the rest were afraid of the wrath of their saint. Nothing happened. In shocked horror they stared as Hester calmly explored every room of the building before sitting for dinner. She stayed at her meal for four hours and, before the evening was finished, the whole mountain was buzzing with gossip about her visit.

Hester had heard from other correspondents that Michael had moved from Vienna to France. Half expecting to find a letter from him waiting for her in Tripoli they pushed on, but when she arrived there was nothing. Upset by his continued silence and worrying that perhaps he was ill and couldn't write, Hester sent off another letter. No sooner had it gone than a letter from Michael arrived; he had written it in September from London. He was already beginning to regret his promise of £1,000 a year. He had decided that he would keep their incomes equal; his fortune was to be £2,500 a year; Hester's was £1,200. By giving her £600 they would both have allowances of similar amounts. It was a lot less than he had promised her in January, when he had thought that he himself would only have £2,000.[34] But Michael had met other women on his travels and was starting to feel unhappy about the commitment he had made to a former mistress.

After a brief stay in Tripoli over Christmas and New Year, the travellers returned to Mar Elias. Michael was intending to return to the East to meet up with Hester, believing that Hester expected it. Hester, struggling to keep her promise to Crauford and aware that London gossips were accusing her of chasing after Michael, wrote that she didn't want him to come. Suspicious that Michael wished to make himself appear the object of Hester's desires to a London society that were shocked, but intrigued, by her exploits.[35] She wrote that he was:

> ... making my conduct appear in a very different light than in which it should really stand, both to your friends and in the eyes of the world and have brought upon me undeserved reproach from the idea that I am the cause of what is called yr losing yr time and forsaking yr duty to live with me in a distant country.[36]

Michael had even spoken to James about meeting Hester again, making Hester worry that the fragile, newly reconstructed relationship with her brother might suffer once more and that he would think her 'half-mad' to hold on to a relationship that would lead to nothing. It was the end of any thoughts or plans Hester might have had to travel to Europe; she did not want to see Michael or his father; she did not want any more scenes. Hester was distraught. She had spent the months since Michael's departure trying to come to terms with her loss. She was emotionally tired and vulnerable; Michael's romantic plans could amount to nothing except more long-term hurt for her, as well as further alienating the one member of her family to whom she was still close. The only way she could have anything to do with him was to be distant friends; emphatically, she did not want to see him.[37]

> My health is not bad, but as usual depends too much upon the state of mind, and I see no end to cross purposes and living for some time to come a life of uncertainty and uncomfort and all this springs from yr playing about after what? ... I wish from my heart to avoid seeing you, it is the truth ... [38]

Hester reiterated this position in other letters that followed in early 1815. Just as she had wished to avoid the society of Granville after her first heartbreak, she now wished to avoid the perpetrator of her second. The scene of their parting at Latakia haunted her. Hester was renowned for her courage, but she was absolutely terrified of seeing her lover, and of losing him again.

10

Treasure, Reunion and Revenge

God bless you, I who have known what the charms of dispation [sic] are, can easily pardon you if that is the cause of yr. neglect, tho' pleasure never I believe ever withdrew my attention from the unhappy, but the love of pleasure was to me a natural not an acquired taste, which makes a difference.

Lady Hester to Michael Bruce, 24 June 1815

Lebanese Palace

By the time Hester and Meryon returned to Mar Elias they were both too exhausted to enjoy the delighted reception of the villagers. But they had only a few hours' rest before a messenger arrived. The news was ominous and sent Meryon into a flurry of concern. A Zaim had come from Constantinople with the express aim of seeing Hester and was waiting in Sidon for a visit. The Zaim was a secretive and powerful position in the Ottoman Empire. The word 'zaim' is derived from the Arabic for leader and these men were just that, chiefs supported by huge sects, all powerful in their respective districts. Hester's visitor came from the court of Mehmet Ali; the arrival of such a man would usually mean a certain arrest, but could also signify a stoning, strangling or beheading. With his customary mix of pessimism and panic, Meryon assumed that the period of goodwill shown to Hester in the East had come to an end, and that they would soon be imprisoned or worse. Hester was told to prepare a party for immediate travel to the coast. The Zaim's rank made it impossible for him to enter a Christian house, but Hester was tired, refusing to go anywhere; she told the messenger to tell the Zaim to come to her. Puzzled and perplexed by Hester's apparent diffidence, Meryon reluctantly agreed to return to his cottage. Towards the end of dinner the curious doctor heard, then saw, numerous riders approaching the convent. The Zaim had arrived. Far from being an imposing figure, the chief was a small grey-haired man in his fifties. His face showed all the strain of his journey, and Hester invited him to eat and drink before retiring with him to the salon for a private conversation.

While Meryon, impatient and unable to contain his curiosity, returned to the convent, Hester was presented with three imperial orders, *firmans*, which would give her, albeit briefly, more power in the Turkish Empire than any European had ever received. The first *firman* was to Hester's friend Suleyman, the Pasha of Acre, the second to the Pasha of Damascus and the last was to the governors of Syria; Hester was to demand, and be given without question or hesitation, any assistance she wanted from each of them in the execution of her newest plan.

Unknown to Meryon, but in collusion with Michael the previous year, Hester had been given the copy of an old document said to have been written by a dying monk. It gave the details and location of an amazing treasure trove of money, supposedly hidden under an old temple in Ascalon. Hester was intrigued and insisted on seeing the original parchment. Convinced of its authenticity, she enlisted the support of the British Ambassador, Robert Liston. Liston spoke to the Sultan, who, respectful of Hester's rank and European connections, sent the Zaim to convey his backing. The meeting was the beginning of the realization of Hester's plan. Meryon's suspense was brief; by the time their visitor left he was completely immersed in arranging the preparations necessary to travel to Ascalon in just ten days' time.

Ascalon is the most southerly resort on Israel's Mediterranean coast. The modern city is a regular commute from Gaza for many Palestinians who were deported there in 1950. It is set apart from the old city, now a huge and busy archaeological site where people try to unearth its glorious history as one of the chief cities of ancient times and the birthplace of Herod. In 1815 it was a part of the Turkish Empire and largely ignored by travellers. Hester, believing that her project to search the little-known area for gold was in the public interest, wrote to John Barker for aid in procuring the necessary finance for the journey. The Ambassador was supporting her; the Sultan was helping her. Feeling she should not use her own money for such a public venture, she asked the still obliging Barker to 'hold 12,000 Piastres ready for me, which I shall consider your advance for public purposes', assuming 'a perfect right to reimbursement' in the future when the whole plan was completed.[1] She informed Meryon that she intended to keep a 'regular account of every article' and then submit her bill to the British government, convinced that the honour she was bringing to Britain by conducting this operation warranted their remuneration.[2] Resistance would be met by attack; Hester would write to every London newspaper and create a scandal.

Obviously the plans had to be kept secret; a sudden rush to find the purported treasure would not benefit Hester's cause. Barker and Meryon were sworn to secrecy. While speedy arrangements were made, locals speculated about the reason for the flurry of activity: perhaps Hester was being made a Turkish queen, succeeding the British Prince Regent, or building ports and castles by command of the Ottoman government, or Porte. Hester, still exhausted from their previous trip, yet anxious to respond enthusiastically and quickly to the Sultan's gesture of support, gathered her travelling companions together. It was a large group: local dignitaries, a troop of horsemen and torch bearers, water carriers and tent men, who would normally be reserved to accompany a pasha, all travelled with Hester. In keeping with the eastern sponsorship of the trip, Hester enforced a regime on her companions that was in keeping with Islam. The women of the party, although not Hester, would be veiled at all times in the presence of men, and their tents would be set up in separate sites; fraternization would be severely punished.

But the grandeur of the procession belied the turmoil and sorrow of its instigator. During the journey Hester wrote again to Michael. He had stayed in England only briefly before heading off again to the continent; for five months she had heard nothing from him or of him. In spite of her protestations of independence and the splendour of her trip, she was sad and pensive:

> I cd hardly have supposed that you wd. have added so many hours of anxiety to my solitary life here by yr neglect, but I forgive you, and hope that no one will ever cause you the same uneasiness, or place you in the awkward situation you have placed me.[3]

On their arrival at the city of Acre, Hester was greeted by the friendly embrace of her former landlord Signor Catafagio, who had been such a good host on her first visit to Acre. She enlisted him as a member of the group. Hester renewed her acquaintance with the Pasha of Acre, and Meryon gained further favour by successfully tending to one of the Pasha's visitors, who suffered from a chest complaint. Surrounded by friends, Hester seemed to relax from her worries about Michael and enjoy both the fine weather and the effect of the *firmans*. The Sultan's orders seemed to be bringing Hester a new and unparalleled degree of attention and respect. The Pasha of Acre provided her with twenty more luxurious tents, one of which had been used by the Princess of Wales. It was magnificent. Green and studded with yellow flowers and stars, it had both an outer and inner section. The latter was draped with heavy silk satin in myriad vivid jewel-like colours, complemented by a resting couch ornately embroidered in gold. Hester was also presented with a tartaravan, in which she might make the remainder of the trip. A gorgeous thing, covered in crimson cloth, six gilt balls hung from it, glittering in the sun. But Hester had not lost her general mistrust of this method of transport since she scorned Michael's proposed use of one on the journey to Palmyra. Out of respect, the tartaravan made the trip with them but, before they left, Hester's favourite grey mare, a present from the French Consul, and a black ass were tethered to it so she could ride as usual.

Everyone struggled to set up camp against a wind that was rapidly becoming a tempest by the time that they reached the western gate of Haifa. Hungry and tired, Meryon and Hester, accompanied by some of their companions, retired to the dinner tent to eat and recover. Their meal was interrupted by the arrival of a strange guest wrapped in a long black Spanish cloak. A dirty-looking man in his sixties, with a grizzled beard and matted hair, he carried a huge bible under his arm. As soon as he spoke to Hester it was obvious from his heavy accent that he was French. She invited him to join the table. General Loustennau was a prophet; his home was a shed in the nearby orchards and he scraped a meagre existence from the alms which villagers gave him. Loustennau may have been insane or may have been very shrewd because he regaled Hester as a queen with a great destiny and prophesied much greatness for her. Hester listened to his prophecies and to the passages of French literature that he was able to quote at length from memory. She arranged for him to be fed and washed, and then invited him to join her entourage.

Drifted sand from the seashore was piled high against the thick city walls of Ascalon so that the forgotten city seemed to be on a different, lower level of land than the surrounding countryside. Layer upon layer of centuries of history, burned and rebuilt, covered and regenerated, contained all the mysteries of hidden treasures and lost civilizations. It was a desolate place where fragments of ancient monuments were scattered across the ground; only an old tomb and some crumbling architectural features hinted at the site of an old mosque.

The men set up their tents amidst this debris of earlier centuries while the women rode to a nearby village to find alternative accommodation.

The huge archaeological dig that then began showed no early signs of success and, after several days of exploration, the only find was a colossal Roman marble statue that was headless and had just a single arm and leg. Although a beautiful, detailed piece of sculpture, showing the ornate breast-plated armour of its subject, it was not at all what Hester had hoped for. Yet it was not disappointment or petulance that provoked her response to the find. The Porte had shown their respect for Hester in her mission to recover their treasure, but she had failed and instead found precisely what most other European travellers were looking to appropriate for their own ends: an antiquity. Hester showed her disapproval of this kind of theft, and her own blamelessness with regard to it, by giving an order to destroy the statue.

Fourteen days into the dig, with no gold pieces uncovered, the travellers prepared to leave and the torso was smashed into thousands of pieces, which were scattered across the site. Writing to General Oakes, Hester said she felt it was the only way she could prevent it being said that she came solely to pilfer foreign works of art rather than to find riches for the Turks themselves.[4] The party that returned to Mar Elias was more subdued. The financial backing they expected to find waiting for them was not forthcoming, so Hester sent a detailed financial breakdown to the Ambassador, reiterating succinctly that the trip had not been for private ends but to bring credit to the reputation of the English in the East.

While Hester was conducting her treasure hunt, Michael's correspondence from Paris with his father was not at all friendly. Michael was angered by the comments Crauford had made about his relationship being 'unfortunate' to them both and upset that Hester was now dismissing any possibility that there might, at some point, be a reunion.[5] Yet, in spite of his indignation, Michael still didn't write to Hester, presumably because he was preoccupied by his new Parisian friends, including a close attachment with the Princess Moskowa, the wife of Marshall Ney.

Politically, France was undergoing yet another massive upheaval. Following his defeat and abdication in April 1814, Napoleon had been exiled to Elba. But less than a year later, accompanied by just seven hundred men, he escaped and landed once more in France. The King sent troops to vanquish him, but the soldiers switched allegiance. With his new force, Napoleon arrived in Paris in the spring of 1815, while the King fled to safety.

Marshall Ney played a dangerous, duplicitous role. He had gained promotion during the first Napoleonic period and been given the title 'Prince of Moskowa' by the Emperor. However, he later gained favour with the Bourbons by helping to persuade Napoleon to abdicate. On first hearing the news that Napoleon had left Elba and landed on the coast, he exclaimed to his Bourbon masters that he would bring Napoleon to Paris in an iron cage.[6] Yet when he received word from Napoleon about his advance as well as the news that the King had fled Paris, he immediately returned to his former loyalties and paraded his troops to cries of '*Vive L'Empereur*'.

Michael was openly enthusiastic about Napoleon's return to Paris and, in spite of his father's worries, elected to stay on in the city and continue to enjoy the company of Madame Ney. The affair between them was not a well-kept secret and led to a repetition of the scandal that surrounded his relationship with Hester. Michael received anonymous letters warning him to leave her alone rather than risk her reputation. But far from restraining himself, Michael found yet another love interest and began dividing his time between both ladies, and it was the other, unidentified, woman who wrote to him, in the middle of his affair with Madame Ney, saying:

> I do not know how to express my desire to see you here, although I have never seen you here every place I go recalls something of you ... [7]

Unaware of all this, but wary of what her former lover was up to, Hester was again settled in the convent and, tired of being without horses, was busy acquiring a small stud of Arabs. By late June she was almost desperate. The hot sun exacerbated her irritation, making her position seem impossible. In all the time since their parting she had received only two letters from Michael and most of her knowledge was coming by way of a third party, often John Barker. Meryon, all the time more impatient with Hester's irascibility, wanted to go home. His parents were elderly and he hoped to complete his medical schooling. Money problems were also a huge worry. Michael's original promise of half of his allowance of £2,000 had diminished to £600 and he had written to Coutts Bank to ensure she drew only that amount. Hester, refusing to believe that Michael would withhold the money he had sworn to give her, refused James's help, aware that he was not wealthy and could ill afford to give it.

It was too hot even to think and, in the hope that the mountain air would give her some perspective, Hester moved the household back to Meshmushy. She appeased Meryon by writing to England to find another doctor to replace him so that, by springtime, he would be able to leave, and she carefully worded a written appeal to Michael's sense of honour. While Hester accepted the likelihood that Michael was seeing someone else, even enjoying 'the charms of dispation', she did not want 'to hear it from others first'. In June 1815, perhaps for the first time since their parting, Hester realized that she had lost Michael not only as a lover, as she had always known she would, but, more painfully and surprisingly, as a friend:

> I was sincere in my wish to give you up for yr. happiness and for yr. pleasure, but I expected I must confess to have ever found you an attentive, an affectionate friend, and one I could have relied upon.[8]

It was a revelation for her; the frequent letters would stop, since her life gave her nothing of interest to say and Michael's indifference made them pointless and sad. And in the same generosity of spirit she had shown to Granville, she wished Michael well, although she went on to confess that she would never understand or empathize with how he had behaved.[9]

Hester's summer was a quiet one. Since the plague, any period of great exertion left her worn out. Ascalon had physically drained her but brought little by way of recompense, and the emotional strain of the past year and a half had not abated. She recuperated as she had at Walmer, but exchanged the controlled landscape of her wilderness garden for the rocks, pathways and magnificent views from Meshmushy. While Hester withdrew, Meryon set off on a trip to Alexandria to tend on Colonel Misset. Misset was an officer of the Eniskillen dragoons, renowned for his diplomatic skill in the East, particularly in the face of his serious physical disability. He suffered from a degenerative disease which would eventually paralyse all of his limbs and which by 1815 had already lost him the use of his legs. Hoping that Meryon might be able to help Misset reduce the inexorable deterioration, Hester urged him to make the journey.

Meryon was not the only guest at Misset's house. Burckhardt and his friend William Turner stayed with the Colonel, and the three men made various sightseeing trips together. In spite of the superficial jollity that existed between them, Meryon was unhappy about the constant remarks made about Hester's eccentricities and his relationship with her, which these other young men saw as bordering on blind adoration. Nevertheless, enjoying the society of Colonel Misset's home, Meryon did not return to Meshmushy until November.

Meanwhile, Hester's health improved and she was consumed by a new obsession. Boutin, the Frenchman whom she had helped to travel across the mountain, was dead. Only one letter had arrived from him in the time he had been away. In his letter to the acting French Consul, Boutin reiterated his intention to cut across the mountain where the Ansary tribe roamed. Weeks passed, then months. Boutin did not return. No one received any word. The initial hopes that the silence meant that Boutin had found some antiquities or stayed with a local tribe gave way to rumours that he was dead. The local authorities did not seem eager to conduct an investigation, so Hester decided to do so herself. During Meryon's absence in Alexandria, an Italian travelling physician had stayed with Hester, and she sent him to Hamah to make enquiries after the young Frenchman. She ordered two of her servants, one of them a Druse, to follow the Ansary trail through the mountains as Boutin would have, to try to glean what they could. Hester, her energy restored by her new preoccupation, rode to neighbouring villages to make personal enquiries. By the time Meryon came to Meshmushy, Hester knew categorically that Boutin was dead, murdered by hostile tribesmen. Her investigative obsession gave way to one of vengeance. She would find the perpetrators and avenge him, as if he had been her own countryman. Meryon was understandably dubious about this proposal, fearing that any crusade would only lead to retribution against Hester and her household. But Hester was intractable. More servants were dispatched, some as spies, to find the identity of the killers.

Michael was still philandering in Paris. When he received Hester's June letter, he wrote to his father stressing that Hester was now only to have £600 from his allowance and acknowledging that, although he was developing a friendship with her brother James, his relationship with Hester was finished. Michael had other concerns.

Napoleon's had been but a brief reversal of fortune. Within three months he was again defeated by the British and Prussian allies and abdicated for the second time. King Louis XVIII returned to the throne. The Convention of Paris in July 1815 ostensibly granted pardons for those who had acted against the Bourbon interest, but Marshall Ney, failing to convince in yet another change in loyalty, was arrested and tried.

Caroline Ney and Michael fought on his behalf, but by December Ney was executed. A compatriot of Ney and an aide of Napoleon, Count Lavalette, had been imprisoned too and, with the help of two Englishmen, Michael managed to rescue him, acquiring a glamorous reputation in the process.[10] Lord Byron, who had rejected Michael's tentative advances at Greece, declared that the rescue made him rank Michael as one of his contemporaries whose achievements he most admired.[11] Caroline, dazzled and now freed from marital obligation, began to take the relationship with Michael more seriously.

In the winter, Hester returned to Mar Elias. Her appeals to local authorities for support in avenging Boutin were futile. The Pasha wrote that the weather was too cold in the mountains and any plans would have to wait until spring. The convent roof was strengthened against the deluges of the rainy season and, with some books that Colonel Misset sent her out of gratitude for Meryon's visit, Hester settled down to wait. As Christmas drew near, for the first time since she came to the East, Hester felt homesick. Lying in her parlour she listened to Meryon read from one of Misset's books: *Tales of Fashionable Life* by Maria Edgeworth. The stories seemed to be filled with references to her situation. The tale of Vivian was a story about Michael. When later she wrote to him she entreated him to look at the shallowness of the hero and his bad end. But it was the end of another story, 'Absentee', that caused Hester to break down in fits of sobbing:

> The young man expressed great regret at leaving her totally unprovided for; but said that he trusted his father would acknowledge her, and that her friends would be reconciled to her . . . [12]

The letter that Hester wrote to Michael was an outpouring of her pain. She expected Michael to have a relationship with a young, single, suitable woman, but his affair with Ney, a woman who offered no more hope of a respectable future for Michael than she herself did, meant her selflessness had been in vain. Michael did not even care enough to be honest with her any more; the loss of his friendship was something so unexpected that she could not conceive it.

Michael's notoriety in Paris did not reach its height until early January, when he was arrested and incarcerated in the Prison de la Force. By the middle of the month the story of his arrest was splashed all over the London papers and Crauford was inundated with letters of sympathy and support for his son. Hester's brother travelled to Paris to see if he could help, carrying the news that Crauford was having financial difficulties. After a discussion with James in his cell, Michael wrote to reassure his father; while he would honour Hester's allowance for 1816 it would be the last payment he would ever make to her. While Michael was treated tolerably in prison, March was to bring a further shock. He was charged with treason – which carried the death penalty.

Hester, unaware that her former lover was in a French jail, suffered through a terrible winter. The rains that had come just a few days before Christmas became violent storms that raged across the country in the first months of the New Year. Meryon was not the only person ill at ease. His annoyance with Burckhardt's remarks about Hester continued, resulting in a progressively acerbic correspondence between the two men.[13] Early complaints from Burckhardt over Meryon's lack of letters grew to peevishness and he arrogantly dismissed Boutin's death, knowing that it was important both to Hester and to the doctor, while whingeing about the fact that Meryon had repeated his derogatory remarks to Hester. Meryon was also in regular correspondence with Hester's former maid, Elizabeth Williams, in Malta. She was still unhappy with her life, and in anticipation of his return to England, which would leave Hester without a companion, Meryon urged her to come to Mar Elias.

In 1815 Elizabeth embarked at Malta, completely alone. During frightening storms in a scene reminiscent of the earlier shipwreck, the vessel sprang a leak and was forced ashore at Rhodes. It was almost three months before the repairs were complete and the ship could resume its course. But the second leg of the voyage was even worse than the first. Captained by a vicious and cruel man, the crew mutinied. While Elizabeth lay below, vomiting constantly as the sea churned, sure that she would never reach Mount Lebanon, swords clashed and voices were raised on the deck above. When they reached Cyprus, many of the crew were arrested, but Elizabeth had no time to recover from her seasickness before the voyage to Beirut. The sailing time was three and a half months. Sick and exhausted, she made it as far as Beirut, where she collapsed at the home of Mr Laurella, a British agent. While she recovered, Meryon travelled out to meet her and bring her home.

Meryon was relieved by the fact that Hester did not seem insensible to her maid's loyalty as she welcomed Elizabeth exuberantly, but Hester's improved temperament also had a secondary cause. Elizabeth's arrival coincided with the arrival of two letters that Michael had written to Hester in August. Hester, reassured that his silence was at least in part due to the vagaries of the postal system, immediately regretted her December lament. Still unaware that Michael was in jail, she replied with the news of Boutin's death and of the crippling inflation which seemed to be bringing the country to a standstill. When, a few weeks later, gossip of his predicament reached her, she began a fevered campaign of correspondence to anyone and everyone she thought could help. Hester's own sympathies were not for the French King; she admired Napoleon and wrote scathingly of allied interference in French affairs, ironically in much the same way her father did. She dismissed English interference as brought about by statesmen:

> ... whose unbounded ignorance and duplicity have brought shame through all Europe, and have exposed themselves, not only to ridicule, but to the curses of present and future generations.[14]

However, with Michael's welfare in mind, Hester sent appeals to her distant relative, the Marquis of Buckingham, who had paid substantial sums to ensure the comfort of Louis XVIII as a refugee in England.

Spring heralded the arrival of European visitors, the first of whom, William Bankes, was warmly received by Hester as being a potentially excellent source of gossip. Bankes was a close friend of Byron, whom he had met and known intimately at Cambridge. Although celebrated for his travelling and collecting, his homosexuality would lead to his eventual exile from England. Meryon eagerly took Bankes on a guided tour of the area, limited only by Bankes's riding ability on the mountainous terrain. Meryon had made a discovery – an ancient sepulchre at Abu Ghyas – and he enthusiastically brought his new companion to share his find, mainly in the hope that he would make some copies of the detailed paintings as a memorial to the monument. Meryon seemed to have changed his attitude since his visit to Palmyra, where he too tried to acquire souvenirs. Like Hester, he now thoroughly disapproved of the European theft of eastern artefacts and he was disappointed in Bankes's reaction when, on completing two sketches, he removed two of the original works with the intention of taking them back to England. Hester, no less vehement in her conviction that antiquities belonged in their native countries, showed her disapproval in a pointed way when Bankes asked for her assistance in reaching Palmyra. The Emir Bashir II had an agreement with Hester: any travellers visiting her on their way to his palace should be furnished with a letter; the letter would be Hester's introduction to Bashir and would be marked by either one or two seals. Two seals was the sign that Bashir should embrace the carrier like family, inviting him to share in all the local customs and treating him with the highest respect. One seal meant only that the bearer should be given safe passage, nothing more. When Hester gave Bankes a letter to take to the Emir to guarantee his safety during the journey to Palmyra, it carried a single seal, an implicit warning that he should not be trusted too far. Bankes, knowing the arrangement Hester had with Bashir, checked his letter after he had left the convent. Peeved that it carried only one seal, he discarded it, with the result that he did not reach Palmyra that spring, after being prevented by Muhana's son. His second attempt would be successful, but on reaching the city Bankes was imprisoned and following his release had to pay large sums of money just to copy an inscription from a ruined wall.

Meryon's shaky relationship with Bankes, following the latter's acquisition, was matched by the tension between him and Burckhardt, which was reaching mammoth proportions. In spring, Burckhardt's final letter to Meryon arrived. It accused the doctor of being 'insidious and vulgar' and acting with 'low, cunning design', all for repeating something that Burckhardt had been quite happy to vocalize in public.[15] Hester was equally annoyed by Burckhardt's remarks and, although the squabbling correspondence between him and Meryon came to an end, Hester continued to send vitriolic missives both to and about him in the months ahead.

Bankes had already gone on his way when a parcel addressed to him arrived at Mar Elias. It came with instructions for Hester to open it should it arrive after his departure. Inside she found a bundle of clothes and personal effects belonging to a Mr Silk Buckingham, a man she did not know but who was well regarded by several of her friends, including General Oakes. Hester immediately invited him to visit the convent, thoughtfully enclosing a letter of credit with the invitation, in spite of the fact it was something she could ill afford, so that he could get by without the possessions that had ended up in her keeping.[16] Buckingham treated her kindness with the gratitude it warranted, later admitting that he was more than a little flattered that such an aristocratic woman would take the trouble. He arrived in the small hours of the morning, suffering from dysentery, dressed as a Turk. Anxious not to wake Hester, he went first to Meryon's house, but the doctor, knowing Hester's late hours, sent him directly to the convent. Hester welcomed him warmly. It was an auspicious beginning to an agreeable stay. Buckingham spent nine long and pleasant days with Hester. After recovering from his illness he took to riding her Arab horses before dinner and conversing late into the night. Believing that her attributes were in part due to the fact that she was away from the 'continual round of frivolities which dissipate the thoughts of half the fashionable world in England', Buckingham found her erudite, intelligent and passionate in her defence of anyone she felt was oppressed.[17] He marvelled at her popularity with local people and found that the reality, for him, matched the tales he had heard on his travels of her 'beauty and benevolence'. He was very sad when he had to leave the convent but departed in improved health, furnished with an excellent mare and accompanied by one of Hester's own servants, bearing presents to the Pachas and Governors that Hester had befriended and to whom she had given him introductions.

It might have been the spring drought or the slight but constant arid wind that brought them but, in April, Mar Elias was besieged by locusts. Huge swarms of them swept over the mountain, devouring every crop in their wake and bringing food shortages that lasted long beyond their infestation. Some villagers, unable to afford the local prices, carried grain in sacks on their backs for more than twenty miles to feed their families. Hester's shaky finances suffered too, and news that Caroline, Princess of Wales, had arrived at Acre made her eager to move and avoid the embarrassment that her pecuniary difficulties would cause should they meet up. Visiting Antioch enabled Hester to keep away from the Princess and to pursue the matter of vengeance for Boutin's death, which as yet remained unresolved.

Crauford Bruce was also suffering serious financial problems and was being constantly harangued by Coutts, Hester's bankers, to send the final payment of money she had been promised. From his prison cell Michael played a careful game, writing to Coutts to assure them he would send the £300 but also to his father to complain about what he called Hester's 'extravagant expenses'.[18] With James, the three men began a mutually supportive correspondence with a recurring theme: Hester should return to England.

While Hester went to Antioch, Elizabeth and Meryon remained behind at the convent to keep the household in order. The initial excitement of being in the East had worn off and Elizabeth was feeling lonely and lost. She spoke no Arabic and was left to pass long hours with native servants, with whom she could not communicate, while Meryon was tending his patients. Moreover, the summer heat, which Hester usually avoided by going to Meshmushy, was intolerable at Mar Elias. In July, just over three months after her arrival, Elizabeth fell ill. Suffering from high temperatures and a rash that spread across her body, she was confined to bed for several weeks, and Meryon, fearful of the severity of her sickness, curtailed his professional duties to remain by her side.

In the meantime, Hester was wreaking a horrible, brutal revenge. Mustafa Age Berber, governor of the Ansary mountains, received her command and his men stormed the Ansary villages in a vicious and barbaric campaign. In what became a massacre to avenge a single death, the villages where the assassins had lived, almost thirty settlements in total, were burned to the ground. The men involved in the murder were decapitated so that fifty-two heads were sent to the Pasha, while their wives were dragged to Tripoli in chains to be sold as slaves. Ansary religious sites were desecrated and vandalized before Berber returned to Tripoli in triumph. News of the attack came to Hester as she stayed in Antioch, along with praise and admiration from the French for her persistence in defence of their countryman. Against local advice, apparently proud of the merciless slaughter, Hester rode into the recently ravaged lands to inspect the damage, remaining unharmed perhaps through fear of what further retribution might occur.

As Hester enjoyed the adulation of the French and the respect of the Ansary, her brother James was growing more concerned about her spending, citing it as an incontrovertible reason why Hester should return to Europe. Michael hinted in a letter to his father that perhaps 'her mind was affected'; his father responded, as Michael hoped, that if Hester was mad it was yet more cause to get her into Europe, or better still to England, where friends could give her 'affectionate attention'.[19] Hester was now an embarrassment to them both. In the East she was free to stir up more trouble and to continue to demand the allowance she had been promised; in England, as an unprotected woman, she would be much easier to control; in England, a mad woman perhaps needing medical treatment was easily kept in her place.

Hester's visitor of the previous year, Bankes, still smarting over his single seal and failure to reach Palmyra, was not helping her reputation. His gossip was petty and spiteful, filled with moralizing over her relationship with Michael and fake concern over the scandal it caused. Both her father's eccentricities and the wretchedness of her situation after Pitt's death were remarked upon. Pre-empting the harm Bankes might do her on his return to England, Hester wrote a vengeful letter to General Grenville with some scathing character analysis of her own. She was livid that the recompense for her hospitality was 'being ridiculed by him and his talking in public about my father's absurdities, my former situation and c.' Bankes was arrogant and mean, his cleverness was that of a swindler and he was insincere to the highest degree imaginable, affecting sensibility over her relationship with Michael and a fit of lamentation over the harm it had done. He had accepted Hester's hospitality and then behaved like a hypocrite. English society should know he was a man not to be trusted.[20]

Having found a new physician for Hester, Dr Newberry, Meryon anxiously awaited his arrival throughout the latter half of the year so that he could return to his family and continue his studies. He was tired and eager to resume his life in Europe. When Hester returned to Mar Elias in November, Newberry arrived shortly after. Meryon started to pack. A winter visitor, Firman Didot, who later published an account of his meeting with Hester and added to her reputation as a powerful eccentric, brought French newspapers. Michael was free from prison and, according to the papers, betrothed. It was untrue, probably no more than a fabrication based on gossip about Michael and Caroline Ney, but Hester had no way of knowing it. Michael had just been released and returned to England in July. He did not yet know the woman who would be his wife. Hester, upset and agitated, wrote what she thought would be her last letter to him. Meryon would carry it with him, thus assuring her of its arrival. Her words would finalize any vestiges of uncertainty that lay between them. A painstakingly detailed letter, it justified each item of expense that Michael's allowance had funded: the acquisition of rare books Michael himself wanted to have and the revenge of Boutin's murder, uses which Hester felt far more worthy than 'frivolity at Paris'. His betrothal she accepted, or said she did, with a combination of pride and inevitability; but she no longer wished to visit the continent or to meet Michael. For all her resignation, Hester felt betrayed. She wrote:

> If those, who have experience of my character, cannot give me credit for honour, disinterestedness, and integrity, without statement to prove I am neither mad nor unprincipled, I must content myself that strangers will be more just to my present conduct as well as to my memory.[21]

Hester had closed her relationship with Michael and, in the small hours of Saturday 18 January 1817, two months before her forty-first birthday, another phase of her life ended. Meryon rested in his home for a few hours before saying goodbye to Elizabeth and Hester. After seven years he was leaving his position. The villagers crowded around his horse, some shouting good wishes, some former patients even in tears. When he stopped briefly to rest and eat a picnic he had been given, he found that Elizabeth had been cooking for days: venison tarts, roasted wildfowl and plum cakes, washed down with local wine. In Beirut, Meryon found passage with a Greek ship that would take him as far as Cyprus. It took him four months by land and sea to reach Marseille. And he did so accompanied by a small, shivering angora greyhound he had fallen in love with on the way.

Of the East and of the West

Through Smyrna's plague-hushed thoroughfares,
Up sea-set Malta's rocky stairs,
Gray olive slopes of hills that hem
Thy tombs and shrines, Jerusalem,
Or startling on her desert throne
The crazy Queen of Lebanon with claims fantastic as her own,
Her tireless feet have held their way,
And still unrestful, bowed, and gray,
She watches under Eastern skies,
With hope each day renewed and fresh,
The Lord's quick coming in the flesh,
Whereof she dreams and prophecies.
From 'Snowbound' by John Greenleaf Whittier

Druse Women

THE YEARS BETWEEN MERYON'S DEPARTURE in 1817 and his third visit to Hester in 1830 are probably the most mysterious, but surprisingly least speculated about, years of Hester's life. The notes and diaries from his first visit form a three-volume account of her travels, while those from his last visits make a three-volume memoir. However, the notes, letters and journal entries from the years between them lie forgotten in an archive in Kent under the heading *Additional Memoirs*. In the first volume of *Memoirs of Lady Hester Stanhope*, Meryon dismisses his second visit with a paragraph:

> ... at Lady Hester's request, I again revisited Syria. But I found that her ladyship had in the meanwhile completely familiarised herself with the usages of the East, conducting her establishment entirely in the Turkish manner, and adopting even much of their medical empiricism. Under these circumstances, and at her own suggestion I again bade her adieu, as I then believed, for the last time.[1]

Yet the yellow-edged, sometimes torn, frequently faded, pieces of paper arranged in careful bundles within dark grey files, give a more detailed, if incomplete, account, as well as the suggestion that Meryon, given the time, would one day have published a third series of books.

Meryon's replacement, Dr Newberry, seemed initially to be a success. He settled into Hester's household with relative ease, placating Hester with his excellent manners and 'little courtesies' and passing many hours in solitary study as he tried to learn Italian. Hester devoted much of her own time to an exploration of eastern religion and mysticism, while struggling with Arabic. Although in time she would speak the local dialect fluently with a heavy English accent, she never completely mastered the writing system and her written Arabic was, and is, difficult to decipher.

Early spring brought news that her father was dead. He had died four months earlier. His last years were spent in poverty as his compulsion for frugality became more and more extreme. Living in the huge house at Chevening, which he refused to heat, its rooms largely emptied of the furniture that he associated with the rank and wealth he rejected, Citizen Stanhope became a famous eccentric and recluse. The bad feeling that existed between him and his eldest son culminated in an acrimonious and protracted lawsuit when Mahon took his father to court for running down the estate, using the protection of his own son's inheritance as justification. Louisa's relationship with her husband had never been easy and, strained by the bitterness of his quarrel with their son and forced to live in ever more spartan conditions, she chose to invite a female acquaintance, Mrs Walburga Lackner, to live with them at Chevening. But rather than provide companionship for Louisa, she became an intimate friend to Lord Stanhope, so that his wife moved out and a deed of separation was drawn up between husband and wife. It was a strange arrangement and in his last years he was heard to praise Wally, as he called Mrs Lackner, for her excellent management of his household. Family friend Lord Carrington wrote to Mahon that Walburga was 'naturally anxious to make a purse'.[2] Sir Joseph Banks believed that the Earl starved himself to death.[3] Always thin, he became almost skeletal and 'lived on soup, on the most meagre diet, on barley water sweetened with sugar'.[4] Hearing of the illness that would soon lead to his death, James wrote to his father asking to see him but, although he was given a paternal blessing, he was denied access.[5] Lord Stanhope's life ended in what had become the shell of a grand home, his body wasted. He was buried as he requested in his will: 'without the least ostentation' as if he had died a 'very poor man'.[6]

∼

Hester's final meeting with her father was ten years before, shortly after Pitt's death, in 1807. Because she was afraid that his politics might adversely affect her own and her brothers' futures, it was the first time she had seen him for seven years.

> Much as I might wish to see him I thought it was my duty to consider
> what might be the consequences to myself and younger brothers

if this interview was to lead to his dictating a line of Politick and general conduct.[7]

The reunion was moving and conciliatory, although her father refused to have anything to do with Mahon or her sisters:

He says he never has ceased to love me and always believed I wd never sanction anything low and mean and that my conduct had been quite different from the others.[8]

In spite of its success, Hester did not repeat the experience, believing that Walburga Lackner, already installed at Chevening, would 'prevent great intimacy'. [9]

The long silence that existed between them did not stop Hester grieving at his death, nor did it prevent her clinging to the vain hope of some kind of inheritance. When she wrote to Michael for the very last time, she said that when she received the money she expected from her father's estate she would repay him every penny he had given her. It was a proud gesture but a futile one; Hester's debt was now spiralling to a point from which she could not and did not recover.

Dr Newberry's initial enthusiasm and courtesy quickly faded as he began to grumble that Hester spent less and less time with him, preferring to tend her small stud of horses and consult local holy men. Her chestnut mare, Lulu, a gift from Ahmed Bey, gave birth to a strangely deformed foal. Layla was tiny with a spine that dipped so that her back looked as if it was shaped like a Turkish saddle. An old local prophecy dictated that a horse which was 'born saddled' would carry the next Mahdi, a kind of Messianic figure, and Hester immediately believed Layla to be the chosen mare.

For many of Hester's subsequent western visitors, and to the local European community, this was seen either as a concrete example of her mental instability or more charitably as a mark of her eccentricity. Yet the belief in the coming of the Mahdi, which Hester strictly upheld, was not unusual or strange amongst natives of her adopted country. An orthodox tenet of Shia Muslims, a belief in the coming of holy men, Mahdi, had been adopted by the Druse. These were spiritual leaders whose arrival did not necessarily symbolize an apocalypse but rather a great, significant and beneficial change to civilization. This common and widely held belief fits much more with Hester's own proclamations of her faith (rather than the accompanying European interpretations), specifically that the coming of the Mahdi might symbolize the downfall of decadent western civilization and a renaissance both for the East and for those who had sought spiritual cleansing in its locale. Fundamentally, belief in the imminent arrival of the Mahdi was not 'exotic and sectarian, reflecting merely extreme views'.[10] Rather than conform to western preconceptions of a native gone eastern, which in themselves were romantic and highly poetic, Hester actually tried to live and become as the people around her. The result was three separate and mutually incomprehensible states: the real Lebanese in their ethnic diversity, Hester's attempt to become Lebanese, and the West's picture of what an orientalized European should be. Hester never formally embraced Islam, claiming that she wished only:

> to deserve the goodness of that God, one and almighty, whose existence my entire soul acknowledges.[11]

But she was outspoken in her criticism of Christianity. Her hatred of it was not new. As a child Hester refused to be confirmed into the Church of England, despite the concerned entreaties of her grandmother and stepmother. When they insisted that it was a way to show love of Christ, she replied that she loved her dead mother but would not show her love for her by digging her up out of the earth and turning 'cannibal in eating a bit of her flesh and drinking her blood'. And as she wouldn't do it for love, 'it must be a disgusting thing to do it for anything else'.[12]

Hester's obsessions made her easy prey for many local charlatans. A village doctor named Metta who was employed casually by Hester from 1815 brought her rumours of a holy book and a passage translated from an accompanying old manuscript:

> A European woman will come and live on Mount Lebanon at a certain epoch. She will build a house there, and obtain power and influence greater than a Sultan's. A boy without a father will join her, and his destiny will be fulfilled under her wing. The coming of the Mahdi will follow, but be preceded by war, pestilence and other calamities.

The Mahdi will ride a horse born saddled; and a woman will come from a far country to partake in the mission.[13]

It was a convenient prophecy for which Metta was well paid. The similarity with Brothers' Bedlam prophecy seemed far too great to be mere coincidence and Hester extended her study to astrology and the occult, consulting an Asian dervish expert to instruct her.

After the birth of the foal, Hester moved General Loustennau to the house where Meryon had stayed, putting him in charge of 'the little horses'[14]. Concerned that the strangeness of her mode of life was proving too difficult for Elizabeth, Hester offered to send her home. But, out of a mixture of loyalty and want of better prospects, Elizabeth opted to stay. Apart from Loustennau, Elizabeth and Dr Newberry, the only European servant who remained with Hester was the elderly servant Anne Fry, survivor of the shipwreck, and it was she who suffered the brunt of Hester's tyranny. Anne could be kept till three or four in the morning with chores, yet still have to rise at seven 'to sew horse clothes, or make a mash for one of the mares'. Then she would have to make broth, knead bread, cook dinner and give instructions to other servants. On bad days these chores would be carried out against a background of insults and reproaches 'heaped on her without mercy' from a foul-tempered Hester.[15] Hester, who had always been meticulously tidy, became obsessively fastidious about the running of the convent; it was an obsession driven by fear of illness, as well as by the emptiness of the days. All food was subject to scrupulous examination and washing. Chickens were bought and coloured ribbons attached to one leg; a note of the date and the colour of the ribbon were made in a ledger and only after twenty days, when it was thought free from any outside contamination, could a chicken be killed. However, if a particular chicken proved difficult to catch and kill, the servants often cheated the system by exchanging the ribbons. Hester's moods and irascibility were also due to what she referred to as 'women's complaints', perhaps the result of early onset menopause – she was in her early forties – or of generally poor health. It was a subject she discovered her new physician knew little about. Newberry's ignorance was hardly surprising. A former ship's surgeon, he was most skilled at dealing with concomitant illnesses such as dysentery and ague:[16]

I found out when he began to practice that a boy of twelve years old knew more of women's complaints than he did. The most common disorder he seemed never to have heard of which is scarcely credible.[17]

Hester treated herself with local medicines but, when Sheikh Bashir Jumblat asked her if Dr Newberry might tend on his wife, the doctor's ineptitude put her into a rage. The Sheikh's wife's periods had stopped completely since her last pregnancy and now, after two years, the bloating and pain were becoming unbearable. Making no detailed oral examination of his patient, Newberry assumed the dysmenorrhoea was symptomatic of a pregnancy and told her husband so.[18] Hester was furious and told the Sheikh that had his wife been pregnant, which she most certainly was not, Dr Newberry would not have been fit to tend on her.

Newberry, less subservient than his predecessor, enjoyed neither the East nor working for Hester. By October, less than a year after his arrival, he made preparations to leave. Faced with the difficulty of replacing him, Hester again turned to Meryon and wrote to England, asking him to return but also to bring some domestic help for her – Swiss maids and a manservant – and to speak to the son of a recently deceased friend, inviting him to join her as a companion.

Meryon was settled in London near Charing Cross while working at St Thomas's Hospital. Much of his free time was spent 'in company with Narcisse, the French lady who lodged in the pension house with me'.[19] Pierre Narcisse was born on 4 October 1791 in a Paris that was recovering from the aftermath of the revolution. Just three years after the pomp and magnificence of Napoleon's coronation in 1804 she made her professional début as a dancer at the Paris Opera. Although Narcisse Gentil, as she became known, remained at the Opera for seven years, her career was troubled and interrupted by bouts of ill health. Given to fainting fits which increased in severity with time, unable to cope with the rigours of the dance, her mother (no mention is ever made of Narcisse's father) took her daughter to England. Narcisse's son would later say that his grandmother took his mother to England 'to sell her'.[20] The 'buyer' was Lord Lowther. Passionately devoted to the opera, and to many of the girls who worked in the chorus, Lowther was fat and unattractive. He was a member of the Prince Regent's inner circle, a patron of the Italian and French opera, known for his obsession with dancing girls. Once installed as his mistress, Narcisse's and her mother's financial position was secure. That is, until she fell pregnant. An apprehensive Narcisse befriended her charming neighbour, the doctor, who helped her during her confinement. On 29 July, Fanny Lowther, much to her mother's relief, was acknowledged as the daughter of William Lowther at her christening in St James, Westminster. Settled, and in receipt of a small pension, Narcisse remained besotted with Meryon and, grateful to him for his friendship in less certain times, she kept up a passionate correspondence with him after he received Hester's letters and set out for mainland Europe.

It took considerable time in Switzerland for Meryon to find serving-women who might meet with Hester's approval. By Valentine's Day 1819 he thought he was successful and wrote that he believed he had found suitable servants. They were four in number: Louis was to be Hester's manservant and seemed good-natured and hard-working; Marie was a spirited and experienced woman; Pauline was distinguished by her thoroughness; while a young girl, Louise, still in her early teens, greatly impressed the doctor with her gentleness and sweetness. Miranda Leander, the son of Hester's dead friend whom Meryon had been asked to contact, was completely overjoyed at the idea of travelling to someone he understood to be a great lady, and Meryon was delighted to have his enthusiastic and entertaining company.

They secured passage on a brig to Cyprus but during the voyage Meryon found that his judgement of the new staff had been over-optimistic. The two older women vomited uncontrollably and continuously during most of the trip, and Meryon found them disagreeable in extreme. Marie was bad-tempered and far too arrogant; Pauline whined constantly – hardly surprising given that she was constantly sick – but Meryon found her accent annoyingly affected and reminiscent of the 'Devonshire drawl'. The only person he could find no fault with was Miranda Leander:

> My only comfort is in Miranda Leander, the son of your departed friend whose intelligence is above his years, whose docility, whose juvenile ardour, coupled with a perceived adoration of your ladyship's talents, whose comely looks speak for him before he opens his lips.[21]

By the time they had docked, Meryon was regretting his harshness. Eventually, he too had been ill during the voyage, able to keep down only light broth and water, so he wrote again to Hester, intending to mollify the misgiving and worries of his last letter. Pauline was thorough and very clean and tidy. Louise had an excellent memory. Louis, the manservant, was very obedient and hard-working. The only real problem was Marie, 'foolish and conceited, always talking about things she doesn't understand, and mouthing her likes and dislikes'.[22] There were donkeys ready to carry the new arrivals to their homes when they reached Abra. Meryon alone received word to go to straight to the convent to see Hester. He found her almost exactly as he had left her, seated cross-legged in oriental costume. But there was one striking difference: she now smoked and frequently puffed the long water pipe, or narghileh, that bubbled beside her. Hester, disappointed with the news he had sent her, as well as suffering from bad health, did not greet him quite as exuberantly as he had hoped. Yet he stayed for several hours, listening to her account of the current situation, interspersed with details of her ailments.

Politically, the country was more troubled than it had been when Meryon left. Bashir II was cultivating the support of Maronite Christians, and in doing so appeared to be adopting many Christian ways. Enmity between Emir Bashir Shihab and Sheikh Bashir Jumblat was growing, the two men struggling for power as the Druse increasingly resented the Emir's rule. The Sheikh hoped to use Bashir Shihab's partial adoption of a new faith to destroy him politically in the eyes of the Ottomans. Accordingly, he wrote to the Porte saying the Emir had neglected all the tenets of his faith and become an infidel. The Porte asked the Pasha of Acre to investigate the whole affair further and find out what truth, if any, there was in the Sheikh's accusation. Suleyman, Pasha of Acre, reacted hesitantly, aware that the unity of his kingdom depended largely on the Emir's success as a ruler, a fact that his successor would overlook to his detriment in the near future. Every year, as a matter of mere formality, the Emir was reappointed by 'the investiture of a pelisse of honour'.[23] The tentative investigation instigated by Suleymen resulted in the ceremony being delayed, so that by the time the pelisse arrived it was three months late. It was accompanied by the letters written against the Emir, which the Pasha of Acre had diplomatically ruled to disregard. Hearing that the investiture would occur after all, Jumblat hurried from Makhtara to Beittedine, about three hours' riding, to offer his congratulations. The Emir confronted him, but the Sheikh made excuses and, after a heated argument, an uneasy and duplicitous truce was agreed. The calm was only temporary; Suleyman of Acre died and was replaced by the twenty-one-year-old, highly ambitious Abdullah Pasha, the son of a senior Ottoman official. He was impatient and lacked the careful diplomatic skills of his predecessor. The alliance between the Jumblats and Shihabs was fragile, and the new Pasha resented the Emir's power. The countryside was filled with murmurings and speculations. War was expected. Hester, caught between both the Sheikh and the Emir, with no wish to offend either, now avoided contact with them both. As she later explained to the English Ambassador:

> I have never seen the Emir or Sheikh since the death of Solomon Pasha for then the intrigue began.[24]

Meryon did not leave Hester until after midnight. Guided by a servant carrying a torch, he made his way on a donkey along the rocky and, at times, precipitous path to find all of the servants and Miranda awake and waiting for him. After a journey of months, they had found that their new homes were bare huts with mud floors and windows without any glass. The roofs, supported by rough rafters, looked as if they might collapse at any minute. There were no chairs or tables, no washing facilities, just dirty rugs on the floor for sleeping. Meryon, feeling guilty that their treatment might be related to his reports of their character, thought their situation 'deplorable'.[25] He was right in his assumption. His bad report of the maids had done them no favours and it was three days before Hester agreed to see them, having first got detailed reports about them from the villagers. The meeting bore out her worst fears. These were silly women who not only looked dishonest but 'were both pinched up in stays', a fashion Hester regarded as indicative of the utmost stupidity, for 'how could they even ride and be active with such horrid things about them'.[26] In the brief audience she gave them, she dismissed their motives for agreeing to come to her household, believing they aimed to serve as short a time as possible before going back to society to gossip about her, scandalizing London with her lifestyle and gaining position for themselves.[27] Moreover, Hester claimed they were incapable of living in the correct way or fulfilling the daily duties necessary for her mode of life. She bathed daily and expected servants to emulate her example, but the women washed infrequently. She enjoyed smoking her narghileh, yet none of the women had any knowledge 'of how to fill, clean or light one'.[28]

Four days after his arrival, Hester finally invited young Miranda Leander to the convent. He had been impatient and anxious, but Hester so completely charmed him that he returned to his hovel content to sing her praises.

Newberry's ineptitude was only one reason why Hester's health was bad. As the days passed, Meryon was upset to find Hester deeply sad, in the way he had only seen her immediately following Michael's departure. Her initial outpourings were filled with condescension and indifference towards family and former friends but, as the long and frequent late-night conversations continued, she confessed her that 'her bosom was corroded to the very core by the neglect of her friends in England'. Meryon later wrote in his journal that:

Reflections to this effect were incessantly the theme of our conversation, and she then would melt into tears, sob and make most piteous lamentations. At other times she would burst out into bitter execrations against them.[29]

After these outbursts, she was usually calm. Recovering her haughty manner, she asked the doctor not to tell anyone how badly off she was when he wrote to anyone from home. Aware of the instability of her own emotions, she lamented her own inability to control them:

May God only grant I may die in my senses; for what can my nervousness be? It is like gunpowder. If anything sets fire to me I go off in an explosion, and am no longer mistress of myself.[30]

Meryon went to the convent almost every day, and each time Hester's passionate outbursts disturbed him. Distraught and inconsistent, one day she would rail against him for having mentioned his return visit to her brother James, the next berate him furiously for not telling her family how badly off she was. Money was, as always, a major problem, especially now that Crauford and Michael were no longer sending Hester any allowance and her English stipend was all owed in debts. But the issue that recurred through her diatribes was her disappointment in her brothers, James and Philip, and how she missed her dearest Charles. She was terrified that if they knew how she lived they might find some way to make her return to live in England, in conditions that would amount to house arrest; she was also deeply incredulous that, if they were aware of her situation, they had not offered help:

> Good God! that people who are millionaires should have let me rot here and not once have offered me any assistance! Never will I go to England! To France I may: but if ever any of them come near me, by God, I'll stab myself or blow my brains out. I have bought a poniard for that. Don't think I am mad when I say so, for I mean it.[31]

She despised what she saw as the hypocrisy of friends and relations who purported to be Christians yet gave her no charity, and used her scorn as fuel for her abiding hatred of the religion itself. In fits of rage she implored Meryon to ensure she was not subjected to Christian rites in death:

> I have written a paper, in which I have declared I neither will be buried among Christians, nor in Christian ground, nor by them. You may tell them so, and tell it to all the world if you like.[32]

Although her tantrums were brief, their severity terrified Meryon. Glasses were thrown against the wall and a pottery bowl narrowly missed him, while Hester screamed hysterically throughout. She was never known as a placid woman but Michael's departure and her subsequent sickness were preludes to a change in the violence and passion of her rages, which all of the household and many local villagers dreaded. Elizabeth lived in abject terror of her mistress's black days and was only relieved that Meryon now seemed to bear the brunt of them.

Apart from a possible hormonal disturbance, in keeping with the menstrual difficulties alluded to by Meryon, another clue as to the origin of Hester's mood is still visible in Lebanon today. Among the ruins of the house where Hester spent her last years is a thorn apple tree. It is a cultivated plant which produces Datura, a drug commonly used among eastern mystics and shamans to heighten religious experience. Some of its many side effects are extreme mood swings and lethargy. Hester spent the years before Meryon's return with eastern mystics, discovering a heightened spirituality which may have been partially induced by smoking Datura in her narghileh, a habit which she took up following her recovery from plague. Hallucinations were yet to become an important part of her perception of what was around her, although they would do so within the next few years, but the drug may have been destabilizing her already volatile temperament.

Miranda alone seemed immune from the rages, and when Hester again summoned him, Meryon, anxious to have an evening of peaceful respite, remained in his cottage. It was a balmy evening. Meryon was relaxing over an informal and solitary candlelit supper when he was surprised by some figures making their way towards his cottage in the half-light. Two servants bore flame torches and a third smaller female figure clutched a shawl around her, more tightly than the mildness of the evening seemed to merit. It was Elizabeth Williams and she was crying. Meryon, fearing another of Hester's moods, welcomed her in, but Elizabeth had not come to escape Hester. Far from relaying a complaint, Elizabeth came because she was worried that Hester's money problems were much worse than she had told the doctor and she wanted him to try to help her put some order into the accounts. Hester was generous beyond her means to visitors and to village people begging for alms. Elizabeth believed she paid dearly, in bribes and gifts, for her friendship with many of the local pashas, saying, 'I put no faith in their pretended worship.'[33] People arrived at the convent claiming kinship or friendship with Muhana or another of Hester's allies, and immediately she took them in, fed them, clothed them and ensured they were well prepared for the next stage of their journey. But now there was no money left to speak of and Elizabeth was afraid that her mistress refused to acknowledge it. Bent over a small wooden table, Meryon and Elizabeth worked late into the night trying to put some order into the hurried accounts and lists of Hester's debtors that Elizabeth had brought.

But Hester was far more interested in religious matters than in money. Meryon was regaled by accounts of her theological concerns and the predictions of old Loustennau, now known by everyone as 'The Prophet'. Dismissive of Hester's conviction that she would know and accompany the Mahdi when he arrived, Meryon grew irritated with Hester's inability to deal with practical matters. One argument ended only when she threw a chair at him, saying he was concerned with foolish fripperies rather than the great events which would soon unfold around him.

In spite of his scepticism, Meryon was asked to help decipher religious texts and to consider certain passages in the scriptures which Hester felt might offer clues as to her role in the coming of the Mahdi. One text referred to the new prophet as St Elias and Hester thought it referred to her home, Mar Elias. Another spoke of a bride of the Druse who would ride beside the prophet, who Hester believed would be her. Her conviction in the imminence of a second coming was unshakeable; her response to Meryon's concerns was that, if it failed to occur, she was safe and that 'her horses would be her fortune'.[34] The eclecticism and fanaticism of Hester's beliefs echoed the tide of Christian revivalism in London and the US. Pamphlets on the imminence of the second coming circulated widely in the West, and female evangelicals such as the New England missionary, Harriet Livermore, immortalized by John Greenleaf Whittier, whom Hester may have met, were devout in their conviction that they had been chosen by God.[35]

Meanwhile, the Swiss maids were kept busy in their hovels with needlework, preserve making, biscuit baking and pastry cooking. During their interview with Hester, they had been warned to eat and drink only lightly because upset stomachs were common amongst newcomers and could lead to more serious ailments. But, while following Hester's advice enabled them to escape diarrhoea and vomiting, it did not prevent them suffering from the other common newcomer's ailment. Every one of them broke out in an eruption of blistery lumps that covered their arms, legs, chests and, most distressingly of all, their faces. Meryon prescribed a diet of fruit and vegetables, but it was already too late. Tormented by constant, agonizing itching, they scratched; the blisters burst and suppurated, oozing thick yellow pus and occasionally blood.[36] Anxious to escape the heat, which exacerbated the condition, the women were relieved when Hester told them they would be moving to escape the worst of the sun.

Once again, the palace in the mountains, more than a day's riding from Abra, was rented. Accompanied by the Swiss women and Miranda Leander, Hester left to set up her summer household in Meshmushy. Meryon remained in the village to supervise the running of the convent and insure that the aged Loustennau was able to care for the horses. The person who most benefited by the arrival of the Swiss was Elizabeth Williams. Pleased with their company, she wrote to Meryon as soon as they were settled in the new place. The women rode tolerably well and the journey had passed without accident. Only Louis was a problem; his effeminacy irritated Hester and he was completely useless at riding, frequently falling off his donkey on the ascent. Within a couple of weeks, Miranda Leander was also meeting with Hester's disapproval. His youthful handsomeness was not benefiting from the inactivity of the summer retreat and Hester decided to send him back to Meryon in the convent, where he would be more active, because he was 'looking heavy'.[37] Eager for male European company, Meryon happily anticipated the arrival of his 'optimistic and enthusiastic' travelling companion, only to be disappointed when an unhappy, complaining Miranda arrived with a report that Hester:

> was alternately moaning, weeping or scolding – that it was impossible to please her – that she found fault unjustly and demanded more from her people than they could possibly do.[38]

He felt as if he was being carefully observed and, although he was given a good horse and a small group of servants, resented Hester's constant criticism and attempts to 'improve' him with daily lectures on what he should 'do, say and be silent upon'. Meryon still felt guilty that the servants he had chosen were so unsuitable, and his first concern was for Hester. Unable to leave the convent and the responsibilities of its household, he sent a rider up the mountain with a note in an attempt at consolation. But the worrying news that reached him shortly after its dispatch forced him to abandon his duties temporarily and ride up the mountain himself. There was an outbreak of plague in Sidon; daily word of casualties came to the convent by way of the village. Expecting to have to reassure Hester, he was surprised to find her unperturbed. Her fervour for Mahdism was matched by her faith in the Christian belief that the plague would pass by St John's Day and they would all be perfectly safe.[39]

Meryon noted that, as the house at Meshmushy consisted of only a small number of very large rooms, Hester used locally made carpets to screen off separate sections and create private areas. She ushered Meryon into one of these so they could speak about the new additions to her entourage. The displeasure Miranda had reported was not exaggerated. Pauline was wasteful and dishonest and constantly complaining of ailments which ranged from toothache to upset stomachs; Marie was far too European in outlook, dress and manner, and because of it, was a constant irritation and reminder of all that Hester wished to leave behind; only Louise, in her youth and eagerness to learn, was proving that she might, one day, make a good maid. Pauline was equally unhappy with Hester and had asked to go home: 'Marie is of no use to me and as Pauline chooses to go I think I shall send Marie with her.' Hester told Meryon that the maids should remain only until arrangements could be made and then should travel accompanied by Meryon himself, for she could think of no other way 'to ensure their safe restoration to their homes'.[40] Seemingly ignorant of Miranda's displeasure, Hester said she would keep him as her particular charge, to 'train him in such a manner as to make him tread in the path of honour and virtue'. Meryon, all too aware of Miranda's unhappiness, said nothing but thought it highly unlikely that the young man would want to stay. Disgruntled by the prospect of such a precipitous departure, Meryon only agreed to the suggestion with a great deal of reluctance. When he retired that night he mulled over Hester's latest resolve. While admitting that she gave him 'a wearisome life', he was loath to leave her. In later years, in his journal Meryon would admit that the apathy which set in every time he travelled home was as much to do with his avoidance of 'the toil and anxiety of a physician's life in London' as it was with his devotion to Hester. Seeing the world was a much more pleasurable pursuit for a young adventurous man, and Hester's moods were a small price to pay for the opportunity her summons afforded him.[41] By the time Meryon managed to fall asleep he had convinced himself that Hester would have changed her mind in the morning.

He was wrong. Hester was resolute. The maids must leave and Meryon would take them, as he was the one who had guaranteed their safety. Pauline, Marie and Louis were told to prepare for their departure. While the days were taken up by making travel arrangements, Hester began to spend the evenings coaching Meryon about exactly what he should say to people on his return to England.

Of crucial importance was what Meryon would say to her brother.

James did not approve of Hester's chosen way of life, believing that if she had to live abroad then it would be more seemly to do so amidst other English people, preferably in western Europe. James thought that France would be a good home for his sister. Hester was less convinced, believing France still far too unstable. Moreover, she confessed to Meryon, the possibility of another shipwreck terrified her. None of her relatives had helped her when her ship was wrecked before; she had no faith in them doing so at any time in the future should it happen again.[42] Meryon was to say that Hester was making a home for herself and that 'had Bruce kept his word' she would have done it 'in two years'. Hester reasoned that if only James could understand why she lived as she did then he would come to accept it. She entreated Meryon:

> Above all you must contrive that James comes out to see me. This invitation for him to come must come entirely from you, and as if unknown to me.[43]

Hester could not be seen to be begging her brother for a visit but Meryon could stress the importance of such a thing without in any way implicating Hester. Tired of 'constant direct and indirect opposition', fully aware of the strictures that would be imposed upon her in her own society, Hester now said, for the first time, that she could not contemplate ever returning to England nor indeed living among other Europeans exiles in the Lebanon:

> If they were to give me £100,000 a year to live among the boot-whipping, silly visiting people of England I would not do it. Here if I sit under a tree and talk to a camel driver at least I hear good sense.[44]

Hester described the English exiles to Meryon as nothing better than fleas, jumping about the floor of a filthy room. While they might bite, annoy and hurt her, just like a flea she could get rid of them by sweeping the floor, but she would never live among them.[45] Resigned, Meryon returned to the convent to gather his belongings and to persuade Miranda to stay. He was unsuccessful. Within days Miranda wrote a letter from the convent informing Hester that he wished to leave as soon as possible. Hester contacted an English Jew living in Sidon, who would soon return to London having completed his pilgrimage to Jerusalem, and he agreed to take Miranda Leander as his companion. And so, on the first of August, less than six months from when they arrived, the group comprising Meryon, Louis, Pauline and Marie were ready to return to Europe. Hester settled back in Mar Elias and the doctor, worrying over how she would cope when the plague returned and she had no physician, left her with a promise to return should she need his services. Hester was going to put her faith in eastern medicine and, although she doubted she would ever wish to consult him, she told Meryon that she hoped she would see him again.

Only Louise Charlton, barely fourteen, remained behind to work in Hester's household.

Passion and Political Unrest

One hour of justice excels a thousand months of devotion.
Emir Bashir II, Arabic inscription at Beittedine

Coffee Service

WITH THE OTHER WOMEN GONE, Louise found herself the sole recipient of Hester's constant verbal criticism. But Hester soon discovered that she had completely misjudged the docility of Louise's temperament. Louise was unhappy and stubborn. She wanted to go home. Two months after the others left, Louise was on her way back to France, accompanied by a French gentlewoman employed by Hester to ensure her safe passage. Within the year, although without her knowing, Hester's initial fears were realized. Louise was established, beautiful and talked about, the star of the Parisian salons with her tales of Hester's eccentricities and her anecdotes of life in the East.

Political instability and civilian disquiet surrounded the convent. The new Pasha of Acre, Abdullah, had made the expected attempts to subdue Emir Bashir, even ordering him to pay an exorbitant sum in honour of his new appointment. Initially, the Emir refused, only acquiescing and sending agents to collect the money from citizens across the country after one hundred and seventy Lebanese subjects were arrested. Rebellion ensued. Unable to control it or to collect the sum, the Emir was forced into exile. The two rulers who took his place were unqualified and incapable of bringing any order into the area, so that violent clashes between the various factions sprang up across the region. Hester maintained her domain at Mar Elias in spite of the fighting around her, establishing a reputation for neutrality by offering sanctuary to refugees from any side that approached her.

But a new arrival at Sidon altered the carefully controlled regime of Mar Elias in early 1820. Mad old Loustennau, 'The Prophet', was still tending the sacred horses when his son, an ex-officer of Napoleon's Imperial Guard, landed in Syria with the hope of finding his father.[1] The Captain, although embarrassed by his father's religious zeal, settled in Mar Elias with Hester. A handsome man, who Hester later said reminded her of Sir John Moore, he nevertheless suffered from a financial situation as bad as

Hester's, although he gallantly borrowed money from a French family named Espagnet to help her. The horoscope that Hester drew up for him showed him to be her perfect mate and they became lovers, spending the summer together at Mar Elias, unable to move to higher ground in the atmosphere of political disquiet. Captain Loustennau, like Hester, was quick to rage. Restless and arrogant, he offended both Christians and Muslims with his rude and overbearing manner. Oblivious to his faults, Hester's moods improved with the affair and the tyrannous regime of the convent relaxed as she wallowed in her newest obsession.

But, late in the summer, Loustennau fell ill with a high fever. Hester again adopted the role of nurse to a loved one and took up his care personally. His recovery seemed assured when a secondary sickness affected him. It may have been something in his food, although unsubstantiated rumours in the household hinted that his unpopularity may have made him a victim of poisoning. Whatever the cause, Captain Loustennau did not recover from the violent and persistent vomiting that forced him back to his bed. His debtors increased their drive to reclaim their money, fearing 'the visit from the famous rabies', but the Captain was dead within the week. Hester grieved 'over his too cruel fate' and, despite her own monetary difficulties, paid off the Captain's debt to Espagnet.[2] Bereaved and inconsolable, Hester buried him with great honour in her own garden, while 'The Prophet', refusing to accept his son's death, sank further into the world of his own madness, a world where his son was still alive and was daily expected to arrive at Mar Elias.

There was a voluminous correspondence between Hester and Meryon in the early 1820s. Letters were filled with deaths, marriages and news of mutual acquaintances. Meryon suffered the loss of his mother and his brother, who was only forty and the father of five children. In the same month, July 1820, Hester became resigned to the fact that James would never visit her, when he married the daughter of Lord Mansfield. Miranda Leander returned to find his guardian bankrupt but managed to secure a position for himself in a good house in Paris, where stories of his time with Hester, like those told by Louise Charlton, guaranteed his popularity. Dr Newberry died of a painful, unknown complaint in early 1821, at the same time as Meryon resumed contact with Michael.

After his Parisian rescue, and because of the rather glamorous image it afforded him, Michael continued to enjoy the company of several women. Notably, in the spring and summer of 1817 he was the confidant of Byron's former lover, Lady Caroline Lamb. The daughter of Countess Bessborough, Hester's rival for the affections of Granville Leveson Gower, Caroline's eccentric pursuit of Byron was scandalous common knowledge. Bessborough was anxious for gossip about Hester and urged her daughter to arrange a meeting with Michael. Caroline, however, was more interested in Michael as a source of information about Byron: 'write everything you hear of Byron'.[3] Her letters to Michael, her 'Bruce of the Desert', hint at the fanatical nature of her obsession:

> What burning flames can be worse. I shall die very soon and when I do – do you remember it and tell them I suffered enough – tell it Byron.[4]

From her next letter it is obvious that Michael was in contact with Byron, or at least had friends in common, and was able to help satisfy her craving for news. Michael's own love life took a more settled turn when he met Marianne Parker, a widow with children by her first husband, and subsequently married her in August 1818. When Meryon visited the Bruces, he found Michael to be a contented family man, his circumstances humbled by the reduction in fortunes brought about by his father's business failures. Meryon found him far more agreeable than he had been on their travels and with a very beautiful little daughter.

Meryon, still grieving for the loss of his relatives, found solace with the dancer he had helped before leaving for the Lebanon. Narcisse's health had improved substantially and she had taken up work, again as a dancer, at the Opera Ballet in London. What had been a supportive friendship burgeoned into a clandestine relationship and when, in 1821, Narcisse fell pregnant again, it was with Meryon's child. But Narcisse was still partially supported by Lord Lowther. Angry at her affair with Meryon, Lowther informed her that if she did not move to Paris, away from her lover and closer to where he himself was spending more time, the allowance for his daughter Fanny would stop.[5] A few months before her due date Narcisse returned to France, leaving what she described to Meryon as 'your wretched country where it's always raining'. In Paris she gave birth to a son whom she named Charles for his father. Meryon received a short written account of her health, which ended, '*Oui, mon ami, tu as un fils*'.[6] Although Meryon had begun to direct his romantic affections elsewhere, he acknowledged his son, registering his birth under his surname, and agreed to help support him. In order to do so, he would need to establish himself in a good position and he wrote to Hester asking for her help, even offering to return to her if she so wished: 'Recall me to your side and I shall think the voyage back as nothing.'[7] But the usual postal delays meant that the impoverished Meryon was obliged to take up a position in the household of Sir Gilbert Heathcote, while anxiously awaiting her response. In spite of the slightly pompous tone in his writing and Hester's condescending disregard, Meryon was successful with women, a fact more understandable when we consider a late photograph of him from the Royal College of Medicine: a small, elderly, but undeniably dapper, figure, his top hat set at a slightly rakish tilt. He was cultivating a new relationship with an English widow, Eliza Gardiner, and as it developed, the letters he sent to Narcisse became more restrained, although he tactfully made no mention of his new attachment. When he married Eliza in 1823, Meryon adopted her son from her first marriage as his own but made no mention of either marriage or adoption to Narcisse. So the dancer's poignant and passionate love letters to the doctor, emotional disclosures interspersed with details of their son's growth, continued to follow the doctor for several years to come.[8]

Hester was still taking in numerous refugees from the skirmishes around the mountain, but Mar Elias was not ideal; it was far too small to act as either fortress or sanctuary should a larger battle break out. One afternoon, when Hester was riding, she noticed a ruined and deserted monastery, set higher in the mountains, close to the village of Joun. The situation was beautiful but the buildings were derelict and ruined. More than half of it was unroofed and, in the rainy season, water poured down from all sides. On making enquiries she found that it was owned by a Damascene merchant, who was happy to lease it to her for a rent of just £20 a year, with the condition that any repairs and improvements she made would be inherited by him or his descendants.

For more than a year, Hester planned and instigated improvements, borrowing money and selling many of her belongings to raise the money to do so. Joun was not a house but rather a series of buildings, connected

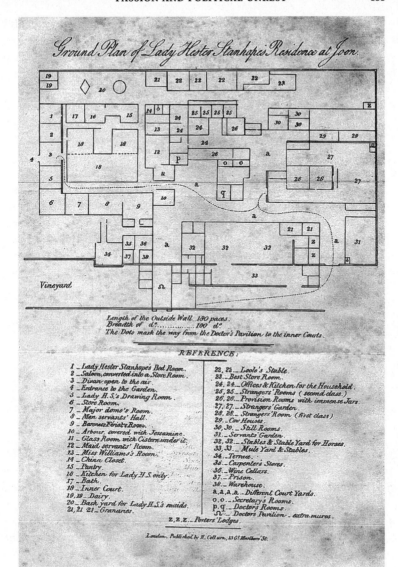

Ground Plan of Hester's home in Joun – the foundations of some
buildings are still visible today

by winding paths and courtyards, some complete homes in themselves where Hester planned to shelter refugees from the great disasters she believed were imminent. The surrounding wall, more than ten feet high on the north and east, and six or seven feet high on the other sides, gave the palace's approach the feel of a prison as much as of a home.[9] Yet Joun became a Wonderland. Hester designed and created a garden, different from any she had made before; it was a garden of the East, watered in such a way that it could sustain plants from Britain too. Covered alleys, winding pathways, summer houses and pavilions covered with big, soft roses gave way to arbours filled with the heavy scent of oleander and jasmine. Orange and fig trees lined pathways, and a new Datura tree was planted close to the main building. But the labyrinthine passages, beautiful as they were, served another purpose. Some provided shortcuts between buildings; others, by way of screens and plants, provided alcoves for eavesdropping which Hester could use to listen to servants or to ensure they were not shirking. The two pavilions contained trapdoors in the ground, behind which lay steep steps leading to a cavernous room underground. This room could be flooded with light when further secret doors on the wall were opened out to the side of the hill, giving views of open country.

When the renovations and preparations to move were complete, Hester, with a small ceremony, reinterred the remains of Captain Loustennau in a tomb in the garden of Joun, the tomb which she wished one day to be hers. Only old Loustennau, 'The Prophet', waiting for a son who could never come again, remained in Mar Elias, tended by a few of Hester's servants.

Calm and serene as the sanctuary of Joun was designed to be, it could not entirely shut out the troubles of the region. In 1821 Abdullah Pasha of Acre, despairing of Lebanese civil unrest, backed an election to reinstate the Emir. When Bashir II again took control of the region he imposed heavy taxes, opposed by both Muslim and Christian villagers. In a move that jeopardized her own neutrality, undoubtedly moved by compassion but also in the belief that her position was in some way inviolable, Hester opened the gates of Joun to escaping rebels, the men who were being hunted down by the new strong alliance. The Pasha of Acre had learned his lesson; he knew his control of the Lebanon depended on his alliance with the Emir. Accordingly, he condemned the villagers, many of whom did not have the means to pay the tax, as 'a few seditious and evil people' who had 'removed from their heads the necklaces of obedience'.[10] Mehmet Ali, aware of the power of the alliance and of its usefulness, cultivated his relationship with both men. Emir Bashir gained confidence and strength from this new ally to the extent that he now felt in a position to defeat his remaining enemies in the region, principally Sheikh Bashir Jumblat.

When the Emir returned from a visit to Egypt, Bashir Jumblat quickly went to Beittedine to assure him of his support and obedience. The Emir was not welcoming; the Sheikh's greetings were met with insults and demands for huge sums of money.[11] Sheikh Jumblat fled the Lebanon temporarily in order to plan his next move. The Emir set Mukhtara on fire and seized the Sheikh's remaining land and property. The Sheikh returned, furious and determined to beat his enemy. In January 1825 he declared a revolt against Emir Bashir Shihab, supported by the Druse population.

Throughout the conflict and in spite of the sanctuary she defiantly offered, Hester was still careful. She had no contact with the Emir or the Sheikh, avoiding 'all social intercourse with great men' and never interfering 'in any of the political concerns'.[12] Now she waited in expectation of 'a scene of bloodshed', proud that she would 'never want courage or forget the duty I owe to my fellow creatures'[13]

Although dense, deep snow covered the whole region, Hester later wrote 'the whole mountain is in a flame'. The revolution had broken out. The Pasha of Damascus gave his support to the Druse, but the Pasha of Acre, mindful of his own dependence on the Emir's control, joined his troops to those of Emir Bashir Shihab. Villagers escaped from the hell of their villages to Sidon and each day Hester received news of miserable people' who aimed to seek refuge with her in Joun if they were 'driven from the asylum they had found. One of her servants brought word that Jumblat's harem was to be invaded by the Emir's men and his children to be executed. Hester, fearing for the Sheikh's wife and five children, although she was 'by no means attached to the woman', sent help to them. It was a gesture that would have far-reaching consequences. Political expedience gave way to compassion as:

Humanity loudly called that I should afford her all the assistance in my power as she was at that period naked, penniless, and flying bare-footed through mountains covered with snow, with five children, the least at her breast.[14]

A servant travelled across the ravaged landscape to give warning to the Sheikh's family. Hester was successful for the time being; the Sheikh's wife and youngest children were hidden, given food and daily necessities by Hester, in the hope that the Emir would show clemency in the aftermath of war.[15]

The Sheikh's revolt failed; the strength of Pasha Abdullah's forces over-whelmed his troops entirely. In the face of insurmountable opposition, Jumblat's men deserted so that he was forced to seek refuge in Damascus with the scattering of loyalists that remained. On his arrival, he was arrested, stripped, bound and thrown in prison. Jumblat appealed to Pasha Abdullah for justice, but the Pasha gave orders for the Sheikh to be executed.[16] His crimes were publicly broadcast as 'sedition and inciting disorder and unrest'. Sheikh Bashir Jumblat was strangled and beheaded; the remains of his body were put on display in Acre as a warning against disobedience.[17]

Hester's hope of post-war mercy for the Jumblat children was naively optimistic. The Emir was terrible in his revenge. Seizing three of the princes, he burnt out their eyes, cut out their tongues and banished them from the country.[18] Hester was angry and appalled; her relationship with the Emir, which had gone from initial fondness to mistrust and diplo-matic avoidance, was now one of hatred. While speaking cordially to the Emir's ally Pasha Abdullah and resuming some correspondence with him, she openly denounced the Emir as 'a dog and a monster' to anyone who would listen. It was the end of Hester's carefully maintained position of impartiality. Acting by stealth in order to avoid any European disquiet, Bashir II began a campaign against Hester's household. Hester prepared to retaliate.

Monetary concerns over how to feed the escapees and the victims of the civil war sheltering in Joun were overtaken by personal tragedy. Hes-ter received a letter. Her brother James was dead. Unable to cope with the sudden loss of his wife, he hanged himself in Kenwood. For the first time in thirty years her sister Griselda wrote to her, but either Hester did not receive her letters or chose not to reply, for she never received an answer. The proximity of the Emir, grief at her brother's death and disquiet in the area all contributed to Hester's reluctance to leave her fortress in the years following the war. Her sole remaining European companion, Elizabeth Williams, became indispensable, acting as Hester's amanuensis as her eyes began to fail. Reluctant to attribute her myopia to her age, Hester blamed her bad eyes on the childhood condition that had given her so many infections, and the spectacles that Meryon thoughtfully sent all lay discarded in a pile in a disused room.

Careful letters in Elizabeth's hand gave Meryon details of Hester's financial difficulties and the ever-increasing loans that she was impelled to take. Then, in 1826, an English traveller arrived in Sidon, claiming to have been sent by the Dukes of Sussex and Bedford and carrying papers to that effect, and with the express purpose of extricating her from her financial difficulties. But when the awaited aid did not arrive, Hester was forced to concede that he was an impostor, although his motivation was impossible to fathom. Meanwhile, the interest on loans she had taken with local businessmen had to be paid and she borrowed again to do so:

As for my debts, it is not, as you think, 25 per cent yearly that I have to pay, but 50 and 95, and, in one instance, I have suffered more loss still. Gold of 28 1/2 piastres, they counted to me here at 45, which I spent at 28 1/2 and am to pay at the Beyrout rate of 45 – calculate that. I am compelled to borrow . . . [19]

People were hungry; she borrowed to feed them. Villagers needed to escape; she paid for their passage or hid them until they could flee. Meryon read her accounts and worried. Aware of her steadily mounting financial difficulties, it cannot have been money that motivated his next decision. He was still fascinated by Hester, and a little in awe of her, a quality that would not have been diminished by her disdain. Flattered by her confidences and ever hopeful that he might at last find favour, Meryon acted in spite of his new familial responsibilities, or perhaps with the intention of escaping at least some of them. When, in 1827, he was freed from his service to Heathcote, he began the long journey to the Lebanon.

The repercussions of Hester's defiance of Bashir II were beginning to take effect. The Emir arrived in Joun with two hundred of his men, demanding an audience with Hester. But she 'positively refused to have any sort of communication with him', feeling that, no matter how much it might be in her own interest, her conscience forbade her 'to have anything to do with such a monster'20 Settled in the house of Jacoub Aga, who had been a corrupt Armenian bishop but was now the Consul for Sidon, Bashir began a campaign of bullying and brutality against Hester's servants. Her water carrier was almost beaten to death and his head 'cut open to the bone'. Dragged from his house by two men, Jacoub Aga then stamped upon the servant's face till he began to suffocate; then, the following day, he tied him up and dragged him to the Emir's palace, where he was bastinadoed, receiving one hundred strikes to the soles of his feet. For the first time in many years Hester appealed to Stratford Canning, now the British Ambassador in Lebanon, for his intervention. The letter, which Canning described as being in 'war like cast', was as much a warning of how she would enact her own retribution if he did not help as it was an appeal for him to do so.[21]

Many of her servants were being threatened and frightened; she advised Canning that she was 'not very likely to bear it quietly'. But she had not yet seen the worst of the Emir's retaliation. The postscript to the same letter, added two days later, was more earnest and even more aggressive than the body of script which accompanied it. The Emir had sent an order to all the villages that Hester's servants were to remain, on pain of death, within the confines of Joun. It was tantamount to a death sentence for the household, as the only water they did not have to carry for almost four miles up the mountain on the backs of mules was from an old and dirty well, which even the animals would not drink. Moreover, the Emir publicly declared that anyone who dared to bring water to Joun 'should be cut into a thousand pieces'. If the Emir persisted, Hester would 'lock up all the women in a room' and take her own chances with the men, with the hope of being able to shock Canning's 'tender heart' with a 'Box full of heads'. In spite of her continued bravado, Hester's position was desperate. Imprisoned with a large retinue and a few refugee families who had been made homeless by the war and remained in Joun, they were without water. When Hester retired she slept fitfully, a knife under her pillow. Anxiously, she awaited Meryon, referring to him in her letters to her banker at Leghorn, who would supply him with money as 'my kind friend' who 'has blasted his own prospects in life by giving up everything to join me in this country'.[22]

The dirty, muddy water of the well dried up with the advent of summer, and with the dearth of irrigation, the beautiful but impractical garden began its slow but inevitable death. Hester's world shrank and fell into disorder as she used fewer and fewer rooms of the rambling building. Stratford Canning did not disappoint her. Sharing her dislike of the Consul, Jacoub Aga, he wrote letters which would effect his removal from Hester's neighbourhood as well as writing a letter to the Emir which he hoped would give Hester 'the best support and assistance that the difficulty of the time has left at my command'.[23] And by July Canning's intervention brought respite, although it was to be but a temporary lull in the conflict.

Hester's reputation among the Europeans of Sidon as a recluse was established as she frequently refused to see travellers and visitors who requested an audience. She remained impervious to the gossip, even remarking in a letter to Meryon on the oddity of being asked to entertain people she had never met, moreover had no wish to meet and who had no connection with her whatsoever. However, her liking for young men and physicians made for some exceptions. Shortly after Aga was dismissed for his conduct, a Dr Madden arrived from England requesting an audience. To his surprise, he was obliged. The same evening, a pair of horses arrived bringing a polite invitation and Madden set off. Joun seemed to him a place of unbelievable contrasts: 'Everything without was wild and barbarous, and all within confessed the hand of taste,' although he was saddened that the 'beautiful garden has gone to ruin for want of irrigation'. And Hester treated him with 'courteous manners', serving him the 'choicest of Lebanese wines' and excellent food while drinking no alcohol and eating only frugally herself. He rewarded her reception by publishing a work rich in admiration and praise, as well as a defence of her mode of life. With an astuteness that many other visitors and contemporary commentators lacked, he attributed her way of life to 'the ambition of governing', acknowledging that, while her influence had diminished greatly recently, she continued to receive the adoration and obedience of many villagers and Bedouin, reminiscent of the *ancien régime*.[24] She regaled him with her mystical interests and convictions but, rather than dismiss them as eccentric ramblings, Madden reasoned that:

> If all those who believed in magic and demonology were to be deemed insane, some of the most celebrated men in modern and ancient times would be called lunatics.[25]

Before his departure, Hester granted Madden a visit to the horses. Layla and Lulu were now cared for by an intricate routine, which included a thorough morning wash in soap and water. Madden left Hester with the firm belief that her eccentricity was a much less important facet of her character than her educative erudition, 'intrepidity of spirit', perfect manners and 'unbounded benevolence'.[26]

Hester in Joun. We can clearly see the bell pull that Hester
used to summon her servants at all hours

While Hester suffered and recovered from Bashir's edict, Meryon, accompanied by his new family and missed by his French one, reached Pisa. But his wife, Eliza, was pregnant and they remained in Italy until September when, accompanied by the newest addition to the family, they found passage for Cyprus on board the Italian frigate *Fortuna*. It was a treacherous time to undertake a voyage. Greece was fighting for independence from the Ottoman Empire and the sea was rife with piracy and mutiny. Many seemingly neutral merchant ships carried a valuable, clandestine cargo comprising weapons and supplies for the Turks. The Greeks did everything they could to prevent this cargo reaching their enemies. For the *Fortuna* there was barely a week of calm seafaring. A schooner hoisting a Greek flag was sighted by the lookout in the distance. Twelve guns and around eighty swarthy, dangerous-looking men faced the frigate, ordering its captain to board their ship. The Captain quickly warned everyone that there was likely to be an ambush and suggested that Meryon's chances might be better if he passed himself off as a consul. Meryon tried to look as distinguished as possible, while the remaining passengers stuffed their underwear with whatever valuables they had. They had very little time; within fifteen minutes the Greeks had boarded the ship. Cyprus was blockaded and they suspected the frigate of carrying supplies to the Turks. They wanted to appropriate the cargo for themselves. They reassured Meryon that, as an Englishman, and therefore an ally of the Greeks, he would be safe, and then went about pillaging the ship. They found casks of wine and drained them; then, drunken and rowdy, they began to torment and threaten the passengers. The Captain's mate had the worst of it. Beaten and bound, they held him over the side of the ship, pressing a knife to his throat. The mate, petrified, screamed an appeal to Meryon to intercede, but Meryon's wife acted first. She was huddling in the quarterdeck, their newest child, a baby girl, in her arms, but on the mate's cry of terror she rushed forward. With a bravery that astonished her husband, she grabbed the Greek's arm, begging him to spare the man's life. The Greek, as shocked as Meryon and, shamed by the woman's appeal, released the man and threw the key of the mate's chest at Eliza's feet.

The pirates did not leave until the evening. Scattered bedding was then replaced on the bunks, a meagre supper of biscuits and water was scraped together and eaten, and the crew discussed what to do next. They needed fresh supplies and so cast anchor at Zante to re-provision. Weary, shaken, too afraid to continue, they returned to Leghorn. Eliza's health had suffered greatly. She was terrified of sailing again and Meryon put off any continuation of their travels until the following spring.

But their ordeal was not the only reason for delaying the journey. England, France and Russia had ordered an armistice in the Greek–Turkish war. Turkey refused, and a large Egyptian fleet, commanded by Mehmet Ali's son, Ibrahim, landed at Navarino, now known as Pylos. The allied fleet commander managed to delay the threatened battle by persuading Ali's son to wait for further orders from his father. However, the Greeks continued to fight and Ibrahim, disregarding the allies, retaliated. On 8 October 1827 the allied ships entered the harbour and destroyed the Egyptian fleet. Mehmet Ali had attempted to support the Ottomans. In spite of his failure he demanded a reward from the Ottoman Sultan and was offered the island of Crete. It was much less than Ali believed he deserved; he demanded Syria. When the Sultan refused, Ali gathered troops to take it by force. News of the Battle of Navarino brought panic to the Europeans of Sidon. Terrified of the revenge of the Ottomans, they flocked to Joun for sanctuary and Hester, in spite of her avowed dislike of the expatriates, took them in until they could find passage, filling her home with the languages of Europe. Again she sold and borrowed to raise the money to do so.

Hester did not learn of the doctor's disasters by sea until the following March. Her eyesight was still bad and Meryon was sent a letter in Elizabeth Williams's handwriting. Hester was growing more and more concerned by Meryon's determination to bring his wife and family. She urged him to leave without them: 'Salute Mrs M., and say I hope no childish feeling will prevent her allowing you to be absent for a little while.'[27] And afraid of yet further delay on Meryon's part, she dismissed the recent outbreak of plague, saying she was sure it would be passed by the time he arrived. In spite of his intentions, Meryon had not set off for Syria again. Eliza's reluctance and his own worries about the political situation kept him in Europe. His French attachments were also pulling on his emotions as little Charles, now six, wrote to him:

Dear Papa I do wish I could see you and give you a kiss its such a long time since I saw you. One day when you can get away please come and have dinner with us, and you'll see our little garden where theres trees almost ripe, redcurrants and plums I love you with all my heart Dear Papa.[28]

At last, acknowledging that it might be better to travel alone, he accompanied his wife and their children to England, with the intention of settling them before embarking on a solitary journey to Hester in yet another year's time, in spring 1829.

The plague which Hester had written of was raging across the country. Most of the European refugees, aided by Canning, had left, so now Hester and Elizabeth Williams, with their greatly reduced household, confined themselves to Joun. However, the plague was not the only sickness that blighted the region; in late summer a second illness, probably yellow fever, swept across Mount Lebanon. It spread rapidly and by the autumn most of the remaining servants were ill, some dangerously so. One Friday afternoon, Elizabeth was doing some needlework with her usual companion, a local seamstress. She shivered slightly and mentioned to the elderly woman that she didn't feel well. The woman thought nothing of it and was pleased when she returned the following day to find Elizabeth apparently recovered. But on Sunday Elizabeth's fever returned more violently. An alternation between good and bad days continued through the beginning of the week, although the symptoms did not seem to worsen. Elizabeth dismissed the illness as trivial and urged her companion not to come to work but to stay at home and care for her daughter, who was also ill. By Wednesday both Hester and Elizabeth were confined to their bed with high temperatures. Hester gave orders to one of the children in her service to give Elizabeth a dose of salts and senna, the 'black dose' that Hester used as a general cure-all. The young maid, having no idea how much of the drug to administer, gave her a generous amount. The effect was terrible.

Senna is a stimulant laxative which prevents constipation by affecting the sodium and potassium balance in the colon. Taken in excess, the significant loss of potassium from the body can cause irregularities in the rhythm of the heart and even coma. For the next twenty-four hours Elizabeth suffered from chronic diarrhoea and cramps. As she lay in agony, her mistress also suffering and helpless in a nearby room, she watched as her few remaining belongings were stolen by servants who then ran away, afraid of catching the disease themselves. The elderly village woman returned to find in a looted, shambolic room what appeared to be Elizabeth's corpse. She sat by the body for a time, mourning the death of her sewing companion, only to find that, instead of becoming cold, the corpse seemed to be retaining its heat. A local doctor who had been summoned at long last arrived and was ushered through to see Elizabeth. Even the doctor was surprised. Elizabeth's cheeks were pink and her blood seemed to be almost 'bubbling inside of her like boiling water'.[29] The doctor asked Hester for permission to open a vein; sick herself as well as distraught at the loss of her companion, she readily gave it. When he took his knife to Elizabeth's foot the blood spurted out; the doctor took out a quantity of blood and bound the foot. If Elizabeth had been in a coma, the blood-letting ended it. By Sunday her corpse was buried in the grounds of a local monastery.

Still unable to move, Hester gave orders from her bed to close up Elizabeth's room, leaving everything exactly as it was. Filled with superstitious terror at the strange prelude to Elizabeth's death, some servants did so but then left Joun taking whatever they could, leaving Hester alone and in deteriorating health. As well as the few belongings that had not been hidden or stolen, the fleeing servants carried tales with them, horror stories that reached the ears of a rich and educated Syrian merchant who lived in a nearby village. In an act of mercy, bringing food, water and some medicine, he headed for Joun to see if he could help any inhabitants who remained. When he arrived, he found Hester, delirious and abandoned, close to death, lying in filth. Cold and starving, she had had no food for fifteen days, subsisting on water and barley water alone. The Syrian immediately tried to feed her. Over the days of his care she gradually regained some of her strength, as well as her faith in the marvels of her own constitution. But she did not recover from the loss of Elizabeth Williams. Hester withdrew further and further into the precincts of Joun, with only a small number of servants to tend her. The few belongings that miraculously remained, having been hidden in anticipation of theft, were either deemed as essential or sold to pay the ever-increasing interest on her debts.

Without Elizabeth to write for her, Hester's most pressing need was for a secretary and she found a Frenchman, Chasseau, who agreed to take the position. Before the end of the year, Meryon received news of Elizabeth's death and began a determined campaign to overcome his wife's reluctance to travel.[30] He made plans to sail to Beirut, in spite of the terrible winter sailing conditions, early in the new year of 1829. But his wife was resolute; not only did she not wish to go with him, she no longer agreed to consign her husband to the plagues, diseases and unknown horrors of the East. Meryon's persistent entreaties did not pay off for over a year until in November 1830 he, at last, set off with his family towards the Lebanon. It was an easy voyage on a French brig, with none of the calamities of their earlier attempt, and by 8 December the Meryons had reached Beirut.

On his arrival, the doctor received a letter from Hester which filled him with consternation because, although she was looking forward to seeing him, she warned that his family should not expect any particular attentions. Meryon brought his family against her wishes and advice. She did not like Englishwomen in general. Moreover, the demands of a wife might significantly reduce Meryon's freedom to attend to her wishes. Meryon had been in the Lebanon just three days and already he was apprehensive.

The cottage in Joun that Hester provided for Eliza and the children was adequate: simple and well constructed, with a small garden. Chasseau accompanied Meryon's family there on donkeys, while Meryon made his way directly to Hester on a horse she had sent for him, still unsure as to how he would be received.

13

Families

In truth, this half-ruined convent, guarded by the proud heart of
an English gentlewoman was the only spot throughout all Syria
and Palestine in which the will of Mehemet Ali and his
fierce lieutenant was not the law.

Alexander Kinglake, *Eothen*

Lady Hester's Garden

THE EFFUSIVENESS OF HESTER'S RECEPTION surprised Meryon. With uncharacteristic demonstrativeness, she kissed him on both cheeks. In the past she had never so much as taken his arm; Meryon was bemused, bashful and more than a little pleased, and his hopes for this new visit resurged. While Hester ordered sherbet, orange water and a pipe for his pleasure, he produced the gifts he had brought. Among them were yet more spectacles for Hester to try, which she politely but firmly refused to do. Yet while he ate the simple dinner presented to him he was amused to see that she produced an old-fashioned pair of spectacles, without arms, which she balanced *pince-nez* style on her nose in order to peer at him from time to time. It was late into the night before Meryon's insistence that he return to see his family was heeded and he was able to depart, with a promise to return first thing the next day.

When he got to the cottage in the small hours of the morning his reception was typical of those to come in the months ahead. Eliza sat in the cottage, her trunks unpacked, fretting that the doctor had been attacked or worse. The secretary had discussed the dangers of the local wildlife and, as the long hours passed, she became convinced that only a disaster would have kept her husband away for so long when they had just arrived.

But Meryon was distracted, shocked by the abject poverty in which Hester now lived. The room where she had greeted him on their reunion was furnished with a plain deal table and two rush-bottomed chairs. Food was served on coarse yellow plates and eaten with the only two spoons remaining from her silver table service. But her bedroom was worse. Her bed was in the eastern style, little more than planks of wood on the floor with a mattress on top. Above it dangled a bell rope, part of a crudely made but effective system of bells that ran throughout the buildings, which enabled her to summon servants to her at any hour of the day or night. Beside her bed lay a large chintz cushion, a testament to her abandonment of her childhood conviction that slavery was evil because it was the bed of her slave, a young girl, Zezefoon, whom she had bought in Sidon. The room itself, where woman and slave girl spent most of their time, was shadowy and cluttered because only one of the three windows permitted any light, the other two having been long since covered. Piles of paper, handkerchiefs and other household paraphernalia lay scattered in muddled heaps across the floor, cobwebs spanning them, dust covering them. The only real furniture was a little stool of rough wood on which was presented a constantly changing array of snacks: aniseed and cloves, almonds and violet syrup, lemons and quince preserve. The household, always strictly run in the past, was now subject to fanatical discipline. Maids complained to Meryon when out of earshot of their mistress that she often found fault with things: the way her bed was made, the way her bread was toasted, their disgusting habits – she claimed that they would use the same towel to clean their noses and the drinking glasses. She used corporal punishment to chastise her staff and, unable to sleep, she expected them to be constantly on call, often requiring attendance in the middle of the night.

Hester's nocturnal habits meant the doctor was often free to spend the daylight hours with his family, but every evening, just before sunset, he would leave them to go to Hester. Her time was occupied with orders and instructions, intricate details of the most trivial of household matters. The doctor listened and later jotted down the substance of her incessant monologues, at times lasting for seven or eight hours, punctuated only by Hester's deep draws on her pipe and by the coughing fits which racked her body at frequent intervals. The doctor lamented that 'social and unrestrained conversation was out of the question' now and that to sit with her was 'to go to school'.[1] Tired out, through long nights Meryon listened to anecdotes, opinions and detailed descriptions of her spiritual and religious beliefs, seeking consolation in the fact that he was compiling them for a book. Hester implicitly believed, following her recovery from both plague and fever, that she was chosen by God, a God who had given her the ability to see into the future and was her friend. She quoted frequently from the scriptures and based her continued conviction that the second coming was nigh on the book of Revelations in the New Testament. The Mahdi would chastise and subdue the Christians and Muslims, changing the world into a harmonious place. Hester's situation and her ramblings were not Meryon's only idea for a publication. His affair with Pierre Narcisse was also a possibility he considered. He planned a novel, in epistolary form, about a French girl and illegitimate baby, so closely based on his own experiences that his notes held a key to relate the fictional characters to the real ones.[2] But Hester's notoriety made her an obvious subject for a Europe becoming eager for information about the eccentric woman who lived in the East.

When the weather was clement, Meryon entertained his family in the countryside during daylight hours, walking in the valleys, admiring the plants and wildlife. Not long after their arrival in Joun, Hester sent an invitation to Eliza to come to see her. But Eliza's enthusiasm for the prospective visit was not shared by her husband. All too aware of Hester's mistrust of her own sex and his wife's strong character, Meryon, as it turned out correctly, anticipated it would be the prelude to a difficult association. It began well enough. Hester was charming and polite, even wrapping Eliza in a long Turkish robe of gold brocade and winding a delicately embroidered turban on her head. It was the only occasion in which cordial relations between them would exist.

When word reached Ahmed Bey, Pasha of Damascus, that Meryon was in the East, he immediately wrote to Hester. He had a close friend suffering from a painful mouth condition that seemed to resist all cures; he wished Meryon to come to Damascus and treat him. Summoning Meryon, Hester told him that she wished him to go. It would be a journey of three or four weeks. Meryon was reluctant. Not only was he worried about leaving his family alone in the cottage, unable to speak Arabic, but he was aware that Eliza would never countenance such a separation. Hester was determined; she would persuade Eliza that her husband had no option but to respond to the Pasha's request. Hester made the same assumption that she had made about Louise Charlton, one that she often applied to European women, namely that she was essentially docile and would be easy to convince. She had not reckoned on Eliza's strength. The woman who had so fearlessly prevented a sailor's death was not going to be worn down by the wheedling of an ageing aristocrat. Hester began by saying that not only would Meryon's reputation among the Pashas be ruined if he did not acquiesce but the British Ambassador in Constantinople would be angry. This had no effect on Eliza's determination to keep her husband at home, so Hester moved on to try to frighten her instead. Dervishes would inflict evil upon her, causing her horrible physical blemishes. An incredulous Eliza remained unmoved, telling Hester that, of course, if her husband wanted to go, he could, but in doing so he would hurt her. They parted in covert hostility, which would remain between them for the rest of the visit. When Eliza returned home she told Meryon what had transpired. He reassured her of his determination to remain with his family and waited on the inevitable summons to Hester. For three days no horse arrived to take him up the mountain, and for three days he anxiously awaited the oncoming storm. Even then the messenger who finally came to the cottage did not bring an invitation for the doctor, but a note asking for his decision. Meryon replied in a letter; he would not leave his wife. The Meryons had been in the Lebanon less than two months and already the atmosphere was strained.

It was not until the next day, while the family were seated at the table taking breakfast, that the first real sign of Hester's fury surprised them. A young maid stormed into the cottage and began to scream abuse at the couple in Arabic about their treatment of her mistress. Eliza didn't understand a word but it was clear from the shouted invective that something was wrong. Meryon listened to the abuse but wasn't provoked, feeling that the girl was probably acting for Hester and would have been unable to do anything else. There was another period of silence, five days in total, before a horse arrived to take Meryon to Joun. The row that ensued between Hester and Meryon was terrible. She accused him of being emasculated by his wife and ranted and entreated him to change his mind; Meryon was unmoved. The only journey he now wished to make was to leave the Lebanon and return home.

The argument did not end. Distracted intermittently by discussions of a plan to build a European garden for Abdullah Pasha in Acre, all conversations returned to the usual theme of why Meryon should make the trip to Damascus. It was not until the end of February that the topic finally ceased to be revived. Meanwhile, the enmity between Hester and Eliza continued to fester. Eliza was displeased with a servant that Hester had sent to them and returned her to Joun. Following the example of Emir Bashir, Hester put word out around the village preventing anyone else working for Eliza, saying that harm would come to anyone who did. Meryon was trapped; in the evening when he visited Hester she treated him with marked kindness. During the day, he walked with his wife along narrow, precipitous paths, looked out across the wintry landscape and agonized with her over how they should deal with their predicament. Hester was not only intent on making their life difficult; she also prevented their escape because no one in the village would allow the Meryons to hire their camels or mules.

Meryon was also losing some of the admiration he had had for his mistress. He was passionately opposed to slavery and disgusted by Hester's use of corporal punishment. Meetings between them became less and less frequent; when they did occur they were tempestuous. On one occasion, after waiting ten days for a horse to be sent only to find the ensuing audience fraught with argument and bitterness, he again voiced their wish to leave. Difficulties in his relationship with Hester were not Meryon's only preoccupation. During the journey East he had sent carefully tied bundles to France – cast-off shirts to be remade for his son, Charles, now nine. Pierre Narcisse, lonely and missing him, did not cut them up but took them with her to bed so she could smell Meryon as she fell asleep.[3] Meryon, feeling guilty, began to wonder if he should tell her he now had a wife and child.

It was not until the end of the winter weather and the advent of April that Hester appeared to relent. While her relationship with Eliza did not improve, she lost the will to oppose their departure. This time the arrangements were quickly made, but before leaving Meryon sat with Hester to try once again to order her financial affairs. The debts were huge, although mostly charitable in nature: for example, money to help the Jumblat family when they went into hiding after his execution, a large sum to aid the destitute wife of a disgraced secretary of the Emir following the decapitation of her husband. The interest on these accumulated borrowings was as much as twenty-five per cent; there was no way that Hester could pay it and Meryon left with a promise to try to raise money in England without compromising her pride. He recommended an Italian doctor resident in Sidon by the name of Lunardi to act as his replacement and returned to the cottage. Hester's farewell gift awaited him: baklava, a hand-carved pipe and some tobacco, which he later described as 'wonderful'. On 7 April the Meryon family left for Sidon in preparation for their sail the following day.

Hester now re-entered a brief period of partial seclusion. Lunardi, unencumbered as he was by any familial loyalties or duties, proved an excellent successor to Meryon. But peaceful solitude was shattered in a matter of months. Before the end of the year political turmoil tore across the landscape of Mount Lebanon; Joun was crowded with refugees and Hester, by her own manipulation and scheming, was at the heart of the crisis as well as, unbelievably, still further in debt.

Having been refused Syria by the Porte as recompense for his failed support against the Greeks, Mehmet Ali sent his son Ibrahim, fresh from defeat at Navarino, to conquer Syria. If Egypt was not to be granted Syria as a boon, she would take her by force. The Jumblat Druse were bitter in their hatred of the Emir, eager for revenge for the death of Bashir Jumblat and well aware of the strong alliance between Mehmet Ali and Bashir II. So hatred of the Emir, rather than any great love for the Porte, moved them to act, but they struck out as if they were the most loyal servants of the Ottoman Empire. Staging a rebellion they attacked Ibrahim's troops. Ibrahim reacted quickly, commanding the Emir to help him. Wary of the consequence, which he believed would be an all-out civil war across the Lebanon, and of openly taking sides against the Porte, the Emir was cautious at first. Mehmet Ali had no patience for indecision; he threatened to invade Lebanon with his full force unless Bashir II supported his son unreservedly. And so the Emir did so, placing all of his men and resources at Egypt's disposal.[4] He was not alone; the Maronites also saw Egypt as an ally. Ibrahim, cannily aware of their support, fostered it by removing the traditional restriction placed on Christians and Jews, to put them on an equal footing with Muslims.

At the end of November Egyptian allied forces besieged Acre. Resistance was strong and initially Egyptian troops only succeeded in occupying Beittedine and Dar-el-Kamar. Abdullah, the Pasha of Acre, did not surrender until after Acre fell on 27 May of the following year, 1832. Then, rich with triumph, the troops proceeded to Damascus. The Pasha fled; Syria was under Egyptian rule.[5]

Hester's continued friendship with Abdullah – the garden they had designed together was now complete – and her open hatred of the Emir meant that Joun was regarded as a haven by refugees from the conflict. Battle weary, battered, starving and mutilated, the refugees rode, walked and crawled to Hester's home begging for safety, pleading for shelter. She would later write:

> After the siege of Acre which lasted 7 months (& sometimes 90,000 cannon ball thrown in one day) 200 people fell upon me at once, what sd I do with the starving & naked & many in fear of their lives.[6]

Oblivious to her financial plight, filled by a sense that God had ordained her to be in the Lebanon for just such an occasion as this, as well as by an aristocratic conviction that it was her duty to offer support to people who looked to her for charity, Hester welcomed them in. Despising the other expatriate Europeans, who refused to help for fear of Ibrahim Pasha's vengeance, she sent water to prisoners of the Sultan's army as they were marched through Sidon. Trading the few things she had left and borrowing more money, she housed, clothed and fed the exiles. Her home was 'like the tower of Babel, filled as well as the village, with unhappy people from Acre of all nations'.[7] One of the Pasha of Acre's wives, remarried to his treasurer, stumbled to Joun, having been stripped to her fine shift, supporting her husband, whose legs and thighs had been skinned by a gunpowder blast. They carried their smallest child, naked, shivering and crying, while guiding the treasurer's private secretary, who had lost both his eyes and his nose to a cannon ball. Hester took them in. Her generosity as great as her temper, wounded Mamelukes came with Druse; a family of eighteen from Acre, all young and helpless; orphans, widows and wounded soldiers straggled into Joun and took up residence in its little rooms and cottages. With no more resources of her own, Hester repeatedly borrowed money from Syrian moneylenders to feed and clothe them. Within a few months of the fall of Acre, Hester was housing seventy-five people within the walls of Joun.

The French poet Lamartine arrived in Lebanon in 1832 and established himself and his family in Beirut. Hester's story, with much embroidery, had reached him. He believed she had lost a huge fortune in a shipwreck, returned to England to sell her property, then used the accrued profit to become a great power in his adopted country. Now impoverished again, her influence with Arab tribes was still renowned. Lamartine believed that a recommendation from her might ease his passage among the Bedouin, so he planned to see her and wrote to request a meeting. Appealing to what he felt was a similarity between them in their appreciation of '*la charme de la solitude*', he sent word to her from Sidon and waited. He did not wait long; her current physician, Dr Lunardi, arrived to conduct him up the mountain.

His impressions of Joun, that it was a 'quaint confused assemblage of ten or twelve little buildings', were limited by the fact that Hester kept careful control of his movements at all times.[8] Many of the refugees from the fall of Acre still lived in the warren of houses and Hester, believing that Lamartine's sentiment was 'all in his pen and not in his heart', wished to keep the poet unaware of them.[9] The visit did not begin auspiciously. Lamartine was accompanied by a little lapdog and it was impossible to decide whether the dog's yapping or the constant affected fussing that Lamartine made over the animal irritated her more. Moreover, Lamartine was not a modest man; proud of his success, his first concern was to establish whether Hester was familiar with his reputation and his work. Ever forthright, Hester replied that actually she had not read them, nor did she have much interest in European literature. The encounter took place in semi-darkness. Hester was dressed in white, a long loose robe and turban, broken only by a thin strip of purple silk wound around the turban with the ends dangling over her shoulders. Lamartine almost grudgingly conceded that she had a look of dignity and grace.[10] He was ushered into a different room to eat alone but after dining joined her again. Smoking together, they discussed the East; then Hester took him out to her garden, a place she normally jealously guarded from outsiders. He was absolutely enchanted by:

un jardin charman, a la mode des Turcs; jardin de fleurs et de fruits, berceaux de vignes, kiosques enrichis de sculptures et de peintures arabesques; eau courantes dans les rigoles de marbre, jets d'eau au milieu des paves des kiosques; voute d'orangiers, de figuiers et de citronniers.[11]

From the garden, Hester led Lamartine to the stables, where he was introduced to the cherished mares: the chestnut mare on which the Messiah would ride and the snowy white horse on which Lamartine believed

Hester intended to accompany him. The meeting which had begun so inauspiciously ended well. When Lamartine left, he did so with the precious introductions he hoped for and with the erroneous conviction, as Hester's following visitor would find out, that he had made a good impression.

The next visitor was a welcome one, although he was just as intrigued by, and romantic about, the enigmatic Hester as his predecessor. Alexander Kinglake was a young lawyer whose maternal family had known Hester at Burton Pynsent. Known initially only as 'the intrepid girl who used to break their vicious horses for them', her travels had made her the 'Queen of the Desert' in Kinglake's childhood.[12] Treasured letters and small exotic presents, such as bottles of attar of roses, sent by Hester were hidden safely away, while bedtime stories filled his early years with awe at the fantastic exploits of his mother's heroine.

When Kinglake asked Hester if he might visit, he mentioned his mother's name, offering to let her know what had happened to 'her old Somerset acquaintance'. The reply was slow, delayed by heavy rain and a brief bout of illness, but welcoming when it came. The drama of the message was not lost on Kinglake and the expectations of his childhood satisfied when:

> A couple of horsemen covered with mud suddenly dashed into the little court of the 'Locanda' in which I was staying, bearing themselves as ostentatiously as though they were carrying a cartel from the Devil to the Angel Michael.[13]

One of the riders was Lunardi, the other a servant who accompanied him. Their message was surprisingly welcoming: Hester would love to speak of his mother, the 'sweet lovely girl' of her Somerset stay.[14] After a few days waiting for clement weather, Kinglake set off for 'the dwelling-place of Chatham's fiery granddaughter'. [15]Lunardi greeted him on arrival and, after a brief rest, Kinglake was served some local food and wine. When the meal was over, Lunardi conducted him through the open courtyards in the still heavy rain to where Hester waited for him. By the time he arrived he was drenched, but Hester gestured to him to take a seat opposite her sofa, where he took stock of the idol of his childhood. She was dressed in a mass of loose white drapery, a robe of linen that reminded Kinglake of a priest's surplice. Kinglake was enthralled. Hester's soliloquy meandered through stories of eastern machination to her religious conviction. But it was not dull; every treatise was broken by moments of 'full audacious fun' when she mimicked the affectations of Byron and Lamartine to their detriment but to Kinglake's delight.[16] Yet she reiterated her belief: the West was doomed; only those in the East would remain to build a new life.

His audience lasted until after midnight. In the morning he intended to visit the horses, but the torrential rain, and a repetition of the previous night's drenching, made the visit seem more effort than it was worth. Just after noon Hester sent for him, catching him by surprise; one of the most pervasive rumours about Hester was her preference for nocturnal meetings. It was a calmer meeting, with Hester asking after his mother and sister. Kinglake left Joun convinced of Hester's sanity, seeing her apparently eccentric beliefs in the eastern context, albeit with a romantic tinge, where she had acquired them. Later, when he wrote about his encounter in *Eothen*, he related the rumour that Mehmet Ali claimed Hester 'had given him more trouble than all the insurgent people of Syria, and Palestine'. Kinglake did not doubt it:

> In truth this half-ruined convent, guarded by the proud heart of an English gentlewoman, was the only spot throughout all Syria and Palestine in which the will of Mehemet Ali, and his fierce Lieutenant was not the law.[17]

In the years immediately following Kinglake's visit, Hester admitted few, if any, other travellers to Joun, living entirely within the walls of her fortress as renewed fighting spread across the region. The Egyptian regime in Syria had begun well enough. The new administration was better organized than that imposed by the Ottoman rulers, and Ibrahim worked to rid the country of the prevalent bribery and dishonesty. The political and social equality of Christians and Muslims, which had begun as a matter of political expedience, was upheld, much to the consternation of the latter. But the benefits were temporary. Years of neglect and corruption had made Syria a poor country; the Egyptian army of occupation was expensive. Impelled to raise money, Ibrahim did so by taxation, and when the money was not paid and there were not enough soldiers or men to collect it by force, a programme of forced labour and military conscription was imposed. Bashir II acted as a puppet of his Egyptian masters. Any semblance of religious tolerance was, ironically, destroyed by each religious group's shared hatred of the new draconian measures.[18] The Maronites believed that, as Christians, they could not be asked to fight in a Muslim army, while the Druse *uqqal* refused to have their young men serve alongside Muslims in case they lost their religious integrity. The Lebanese peasantry revolted against a political move that took men from working on their land to fight wars in which they had no interest.[19]

Two years after Kinglake visited Hester, revolts were breaking out across Syria, and Bashir II fought alongside the Syrians to quell the rebellions. They were successful but the years of fighting took its toll on the army. Ibrahim gave orders to the Emir to conscript one thousand six hundred Lebanese Druse, who would serve in the Egyptian army, for a term of fifteen years. For the first time Bashir II baulked at his command, pleading that the number was too high. Consequently, it was halved, but when the Emir summoned the Druse to comply, they refused. A rumour spread across the mountain that Ibrahim would soon begin conscripting the Maronites. Their reaction was immediate: any attempts at enforced conscription would be met by an appeal for French intervention. European consuls throughout the region quickly took up the appeal of the Christians, leaving the Druse even more vulnerable. But Joun became their refuge. While the sepulchres in caves tunnelling through the ground below Sidon became hiding places for young men, Hester's servants and people living within the walls of her home were exempt from the conscription. The English Consul in Beirut granted her protection for sixteen male domestics, but by July 1834 Mehmet Ali himself had lodged an official complaint through his agent. Hester had 'given protection to many followers of Abdullah Pasha, late Pasha of Acre'; moreover, she 'had granted protection to 77 people with the families of such as were married', claiming that they should be exempt from all taxes and 'entirely considered as withdrawn from under the jurisdiction of the authorities of the country'.[20] Hester, ignoring any such complaint, was more constrained by her lack of resources than by any threat from Mehmet Ali. As her home became the epicentre of political refuge and defiance, Hester finally regained something of the position she had known in London by her uncle's side, and with it the reputation as a saviour of the Druse.

While the Emir's reproach had no effect, it was not his only method of attack; his other attempt, while slow to take effect, would have much more damaging consequences. One of the moneylenders to whom Hester owed a substantial sum appealed to Mehmet Ali for his help in recovering the money. Seeing an opportunity to exact some revenge, Ali took up the case and appealed to the English Consul General, Colonel Campbell, for aid. Campbell immediately applied to the English government, namely the Duke of Wellington, for permission to force Hester to pay. Wellington refused to grant it saying that:

> as the pecuniary transactions referred to here appear to be entirely of a private nature, his Grace does not conceive that you can inter-fere in any official or authoritative manner with respect to them.[21]

The matter was forced to rest there, but only temporarily until Campbell appealed to the Foreign Office again a year later in 1835 and was again rebuffed. But by the summer of 1836 it seemed that Hester's financial difficulties might be resolved; she received word that she stood to inherit an Irish estate. Sceptical at first, Hester was convinced of the truth of the bequest by a young Irish lawyer who wrote to her. Colonel Needham had bequeathed his estate to her uncle, William Pitt. When Pitt died prematurely the estate fell to his heir-in-law, Lord Kil-morey. Kilmorey, dying childless, had supposedly asked that the Colonel's wishes be carried out, namely that Hester, as Pitt's heir, should inherit the land. Hester immediately wrote to the French Con-sul at Beirut to ask for his help in the matter and to Lord Hardwicke in England to see if he would enquire into the truth of the affair. Opti-mistically accepting that the inheritance was real, Hester borrowed again and again from local moneylenders, this time with the confi-dence that she would clear her debts imminently. But her health was deteriorating; the coughing fits of the previous winter grew more severe and were accompanied by 'a throttling sense of suffocation'. Already thin from her meagre diet, Hester lost even more weight. Ema-ciated and racked by her hacking cough, even she was alarmed when she vomited blood several times over a seven-day period. She pretended nonchalance over the incident and wrote to Meryon not to 'be uneasy about my health', but the letter was, nevertheless, a plea for him to rejoin her:

> I hope I shall not claim in vain the assistance of an old friend, at the moment I most require one I can depend upon, to settle the business of my debts, &c., now made public.[22]

When no replies to her queries over her supposed inheritance were forthcoming, Hester, relying on the doctor's honesty and loyalty, appealed to him to help her pursue the matter. Meryon was enjoying an unprecedented period of domestic harmony. Narcisse, aware of his marriage since his return from Syria, accepted her position in the extended family with hurt graciousness. The teenage Charles was made aware of his own position and invited to join the legitimate Meryon family on a tour of Europe in 1834, which he duly did.

However, on their return, Meryon was unable to find a suitable position. He responded to Hester's summons by employing a governess to care for his daughter, as well as to be a companion for his wife 'in the long evenings during my sittings with Lady Hester Stanhope' in an attempt to avoid the loneliness-induced scenes of the previous visit.[23] In May 1837 the family group left Marseille for Beirut.

14

Final Farewells

I have done what I believe my duty, the duty of everyone of every
religion; I have no reproaches to make myself, but that I went rather
too far; but such is my nature, and a happy nature too, who can
make up its mind to everything but *insult*.
Lady Hester to Lord Hardwicke, Joun, 6 June 1839

Meryon and Hester in Joun

Hester was far from pleased when the Meryons arrived. The doctor had again ignored her express wish that he come alone; not only did he have his wife but also his daughter Eugenia and their maid. She immediately wrote to Beirut, entreating him to travel south by himself, arguing that it would give him the opportunity to find suitable accommodation for his family while allowing her and Meryon 'to well understand each other' before his family joined them.[1]

But the impropriety of leaving his family at a Beirut inn moved Meryon to ignore Hester's request. So after only two days' rest in the city, the whole group set off for Sidon, travelling in the cool twilight hours to avoid the ferocious heat of the July days. From Beirut Meryon had arranged a house for his family in the vicinity of Sidon, but an earthquake the previous year had meant that accommodation was scarce; the house the Meryons were supposed to occupy was still inhabited by a Turkish family who refused to move. Reluctantly leaving his family temporarily ensconced in a tent, Meryon set off for Joun alone. It was late when he arrived, but in spite of the hour, his long journey and the fact that it was their first meeting in seven years, the whole of that first night was spent in semi-darkness, debating with Hester as to whether or not he should have left his wife and child in Beirut. His family fared no better. When the doctor returned to them the next morning he found Eliza in tears. During the night an army deserter had entered her tent as she lay asleep. Only half awake, Eliza saw a soaked and filthy man standing at the foot of her bed. Her screaming caused the children and governess to rush to her. But the local servants who came with them were far from angry. Recognizing that the man was fleeing from the conscription order, they sympathetically directed him to a lane that led to the mountains, where he might find caves to hide in. With the arrival of her husband, Eliza's panic turned to misery and Meryon guiltily set about trying to find them somewhere more solid to shelter.

Their former home at the convent of Mar Elias had also been partially damaged by the earthquake. Hester's old room and the kitchen had caved in completely; only the chapel with its smell of decaying flesh, General Loustennau's room, another large room as well as some small adjoining ones and the bath had escaped damage entirely. But it was better than a tent. The old general still lived there waiting for his son, with a single servant girl of Hester's who attended to his needs, but there was plenty of unoccupied space, so the doctor settled Eliza and Eugenia with their maid, hired some local people from Abra to tend to them and made sure they felt safe and comfortable before returning to Hester for the evening.

The interminable evenings began where they had left off. Meryon sat listening to Hester's monologues, rambling stories from her childhood and her belief in Armageddon, which had neither deviated nor diminished from her earlier conviction. But the reminiscences were the foundation of a continuing myth which began with Meryon's reproduction of them in the first of his *Travels* books. Either they were misremembered or misreported, but many details of the story which was to become accepted as Hester's early life were factually untrue.

Her father's Jacobin tendencies, the cause of so much conflict in later years, became blamed for the supposed stringencies of the childhood that Meryon described:

> My father always checked any propensity to finery in dress. If any of us happened to look better than usual in a particular frock or hat, he was sure to have it put away the next day, and to have something coarse substituted in its place.[2]

Yet Hester's paternal grandmother Grisel took great delight in Hester's clothes and often wrote about her granddaughter's taste in fashion: the dark brown gown she wore around Chevening which so set off her midbrown hair and almost white complexion; the pale green silk which shimmered in the sun. Moreover, by the age of sixteen she was a regular attendee of balls in Kent and London; dressed in a pink and gold spangled dress with a train and a cap with four white feathers she attracted admiration at Gloucester House on an occasion she nevertheless found dull.[3] The young Hester was not a housebound recluse, guarded by an austere father who refused to let her socialize, but a witty teenager who enjoyed balls in the Pantiles at Turnbridge Wells and balls in neighbouring stately homes: 'the three dancing away; every week of late at one or two balls, I hope to their hearts' content'. And the revelries went on until three or four and sometimes even seven in the morning, when they were brought back by their father, who minded the irregular hours less than anyone else.[4]

Perhaps at times it was too painful for Hester, from the dereliction of her Lebanese home, to recollect past gaiety and so she dwelled on later, sadder years, which Meryon mistook as describing her entire childhood. But it was not always so. Hester regaled Meryon with details of the feasts in her grandmother's house, occasions where scarlet-liveried servants attended on upwards of a hundred tenants. Huge oak tables were draped with tablecloths of the finest damask, embroidered with intricate, exquisite designs. Sides of beef were dressed in extravagant ways; huge plum puddings were carried to the table with great ceremony by two servants at a time. Wine was ordered and consumed in great quantities and, after the food, musicians would arrive to entertain the guests and dancing and merriment would go on till the small hours. Her accounts, unlike those of her hardship, were not exaggerated and the detailed household accounts of Grisel Stanhope show not only the lavishness of the entertainment but the vast expenditure it incurred.[5]

The regime of Hester's own household remained as hard and inviolable as it had on Meryon's last visit; at least five servants were on constant call, day or night. Meryon acknowledged that no European employee would put up with the complete lack of any free time and long hours that Hester enforced upon her servants, yet she was constantly unhappy with their ineptitude and disobedience. Unmarried male and female workers, in keeping with Islamic custom, were strictly segregated, the latter being confined to the harem or inner court for their living quarters. One cause of Hester's incessant complaints was the attempts of the servants to sneak into each other's rooms. Hester tried to enlist Meryon's help in her crusade against what she deemed the servants' immorality, but while he was 'most happy to lend his assistance' he baulked at doling out any kind of corporal punishment to offenders.[6] Hester frequently used a korbash to discipline her maids, and Meryon's disapproval of the method met with her ridicule and 'a never-ending battery of abuse'.[7]

Meryon had secured the services of an Italian woman to join the staff at Joun as Hester's housekeeper in the hope that, given her poor circumstances, she might persevere in the household. It was August when she arrived and was welcomed initially by the Meryon family to Mar Elias. But she was ill: the difficulties of the trip, compounded by the sweltering heat, had resulted in a brain fever with the most bizarre symptoms. Signora L, as she is only known, wandered from room to room, partially dressed, exposing herself to anyone in the vicinity. She cut her hair close to the roots and sang and danced without pausing to rest. Hester sent a surgeon barber from Sidon to her with instructions that she should be bled. She was, but to no effect. With the idea that air and space might calm her, the woman was moved to the chapel and bled continuously until she fainted. Meryon protested but Hester's faith in eastern medicine was unshakeable and she refused to countenance any of his suggested treatments. Waking from her swoon, Signora L began again to rant and rave, although now she was physically wild. Her arms flailed and her hands tore everything they could touch – a parasol, bedclothes, bandages, garments – while she sang plaintive Italian songs. Eventually Meryon realized that he would have to restrain her and he made a kind of straitjacket to prevent her doing damage to herself. Meanwhile, much to Meryon's annoyance, Hester's barber administered sachets of unknown substances. The poor woman began grinding her teeth and foaming at the mouth, and at last a priest was sent for. Within a day of receiving extreme unction Signora L was dead, and Hester immediately arranged for her burial at the Catholic burial ground in Sidon.

Haunted by the woman's final days, Eliza and her daughter now refused to stay in Mar Elias. In the night they thought they heard the frantic, manic laughter of the dead woman. Entreating Meryon that anywhere, even the poorest hovel, would be better than a haunted house, they insisted he find an alternative. Hester's animosity towards them had not diminished; she was adamant that they could not have even one of the empty cottages of Joun. The doctor persisted, but Hester refused to relent. In the end, she suggested that, as she was still waiting for news of the inheritance, it would be as well if Meryon settled with his family in Beirut or Cyprus until she did have word, and only then returned to her. The French Consul obliged by looking at some prospective properties for the Meryon family while he was in Beirut. But the matter was settled when a house in Abra was found that met with Mrs Meryon's approval, so that Hester and the doctor were able to continue as before.

As Hester impatiently sent servants to check each arriving ship for news of the money she expected, an old battle had resumed without her knowledge. In September 1837 Colonel Campbell, still the British Consul General, received yet another appeal from Mehmet Ali to facilitate the repayment of Hester's debt to the moneylender, Homsy. This time Campbell wrote to Lord Palmerston, who had recently replaced Wellington in the Foreign Office. Palmerston was much more sympathetic and agreed to help, but he deliberated over the best method of doing so. There seemed to be only one possibility: Hester's pension, the one that had been made by the state in response to her uncle's deathbed wishes, must be confiscated and used to clear the debt. It would not be a straightforward solution to impose. Hester had long since ceased contact with the English Consul and validated the quarterly declaration which enabled her pension to be sent from England with the signature of the French Consul, M. Guys. Nevertheless, Campbell wrote to Hester to advise her of Palmerston's decision. She did not receive his first letter but the second arrived early the following year; the British would no longer accept the autograph of the French or any other foreign consul, and the British Consul would refuse to sign until all her debts to Homsy were honoured. Hester treated it with scorn and said she would write to Queen Victoria. Her outward fight could not conceal the true effect of the letter. Her health, which was poor, deteriorated further. Again a violent cough racked her emaciated body; her servants murmured about consumption, and she vacillated between rages at her physical weakness and the treachery of the English and moments of pure exhaustion when she struggled to breathe as paroxysms of coughing left her helpless. As she dictated the letter to the Queen, Meryon noted and later described her bent back, the bones jutting through her papery vein-laced skin. Her eyes, while still a shade of blue that seemed to pierce rather than soothe an observer, were sunken and black-ringed from tossing and turning at night. Sleep came only fitfully and only after settling in the one position that allowed respite from the pain of her back and the continual coughing. She was, she said to Meryon, 'like those little figures of tumblers; place her as you would, she rolled over to the left side, as if there was a weight of lead there'.[8]

In spite of all, the letters she dictated were defiant and proud, with a simple message: she would never allow her pension to be stopped by force but she would give it up for the payment of her debts and 'with it the name of English subject'. She wrote letters to the Speaker of the House of Commons, Mr Abercrombie, and to Sir Edward Sugden in the House of Lords.[9] She and Abercrombie had played together as children, but a brief mention of this gave way to Hester's despair and anger at a queen 'who made me appear like a bankrupt in the world, and partly like a swindler'.[10] Hester would not be put under 'consular control'; again she stated she would resign the name of an English subject. Her letter to Sugden was longer, reiterating her position, but railed against the English, a people who had 'lost their national character' and had an aristocracy that was a 'proud, morose, inactive class of men' with no great principles but full of egotism. The message behind each of her letters was clear. She admitted to the debts but again and again attributed their cause to the aftermath of Acre, the housing and protection of the refugees and to the humanitarian aid she had given to the Druse.

It had been a terrible winter; the lower regions were buffeted and flooded by torrential rains while, on the mountain, heavy snow fell in tremendous, bitter storms. At the end of 1837, impelled by disorder and dirt, Hester finally attempted to leave her bedroom for an adjoining salon, but the floods had meant it was piled high with cushions and fabric to shelter them from the rain, so she returned to her confinement, often dictating from her bed, as large numbers of animals inexorably took over the rest of her home. As many as thirty cats with their kittens roamed around the courtyards, the ruined garden and the outhouses where the refugees had hid and waited. These cats were as protected by Hester's wrath as the refugees had been; it was absolutely forbidden to harm them and all infractions were punished with severity. As spring approached, Meryon's careful attempts to write her correspondence became a constant struggle to hear over the wailing and yowling of animals, but Hester remained adamant in her refusal to move or hurt them. With the amelioration of the weather, her imprisonment to a single room relaxed and she was able to pass time again in what remained of her garden. Her cough lessened, some of the plants – jasmine and periwinkle – bloomed and seemed to please her excessively and, by March, the month in which Hester became sixty-two, Meryon found her better on his visits than she had appeared to be for some years. Then a letter came: the German Prince Puckler Muskau was in Sidon and requested an audience. In spite of its flattering tone, the letter was insistent: Meryon would need to go to see him; she was still too ill and too reduced to poverty to entertain anyone, much less a prince. She sent a gentle refusal by messenger and discussed travel arrangements for the doctor. But in the interim more letters came. The Prince was unrelentingly persistent in his insistence that Hester see him. Finally, she wrote an uncharacteristically plaintive letter questioning whether he intended to discuss philosophy or merely 'to laugh at a poor creature, reduced by sickness to skin and bone, who has lost half her sight and all her teeth' but relenting to receive him after some further days when the spring weather had mended her health a little and she was able to speak at length without coughing.[11] Meryon was sent to visit Puckler Muskau so he could report back to Hester in advance of his arrival. While the Prince was very taken with Meryon's amiable nature, the doctor was initially less enthusiastic, especially at the Prince's constant distraction by his pet chameleon. Listening to his endearments and his solicitous '*Ou est mon petit bijou?*', Meryon dreaded 'a second edition of M. Lamartine and his lapdog'.[12]

Yet Meryon returned to Joun the same night with a report of his meeting that was not entirely negative. Prince Puckler Muskau was wise and courteous. Although Hester's spirits were markedly better, the reality of the financial injunction against her was beginning to take effect. No letter had come from her banker Sir Francis Burdett or anyone else about the awaited inheritance, but her pension was indeed suspended.

The Prince duly made his visit on Easter Sunday, 15 April, accompanied by four mules laden with luggage.[13] The garden had recovered from the drought created by the Emir; the roses grew as abundantly as wild flowers, and the pavilion, which was to be the Prince's home for eight days, was covered with climbing plants. Meryon warned the Prince about Hester's nocturnal habits, but he replied enthusiastically that receptions in the dark befitted the land of the thousand and one nights. When Hester finally received him for the first time it was as late as expected. Dressed in a white robe with a scarlet turban and baggy trousers, Puckler Muskau found her impressive but 'almost too masculine'.[14] She regaled him for hours over the merits of astrology, a process that continued throughout the following nights, but far from finding her tedious, the Prince 'felt more drawn to her' as a result of the conversations. Like Lamartine, Puckler Muskau was treated to the sight of the sacred mares. Used now, for many years, to being spoiled and pampered, they behaved 'like spoiled princesses', so that the Prince remarked that Layla seemed more devilish than holy. On what should have been the last evening Hester and the Prince enjoyed the view from the terrace at Joun: a fantastic sight of mountains and, in the distance, the sea.

However, Puckler Muskau's departure for the Emir Bashir, who had also granted him an audience, was delayed twice, the second time on the pretext of ill health, a guise the doctor felt sure he would have avoided had he been aware of Hester's black dose. This was a favoured cure-all which the Prince was forced to take and suffer the purgative effects of following his declaration. Meryon had been fully employed during the Prince's stay as Hester had instructed him to make a copy of all of the correspondence relating to her pension and give it to Puckler Muskau before his departure, so he could arrange to have it published on his return to Europe. Fully convinced that public sympathy would gain her support in Britain, Hester felt that her next strategy should be to publicize her treatment at the hands of the authorities. It was a mistake. Puckler Muskau did not help to publish the letters after he had read them, believing them contentious and, on Hester's part, too disrespectful in tone to be involved with.

The political situation in the region was still dangerous. The continued conscription met with more and more retaliation from the Druse, and it was increasingly difficult to travel at all in the area. An insurrection instigated by a makeshift Druse army of deserters and defaulters swept over the valley so that, by the end of April, local villagers were once again preparing to leave or barricade themselves in for fear of reprisals. An obtuse letter from Palmerston arrived, which seemed to say nothing in particular beyond what Hester already knew, namely that the Queen was aware of her situation and that his own motivation was to save Hester 'from embarrassments which might arise' from non-payment of her debts.[15] Unconvinced by his sudden concern, Hester's reply was acerbic and threatening. She thought his meaning obscure and told him so.

Moreover, she had decided on a plan of action. If she had no immediate word, by the next delivery, both that she was 'cleared of aspersions, intentionally or unintentionally cast upon me' and that her financial affairs were resettled, she would:

> Break up my household, and build up the entrance gate to my premises, there remaining, as if I were in a tomb, till my character has been done justice to, and a public acknowledgement put in the papers, signed and sealed by those who have aspersed me.[16]

It was not a statement made merely from bravado. Hester's money and all possible lines of credit had completely run out. The servant who took the letter for Palmerston to the English steamer in Sidon returned with a package. It was the long-awaited reply from Sir Francis Burdett. There was no Irish inheritance; Hester was destitute. She was calmer than Meryon could have believed possible. She told him that she had absolutely nothing with which to run a household; he and all of the others would have to go. Her reply to Burdett confirmed what she had written to Palmerston. She told a story of a lion in a net, calling in vain for help from the other animals, who was rescued only by a field mouse gnawing the huntsman's knots to let him break free. Her aristocratic friends were as ineffectual as the other animals. She would immure herself within her fort until either she died or, perhaps, it pleased God to send her a 'little mouse' of her own. Her health was better, although Meryon was surprised that she survived the winter and doubted that she could live another, but the valley was impassable and torn apart with bloody fighting. However, even if it had not been, she had nowhere else to go. Before the arrangements for his departure in August were made, the doctor transcribed as many letters as she wished. Meryon later admitted that he had no doubt that he would have helped her considerably by prolonging his stay but 'she would not allow me to do so, and insisted on my departure on an appointed day'.[17]

Meryon saw her wall up the gate to Joun before he left, the only opening left just big enough for a mule bringing water from the supply some miles below to pass through. Within days of the doctor's departure, more bad news caught up with him: suddenly and unexpectedly, Narcisse was dead.

The letters that Hester wrote in the months that followed were few; she no longer had Meryon to act as an amanuensis and she struggled with headaches and failing sight. Her dream of someone helping her escape was carried by Meryon when he published, as Puckler Muskau had failed to, all the correspondence relating to the government's edict in *The Times*. But their appearance in print, at the end of the year, led to derision, not celebration, over Hester's situation. *The Times* itself did everything to defend her cause, even criticizing Palmerston for instigating 'his agent to persecute the nearest living relative of the greatest statesman whom England ever produced', while the *Morning Herald* felt that the publication of the letters would benefit Hester's reputation.[18] But the response from the public was less encouraging. On 29 November, just two days after the letters were published, a retort appeared in the *Morning Chronicle*; it was anonymous, signed D, and with an address simply of the Oxford and Cambridge Gentleman's Club. Hester was a spendthrift, the writer claimed, whose reputation in Syria was for extravagant spending and huge debts long before the siege of Acre, and whose penury was not the result of 'charitable propensities'.

Hester sent an angry and indignant reply to the *Morning Chronicle*, which was published in *The Times*, prefaced by a statement of gratitude to its editor and that of the *Morning Herald*. As 1838 came to an end just one voice spoke out in defence, that of Sir William Napier, who had known her in Downing Street. Napier respected her vast influence 'with the Arab tribes', defended her against the charge of being a 'crack brained lady', as other papers had asserted, and warned that 'the extent of her power and resolution may be understood too late'. Moreover, he pointed out the hypocrisy of 'those, who now insult her', who would 'have been too happy to lick the dust from her shoes' when she was Pitt's hostess.[19] On 6 December the government made its only retraction, but in the form of a denial: they had never intended to deprive Hester of her pension. It proved to be no more than words; Hester never received the rest of her money.

From her self-imposed confinement, Hester suggested the only possible solution – that her pension and the annuity from her brother be sold – and enlisted the help of Lord Hardwicke. Meanwhile, daily life at Joun moved on. Loustennau, 'The Prophet', was moved from Mar Elias in the midst of the increasingly dangerous landscape and settled within Joun. Even in her penury, Hester made him comfortable with a new sofa and some shrubs around his outhouse. Meryon's letters to her were filled with guilt that he had not stayed with her, but her replies stated unambiguously that she would have had it no other way: 'Do not reproach yourself about leaving me; it did not depend on you to stay.'[20] It was to be her last letter to him, and it ended with a poignant, almost apologetic, sentiment: 'I have written a sad, stupid letter, but I have no news – shut up.'[21]

Hester lived for another month, attended by no one who could report her condition, slowly wasting away, so like her father in his last days at Chevening: a fading spectre in the shell that remained of a once great house. When her body was found it was decomposing and already beginning to smell in the summer heat, but her expression was calm, as if she had been waiting to die and done so peacefully.

The two riders who approached Joun after an eleven-hour ride in intense heat were understandably weary. They wound up the mountain in the pitch-blackness, travelling beyond the village to Hester's domain. The effect of the building was forbidding – with its thick surrounding walls more like a fortress than a home and, once beyond them, like a maze in the darkness, ramshackle buildings clustered together on a mountain eyrie. Around midnight the English Consul and the American missionary dismounted, barely illuminated by the light of torches held by the servants who gathered around them. Cats yowled, cried and brushed past their legs. They found Hester's room near the entrance. It was dilapidated and disordered, cluttered with candle ends, paper and paraphernalia, crowded with cats and kittens and rank with their smell; in the far left-hand corner was the eastern-style bed where Hester's body lay. Fearful of the heat and not waiting for the light, the servants led the way to the garden and the vault where their mistress had asked to be buried, and opened it. The bones of her last lover were removed and then replaced at one end. Meanwhile, a group of retainers carried the body, in a plain deal box, guided by a mixture of lanterns and firelight, from her room through the alleys and alcoves of the garden. The young missionary took a wrong turn in the dim light, crying out in shock when he literally fell upon the arbour of the crypt. The first thing he saw was a pile of bones with a skull on top, a lighted taper flickering through each eye socket, grinning at him amidst the shadows of plants and trees – a grotesque arrangement made by the servants.

There was little ceremony, yet the two simple observances denied both of Hester's express wishes, namely that she should be disassociated both from her country and from the Christian religion. The coffin was draped with a British flag and the missionary performed the funeral rite of the Church of England. Hester was buried and the small party returned in silence, through the winding alleyways of roses run wild, to the decaying palace with its thirty-five rooms, all filled with scavenging cats.[22]

15

Aftermath

It was her legacy to me, for she had nothing else to leave me.
Meryon, letter to Philip Mahon

Dr Meryon in Arabic dress. He sent this drawing to
his illegitimate son who kept it with him

MERYON RETURNED TO ENGLAND with his English family to support, as well as his illegitimate son. Financially, things were not
easy. The newspaper articles and the controversy surrounding Hester's
death suggested a possible way to alleviate his situation. It had always
been Meryon's intention to publish a book about his travels with Hester,
and now was the ideal time. He frantically began collating his notes and
letters, transcribing and arranging them. By December it was ready for
publication.

However, Hester's eldest half-brother, Philip Mahon, now the fourth
Earl, intervened. Motivated more by concern for his own reputation and
fear of any public revelation of his own difficult relationship with his
half-sister, he wrote to Meryon begging him to reconsider:

> I am convinced, from all that I know of your character that you
> would deeply regret if you were to be the instrument of wounding
> the feelings of Lady Hester's relations and friends by a disclosure of
> family anecdotes and domestic dissensions which ought to remain
> unknown in the world.[1]

The doctor replied stating the difficulties of his financial state, arguing
that he had followed her for the best years of his life, 'guided by his sense
of devotion and attachment to her', and that he was writing the book in
compliance with Hester's own wishes: 'It was her legacy to me, for she had
nothing else to leave me.'[2] He felt that the material and anecdotes he had
collected would bring honour rather than shame to her name. Lord Stanhope was not so easily appeased. His reply continued to protest against
the forthcoming volumes and expressed his intention to take legal action
if the character and conduct of any person was assailed. Stanhope's intervention only delayed the process and, in 1845, the three-volume *Memoirs
of Lady Hester Stanhope* was finally published. It was the beginning of the
mythologizing of Lady Hester. A year later the three-volume *Travels of*

Lady Hester Stanhope appeared, advertised as the completion of the first trilogy. In these books, the Boswellian Meryon, a man whose fortune was so inextricably linked with his idol, had created a story about Hester, part fact, part fantasy, that would be read and largely believed for centuries.

In spite of the effect they would have on future generations, at the time the books were received with criticism. The *Quarterly Review* of September 1845 stressed the particular inappropriateness of the remarks being disclosed by a '*medical gentleman* [italics as original]'.

Financially, Meryon's life was improved by the publication of the books; he even started on a third trilogy of *Additional Memoirs*, the notes for which are still to be found in the archives in Kent. He also drew up plans for a book based on his liaison with Narcisse, the Opera dancer, carefully changing the names of the protagonists and translating the correspondence between his son, Charles Meryon, now a young man with considerable skill as an artist, Narcisse and himself into English. These are all in the British Library. But in spite of his small literary success his final years were troubled.

The years he had spent serving Hester came back to haunt him when his illegitimate son Charles accused him of neglect and blamed his gradual descent into insanity on his father's absence and his own inability to cope with the stigma attached to his birth. Late in 1840 Charles wrote to his father:

> As things are now you don't belong to me, I don't belong to you, in the eyes of society we are not even related.

Posthumously, Charles Meryon was recognized as a world-class engraver, described by Van Gogh as someone who 'puts into his etchings something of the human soul, moved by I do not know what inner sorrow',[3] but his life was blighted and destroyed by severe mental illness. He travelled even more extensively than his father and created representations of, at the time, hardly known worlds, carefully drawing Maori warriors and Antipodean fauna, as well as the Parisian scenes which eventually brought him fame. But the father could take no pride in his son. Their correspondence became more fractured and troubled in the years following Dr Meryon's literary début, until his son was committed to a French asylum at the age of just thirty-six. He died there ten years later, in 1868, outlived by his father, having spent his last weeks in a sad tableau, reminiscent of the woman who had occupied so much of his father's time, claiming he was the Messiah. Dr Meryon was left with regrets and received public blame for his son's end. His nephew was still defending him in 1892, when he protested that the engraver's biographer, Frank Wedmore, had erroneously blackened his uncle's character.[4]

But Dr Meryon would not achieve his greatest fame as his son's father. It was Hester and his books that would bring him too a kind of immortality. He was the ultimate fan, even if he was not always complimentary to his idol. He followed Hester on a series of difficult travels, enduring abuse and receiving little remuneration, yet still, in spite of his understandable occasional gripes, seemed to maintain his initial impression that she was in some way 'the best lady who ever breathed'.

Ten years after her death he wrote to Michael Bruce, with what was more than a tinge of reproof. The letter was obviously unexpected and began by wishing him a happy birthday for the following day, adding, 'Do you not wonder how I recollect your birthday?' It contained the reason for his memory. On the verso of the page were the verses comparing Hester to a poppy, which he had written for her thirty-seven years ago when she was missing Michael at Mar Elias. They had been a gift, Meryon pointedly told him, 'to console a forlorn and weeping lady, the recollection of whose virtues shall ever be embalmed in my memory, whatever her so called eccentricities may have been'.[5]

While Meryon did not omit Hester's later bizarre behaviour from his books, he retained the essence of her strengths. His impressions and opinions largely created the image of the woman from which subsequent imaginations would develop their own interpretation.

Epilogue

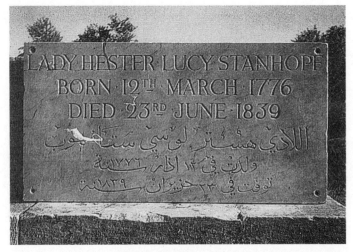

LADY HESTER LUCY STANHOPE
BORN·12ᵀᴴ·MARCH·1776
DIED·23ᴿᴰ·JUNE·1839

اللّادي هستر لوسي ستانهوب
ولدت في ١٤ آذار سنة ١٧٧٦
توفيت في ٢٣ حزيران سنة ١٨٣٩

Hester's original grave in Joun

Meryon's books, which had met with such a mixed reception, found popularity after their author's death and gave their subject prominence as a referential figure in the following century. The Victorians tended to see her as an eccentric heroine, possessing an abundance of 'patience and fortitude', virtues that were so desirable in women at that time.[1] Her love affairs and more scandalous behaviour were left unmentioned, no doubt out of deference to the fact that she was 'a lady of high rank'.

Later Hester was portrayed in a contradictory collection of guises by famous people, but often in ways so far removed from each other, as well as from any factual history, as to seem to be a description of someone else entirely. By the early twentieth century Lady Hester began to figure as a classic example of what could go wrong in the upper classes. In 1919 Lytton Strachey saw her as an emblem of eccentric aristocracy:

> There has always been a strong strain of extravagance in the governing families of England; from time to time they throw off some peculiarly ill-balanced member, who performs a strange meteoric course.[2]

For him she was a preposterous woman 'of wild ambitions, of pride grown fantastical', who died 'lying back in her bed – inexplicable, grand, preposterous, with her nose in the air'.[3]

It was an image that the poet W. H. Auden repeated in an essay in 1941, but stressing an altogether different attribute:

> For myself, I either don't know or won't say. But I think often of ridiculous, crazy, incompetent old Lady Hester Stanhope whispering, 'It's all been very interesting,' and then dying far from home with her nose in the air. If when my time comes, I can show even half as much courage, the mortician may paint me all the colours of the rainbow, the columnists come out every morning with an entirely new explanation of the World Crisis, and the telephone bleed to death under the stairs, but I shall not care.[4]

In James Joyce's *Ulysses*, she makes an appearance as Hester Stanhope, Molly Bloom's friend, but whenever Molly wears or imagines Arabic dress, her image merges with that which Meryon gives of Hester, down to the scarlet trousers and yellow slippers he sees her wearing on his penultimate visit.[5] For Molly, and for Joyce, the image of Lady Hester is inextricably linked to a concept of the romantic East, just as it would be for popular romantic novelists later in the twentieth century.

These contradictory and powerful images of a reclusive eccentric and romantic heroine fuelled my own interest. I found Joan Haslip's 1934 biography on a wet May afternoon in a second-hand bookshop on Lon-

don's Charing Cross Road. About to fly to Istanbul to spend some time
with a colleague there and carry out some research, I thought it would be
ideal reading. It was my first time in the East. Living in an exclusively
Muslim suburb of the city, waking to the muezzin's cry then hearing the
shouts of market traders from the quay of the Bosphorus just below the
apartment, I would read until the gentle pad of my friend's slippers in the
hallway indicated that he was awake. The romance of Hester enchanted
me, but I was also a little afraid of her. I was curious about her relationship with Meryon, by far the longest and most enduring association of
her life. In the notes and volumes scattered in various parts of the United
Kingdom and abroad, it was possible to learn about Hester as much from
what he had omitted from his books as from what he had included. Arabic manuscripts in Kent hinted at Hester's domestic concerns; her letters
to her many correspondents showed her progression from giddy girlhood
to maturity. And there were the treasures of the East, stories to be listened
to in Ascalon, ruins and old documents to be explored and studied in
Joun, Palmyra and Beirut.

Then, in the final days of research, I visited a house at Meshmushy, in
southern Lebanon, reachable only by roads flanked by unexploded land-
mines. There I took tea and chatted about Hester as if she were some long
lost, slightly batty family member, to be indulged by memory and honoured in death. My host's stories were proud and fearful; Hester had treated one of his forefathers with a great deal of cruelty yet saved another from
conscription and likely death. Amidst his family memories there was, at
last, a glimpse of the iconoclastic Hester, the woman who had inspired
Picasso, a powerful, political figure who took and spared lives, and valued
the opportunity to do so. Here in her adopted home she was truly a heroine,
an idol, something more than all she had been, she who had been so many
things.

Select Bibliography

MANUSCRIPT SOURCES

Birmingham University Special Collections
STA 143

A
Ad
Add

Centre for Ken
Stanhopes of Chevening MSS UI590

Chevening Library
Letters (given to me by Colonel Brooks)

Cumbria Record Office
Lowther Family Papers

Deir Moukhalles Monastery papers

Herefordshire Record Office
AC40/9528
AC40/9564

Public Record Office, London
PRO 30/8/5
PRO 30/8/14
PRO 30/29/6
PRO 30/58
PRO 30/70/6

Victoria and Albert Library
Forster Collection

Wellcome Library, London
The Meryon letters MSS 5687–9

West Sussex Record Office

PRINTED SOURCES

Newspapers and Periodicals
Covent Garden Magazine
Daily Advertiser
Gentleman's Magazine
Kentish Gazette
Kentish Herald
London Chronicle
London Evening Post
London Gazette
Morning Chronicle
Morning Herald
Morning Post
New Monthly Magazine
Oracle and Public Advertiser
St James Chronicle
The Times

Books

... of a Babylonian Princess (London, 1844).

... Last Five Sultans of Turkey, Being

Physician, in *Bulletin of the John Rylands Library University of Manchester*, Vol. 55, No. 1 (Manchester, 1972).

Brothers, Richard, *Further Testamonies of the authenticity of the prophecies of Mr Richard Brothers* (London, 1795).

Brownrig, Lady Beatrice, *The Life and Letters of Sir John Moore* (London, 1923).

Bruce, Ian, *Lavalette Bruce* (London, 1953).

Bruce, Ian, *The Nun of Lebanon* (London, 1951).

Bucke, Charles, *Ruins of Ancient Cities*, Vol. 2 (London, 1840).

Buckingham, J. S., *Travels Among the Arab Tribes Inhabiting the Countries East of Syria and Palestine* (London, 1825).

Burty, P., *Charles Meryon et Son Oeuvre* (London, 1879).

Carne, John, *Letters from the East*, Vol. II (London, 1830).

Coke, Lady Mary, *Letters and Journals 1886–1896* (London).

Collins, Roger, *Charles Meryon, A Life* (Wiltshire, 1999).

Crossley, C. and Small, I., *The French Revolution and British Culture* (Oxford, 1989).

De Lamartine, Alphonse, *Souvenirs, Impressions et Pensées Pendant un Voyage en Orient* (London, 1841).

Dickinson, H. T. (Ed.), *Britain and the French Revolution 1789–1815* (London, 1989).

Dodwell, Henry, *The Founder of Modern Egypt: A Study of Mohammed Ali* (New York, 1977).

Duchess of Cleveland, *The Life and Letters of Lady Hester Stanhope* (London, 1914).

Miss Edgeworth, *Tales of Fashionable Life*, Vol. VI (London, 1812).

Eliade, Mircea (Ed.), *The Encyclopaedia of Religion*, Vol. 9 (London, 1987).

Emery and Emery, *History of a Genetic Disease, Duchene Dystrophy or Meryon's Disease* (London, 1955).

Firro, Kais M., *A History of the Druses* (Leiden, 1992).

Flaxmer, Sarah, *Satan Revealed* (London, 1796).

Granville, Lady, *The Private Correspondence of Lord Granville Leveson Gower* (1916).

Hamel, Frank, *Lady Hester Lucy Stanhope* (London, 1913).

Haslip, J., *Lady Hester Stanhope* (London, 1945).

Heneine, Alice, *Lady Esther Stanhope et le Liban* (Beirut, 1983).

Hibbert, Christopher, *George III* (London, 1998).

Hitti, Philip K., *A Short History of Lebanon* (London, 1965).

Joyce, Jermiah, *Sermon to Which is Added an Appendix Containing an Account of the Author's Arrest* (London, 1796).

Kinglake, Alexander, *Eothen or Traces of Travel* (London, 1845).

Kubler, George A., *The Era of Charles Mahon, Third Earl of Stanhope, Stereotyper* (New York, 1938).

Lever, Sir Tresham, *The House of Pitt* (London, 1947).

Lewis, Norman, *Nomads and Settlers in Syria and Jordan 1800–1900,* (Cambridge, 1987).

MacCarthy, F., *Byron: Life and Legend* (London, 2002).

Maccoby, S., *English Radicalism 1786–1832* (London, 1955).

Madden, R. R., *Travels in Turkey, Egypt, Nubia and Palestine* (London, 1829).

Makdisi, Ussama, *The Culture of Sectarianism: Community, History and Violence in Nineteenth Century Ottoman Lebanon* (University of California, 2000).

Marsot, Lufti al-Sayyid, *Egypt in the Reign of Muhammed Ali* (Cambridge, 1984).

Napier, Sir W., *The Life and Opinions of General Sir Charles James Napier* (London, 1857).

Newman, A., *The Stanhopes of Chevening* (London, 1969).

Plowman, Stephanie, 'Lady Hester Stanhope: A Family Affair', in *History Today 4,* pp. 844–50, (London, 1954).

Price, Rev. Thomas, *Literary Remains* (Wales, 1856).

Reilly, Robin, *Pitt the Younger* (London, 1978).

Roundell, Mrs., *Lady Hester Stanhope* (London, 1909).

Salibi, Kamal S., *A House of Many Mansions* (London, 1988).

Salibi, Kamal S., *The Modern History of the Lebanon* (London, 1965).

Stanhope, Earl, *Miscellanies* (London, 1863).

Stanhope, Earl, *Notes and Extracts of Letters referring to Mr Pitt and Walmer Castle* (Printed for Private Circulation, 1866).

Stanhope, Earl, *The Life of William Pitt in Three Volumes* (London, 1879).

Stanhope and Gooch, *The Life of Charles, 3rd Earl of Stanhope* (London, 1914).

Stein, Stephen J., *The Encyclopaedia of Apocalypticism*, Vol. 3 (New York, 1999).

Thomson, W. M., *The Land and The Book* (London, 1859).

Warburton, Eliot, *The Crescent and The Cross* (London, 1845).

Watney, John, *Travels in Araby* (London, 1975).

Webb, K. G., *Stanhope Impressions* (Oxford, 1966).

Wedmore, Frederick, *Meryon and Meryon's Paris* (London, 1879).

Endnotes

Abbreviations

BL	British Library
Bod	Bodleian Library, Oxford University
Kent	Centre for Kentish Studies
PRO	Public Record Office, Kew
V&A	Victoria and Albert Museum Foster Collection

Prologue

1. See Penrose, *Picasso: his life and work*, London, 1981.

Chapter 1

1. Meryon, *Memoirs*, Vol. 2, p. 79.
2. See BL Add 42772 ff. 266–312 for various letters on Pitt's health, as well as *Pitt the Younger*, Reilly, p. 342.
3. From an account given by James Stanhope, quoted in *The Life and Letters of LHS*, Duchess of Cleveland, p. 69.
4. Canning to GLG, 29 Jan 1806, PRO 30/29/8/3.
5. Meryon, *Memoirs*, Vol. 2, p. 5.
6. Kent UI590 S6/2/5 Journal Chapter Five, 9 April to 9 May 1919.
7. See *Chevening*, booklet published by the Chevening Estate, p. 16.
8. LHS to Lord Glastonbury, 19 March, Kent UI590.
9. *Ibid.*
10. *Ibid.*
11. *Ibid.*
12. Hibbert, p. 306.
13. LHS to Lady Chatham, Weymouth, Monday 28 September 1801, PRO 30/70/6.
14. LHS to T. J. Jackson, 18 Oct 1801, Kent UI590.
15. LHS to Lord Haddington, 23 Oct 1802 (quoted in Newman, A., *The Stanhopes of Chevening*, 1969).
16. See Stanhope & Gooch, p. 45, letter from Earl Stanhope to Mahon, 10 June 1803.
17. LHS to T. J. Jackson, Walmer Castle, 19 Nov 1803, Kent UI590.
18. *Ibid.*
19. 4th Earl Stanhope to Lord Carrington, 12 Oct 1803, Kent UI590 (quoted in Newman, *The Stanhopes of Chevening*).

Chapter 2

1. *Additional Memoirs*, Kent UI590 6/2/5.
2. Meryon, *Memoirs*, Vol. 2, pp. 36–7.
3. Moore to LHS, 23 Nov 1808, cited in *Stanhope Miscellanies*, pp. 61–4.
4. Moore to LHS, 16 Oct 1808 Kent UI590.
5. LHS to unknown, Monday night, quoted in Cleveland, pp. 73–4.
6. LHS to Grenville, 25 Jan, Montagu Square, Kent UI590.
7. *Gentlemen's Magazine*, February 1809, Vol. 79, p. 185, London.
8. *Ibid.*
9. *Additional Memoirs*, Kent UI590 S6/2/5.

Chapter 3

1. LHS to T. J. Jackson, Walmer Castle, 14 Jan 1804, Kent UI590.
2. *Memoirs*, Vol. 2, p.30.
3. *Ibid.*, p.32.
4. *Gronow's Reminiscences*, Vol. 1, p. 269 (1889).
5. LHS to GLG, Dec 1804, PRO 30/29/6/2.
6. LHS to Adams, Walmer Castle, Sunday 1805, Kent UI590.
7. Lady Granville, *The Private Correspondence of Lord Granville Leveson Gower*, 1916, p. 458.
8. *Ibid.*, p. 462.
9. Ibid.
10. 6. LHS to GLG, Dec 1804, PRO 30/29/6/2.
11. The actual note does not exist but there are various references to it in Granville and Bessborough's letters – see Leveson Gower book, Vol. 1, p. 466, Vol. 2, p. 48, and in Hester's own PRO 30/29/6/2.
12. LHS to GLG, 27 Dec 1804, PRO 30/29/6/2.
13. Cited in MacCarthy, p. 173.
14. LHS to T. J. Jackson, Walmer Castle, 19 Nov 1803, Kent UI590.
15. LHS to T. J. Jackson, Walmer Castle, 3 Feb 1805, Kent UI590.
16. *Ibid.*
17. *Ibid.*
18. Canning to LHS, Kent UI590 C419/12.
19. LHS to T. J. Jackson, Walmer Castle, 3 Feb 1805, Kent UI590.
20. *Memoirs*, Vol 2, p. 66.
21. *Ibid.*, p. 67.
22. Lady Granville, *The Private Correspondence of Lord Granville Leveson Gower*, 1916.
23. Rev Thomas Price, *The Literary Remains Vol. 2*, Wales, pp. 28–9 (1855).
24. LHS to TJ Jackson, 17 July 1803. Kent UI590 S90.

25. In a BL manuscript letter dated 6 July 1862 Meryon's other child refers to her as *'une petite fille . . . de votre premier mariage'*. While no marriage record exists, I have accepted in the absence of evidence to the contrary that he was indeed married to poor Elizabeth.

26. Meryon to his sister, 10 Feb 1810, Wellcome Foundation, MS 5687. In this letter to his sister he writes that he is afraid the 'family malady' might never 'be eradicated'.

27. Meryon to his sister, Gibraltar, 12 March, 1810, Wellcome Foundation, MS 5687.

Chapter 4

1. *The Letters and Journals of Lady Mary Coke Vol. IV*, p. 447 (Edinburgh, 1896).

2. Countess Grizel Stanhope to Lady Chatham, Queen Anne Street, 14 March 1776, Kent UI590 S5.

3. *Ibid.*

4. Countess Grizel Stanhope to Lady Chatham, 14 Aug, 1788 & 5 Sept, 1791, Kent UI590 S5.

5. Countess Grizel Stanhope to Lady Chatham, Dec 1776 Kent UI590 S5.

6. Hester Pitt to Lady Chatham, 24 April 1780 PRO 30/70/5.

7. Countess Grizel Stanhope to Lady Chatham, 15 April, 1780 & 15 may, 1780 Kent UI590 S5.

8. Countess Grizel Stanhope to Lady Chatham, 27 Oct 1783 Kent UI590 S5.

9. Countess Grizel Stanhope to Lady Chatham, 27 Oct 1783 Kent UI590 S5.

10. Countess Grizel Stanhope to Lady Chatham, 13 Oct 1787 Kent UI590 S5.

11. Newman, p125.

12. *Additional Memoirs*, Kent UI590, S6/4/1.

13. See the account in the *Additional Memoirs* chapter 'Scenes from the High Life', Kent UI590 S6/4/1.

14. *Memoirs Vol 2*, pp. 24–6.

15. LHS to Lady Chatham, 6 Jan, 1801 PRO 30/70/6.

16. PRO 30/7/6/34.

Chapter 5

1. Meryon to his mother, Gibraltar, 12 March 1810, Wellcome Foundation MS 5687.

2. *Ibid.*

3. *Ibid.*

4. *Ibid.*

5. Meryon to his sister, Gibraltar, 12 March 1810, Wellcome Foundation MS 5687.

6. MB to CB, Salamanca, 12 Dec 1808. Quoted in Lavalette Bruce, p.44.

7. Byron to Hobhouse, Athens, 23 Aug 1810, BL.

8. Meryon to his brother-in-law, Gibraltar, 18 March 1810, Wellcome Foundation MS 5687.

9. Meryon to his mother, Malta harbour, 21 April 1810, Wellcome Foundation MS 5687.

10. Meryon to his brother, Valetta, 30 April 1810, Wellcome Foundation MS 5687.

11. *Ibid.*

12. Meryon to his sister, 8 June 1810, Wellcome Foundation MS 5687.

13. MB to CB, Malta, May 1810, Bod MSS.Eng.C.5740.

14. *Ibid.*

15. Meryon to his father, 8 June 1810, Wellcome Foundation MS 5687.

16. Meryon to his brother-in-law, Valetta, 24 April 1810, Wellcome Foundation MS 5687.

17. Meryon to his brother-in-law, 5 June 1810, Wellcome Foundation MS 5687.

18. Meryon to his father, 8 June 1810, Wellcome Foundation MS 5687.

19. Meryon to brother-in-law, 15 June 1810, Wellcome Foundation MS 5687.

20. Meryon to brother-in-law, 15 June 1810, Wellcome Foundation MS 5687.

21. Meryon to brother-in-law, 28 June 1810, Wellcome Foundation MS 5687.

22. LHS to CB, St Antonio, June 1810, Bod MSS. Eng.C.5744.

23. MB to CB, Malta, 27 June 1810, Bod MSS. Eng.C.5744.

24. Meryon to his sister, 10 Feb 1810, Wellcome Foundation MS 5687.

25. Meryon to his mother, 15 July 1810, Wellcome Foundation MS 5687.

26. Meryon to his sister, 14 July 1810, Wellcome Foundation MS 5687.

27. Meryon to his mother, 15 July 1810, Wellcome Foundation MS 5687.

28. Meryon to his sister, 14 July 1810, Wellcome Foundation MS 5687.

Chapter 6

1. Meryon to his brother, Zante, 18 Aug 1810, Wellcome Foundation MS 5687.

2. Cited in *The Nun of Lebanon*, p. 67.

3. A long garment very similar to a burkha.

4. Meryon to his father, Pera, 23 Nov 1810, Wellcome Foundation MS 5687.

5. Meryon to his mother, Athens, 15 Oct 1810, Wellcome Foundation MS 5687.

6. MacCarthy, p. 128.

7. Meryon to his mother, Athens, 15 Oct 1810, Wellcome Foundation MS 5687.

8. Meryon, *Travels 1*, p. 43 and MacCarthy, p. 128.

9. Meryon to his sister, Pera, 27 Oct 1810, Wellcome Foundation MS 5687.

10. Meryon to his sister, Pera, 23 Nov 1810, Wellcome Foundation MS 5687.

11. Byron to Hobhouse, Patras, 4 Oct 1810, BL.

12. Meryon, *Memoirs.* Vol. 3, p. 218.

13. Byron to Hobhouse, 19 June 1811, BL. See also Crompton, Louis, *Byron Greek Love,* pp. 172–3, Faber and Faber (1985) and MacCarthy, p. 130.

14. Transcript letter Hobhouse to Byron, Malta, 31 July 1810, BL.
15. Meryon to his sister, Pera, 23 Nov 1810, Wellcome Foundation MS 5687.
16. CB to LHS, 3 Sept, Bod MS 5749.
17. CB to MB, Taplow Lodge, 20 Aug 1810, MS 5749.
18. CB to MB, Taplow Lodge, 3 Sept 1810, Bod MS 5749.
19. CB to MB, Taplow Lodge, 3 Sept 1810, Bod MS 5749.
20. LHS to CB, 12 Dec 1810, Bod MS 5759.
21. The exact date and nature of the proposal are unknown. Several references are made to it afterwards in letters and I have tried to date it with reference to these.
22. Meryon to Smith, Therapia, 20 Jan 1811. Wellcome Foundation MS 5687.
23. This letter is quoted from in a reply from Michael dated 24 Dec, Constantinople, Bod MS 8749.
24. MB to James Stanhope, Constantinople, 24 Dec, Bod MS 2835.
25. LHS to MB, Therapia, 17 Febry [sic] 1811, Bod MS 5759.
26. LHS to General Oakes, V&A Forster Collection.
27. LHS to CB, 28 July 1811, Bod MS 5759 & BL Add 42057.
28. Meryon to his mother, Brusa Capital of Anatolya, 30 May 1811, Wellcome Foundation MS 5687.
29. Sligo to MB, Malta, 11 June 1811, Bod MS 2835.
30. General Oakes to LHS, 22 June, V&A, Forster Collection.
31. LHS to General Oakes, Bebec, 27 Aug 1811, V&A, Forster Collection.
32. *Ibid.*
33. See *The Nun of Lebanon*, p. 119–121.

Chapter 7

1. I am grateful to Odysseus Koranitov for his expert knowledge of the maritime.
2. Meryon to his mother, Bebec, 12 October 1811, Wellcome Foundation MS 5687.
3. The slaughter on Chios did not take place until 1821 and the island would at this time be enjoying an unusual period of prosperity and calm under their Turkish conquerors.
4 MB TO CB, 10 Dec 1811, Lindo Bod 5741.
5. Meryon, *Travels*, Vol. 1, p. 97.
6. The description of the shipwreck and its immediate aftermath are taken from: Meryon to his sister, 15 Dec 1811, Wellcome Foundation MS 5687; LHS to General Oakes , 'early in Dec' 1811, V&A, Forster collection; MB to CB, 10 Dec 1811, Bod MS 5741; LHS to CB, 'early in Dec' 1811, Bod MS 5759; Meryon, *Travels*, Vol. 1, pp. 95–102.
7. MB to CB, 10 Dec 1811, Bod MS 5741.

8. Meryon, *Travels,* Vol. 1, p. 101.

9. LHS to SC, 28 Aug 1827, PRO 352/19.

10. *New Monthly Magazine, 67,* Vol. 1, p. 228.

11. LHS to General Oakes, 2 Jan 1812, Kent UI590.

12. Meryon letter, 10 April 1812, Grand Cairo, Wellcome Foundation.

13. Dodwell, Henry, *The Founder of Modern Egypt*, 1931.

14. LHS to CB, 2 May 1812, Bod MS 5741.

15. Wynn was the nephew of Lord Grenville.

16. See *Brothers*, 1795, Halhed (The Second Speech. . . 1795) and Halhed Testimony 1795).

17. See *Oracle and Public Advertiser*, 6 March 1795.

18. Flaxmer, Sarah, *Satan Revealed,* 1795, BL.

19. *Oracle and Public Advertiser*, 6 March 1795.

20. *Additional Memoirs*, Chapter 5, 9 April to 9 May 1919, Chevening. Meryon used this remark anecdotally in *Riding Habits and Habit*, published under the pseudonym Chevalier Califourchon.

21. MB to CB, 20 April 1812, Bod MS 5741.

22. LHS to CB, 8 May 1812, Bod MS 5758.

23. Meryon to his parents, 28 July 1812, Wellcome Foundation MS 5687.

24. Meryon to his parents, Sidon Coast of Syria, 28 July 1812, Wellcome Foundation MS 5687.

25. Meryon, *Travels*, Vol. 1, p. 271.

26. Sim, *Desert Traveller,* p. 127.

27. 25 Jan 1816, BL.

28. 3 Jan 1817, see Duchess of Cleveland, p. 205.

Chapter 8

1. See Makarem, Sami Nasib, *The Druse Faith*, p. 53 (New York, 1974).

2. Betts, Robert Brenton, *The Druse*, p. 44 (Yale, 1988).

3. Churchill, Colonel, *Mount Lebanon, A Ten Years Residence*, Vol. 2, p. 236 (London, 1858).

4. Salibi, Kamal, *A House of Many Mansions,* p. 109 (London, 1988).

5. Betts, Robert Brenton, *The Druse*, pp. 38, 42–3.

6. LHS to General Oakes, 30 Sept 1812, V&A, Forster Collection.

7. Makdisi, Ussama, *The Culture of Sectarianism,* p. 24.

8. Meryon to his parents, 30 Sept 1812, Wellcome Foundation MS 5687.

9. Meryon to his sister, 12 Oct 1812, Wellcome Foundation MS 5687.

10. LHS to CB, 24 August 1812, Bod 5744.

11. LHS to CB, 23 Sept 1812, Bod 5744.

12. Lewis, pp. 8–9.

13. *Travels,* Vol. 2, p. 67.

14. LHS to General Oakes, November 1812, V&A, Forster Collection.

15. Meryon to his parents, 19 Dec 1812, Wellcome MS 5687.

16. Addison, Charles G., *Damascus and Palmyra* (London, 1838).

17. LHS to General Oakes, 25 Jan 1813, V&A, Forster Collection.

18. Meryon to his parents, 15 March 1813, Wellcome Foundation MS 5687.

19. Meryon to his brother-in-law Latikia, 11 June, Wellcome Foundation MS 5687.

20. CB to MB, 22 Jan 1812, Bod MS 5741.

21. LHS to CB, 27 Jan, Bod MS 5759.

22. LHS to General Oakes, 25 Jan 1813, V&A, Forster Collection.

23. Meryon, *Travels,* Vol. 2, pp. 188–9, and 11 June 1813 Wellcome Foundation MS 5687.

24. Description of the trip to Palmyra from Meryon to his brother-in-law, 11 June 1813, Meryon to his parents, 12 June 1813, Meryon to Sligo, 22 June 1813, Wellcome Foundation MS 5687.

Chapter 9

1. Cited in MacCarthy, p.113.

2. LHS to Mary Rich, 12 July 1813, BL EUR C740.

3. Meryon to Sligo, 29 Aug 1813, Wellcome Foundation MS 5687.

4. *Ibid.*

5. These letters are (so far) lost, but their content can be inferred from letters in the Bodleian Bruce collection. Cf. 3 Oct 1813, 5 Oct 1813.

6. In *The Nun of Lebanon* this is seen as being critical of Michael. I find the tone a little motherly, but not harsh. Her PS does go on to say 'a purer heart never existed'. MS letter, 5 Oct 1813.

7. MB to LHS, 4 Jan 1814, Bod MS 578.

8. MB to LHS, 20 Jan 1814, Bod MS 5742.

9. LHS to MB, Undated Bod MS 5758.

10. LHS to MB, Saturday the ninth, Bod MS 578.

11. *Ibid.*

12. *Ibid.*

13. Letter from Miss Williams is lost but see the response, 2 Dec 1813, Wellcome Foundation MS 5647.

14. 31 Dec 1813, Wellcome Foundation MS 5687.

15 Meryon to Miss Williams, December 1813.

16. Meryon to Lord Sligo, 1813, Wellcome Foundation MS 5687.

17. Meryon to his sister, 12 March 1814, Wellcome Foundation MS 5687.

18. *Ibid.*

19. Transcript letter LHS to MB, 12 May 1814, in Hogg (ed.) 1988, henceforth,

transcript letter 12 May 1814.

20. MS letter, 10 Jan, Bod.

21. Cited in *The Nun of Lebanon*, p. 242.

22. *Ibid.*

23. LHS to MB, 12 Dec 1810, Bod. 'A man in no age has ever suffered in the public opinion by his intimacy with a woman who had his real interests at heart . . . etc.'.

24. Transcript letter, 12 May 1814.

25. *Ibid.*

26. *Ibid.*, section dated 23 May.

27. Cited in *Lavalette Bruce*, p. 326.

28. *Ibid.* section dated 4 June.

29. LHS to CB, 25 June 1814, Bod MS 5744.

30. *Ibid.*

31. *Ibid.*

32. LHS to MB, 7 Sept 1814, Bod MS 5758.

33. In *Travels*, Vol. 3, p. 3 Meryon states 'the party consisted of Lady Hester, the dragoman, myself, eight men-servants, four women and a black female slave, making altogether fifteen'. His arithmetic was wrong!

34. *The Nun of Lebanon*, p. 320.

35. In Vienna Michael had rented a house 'to bring a companion from Paris to Vienna'. His father paid the bill although he did not use it. If the house was meant for another woman he may have used Hester as an excuse when getting his father to pay the bill as his father, while not happy about LHS, acknowledged his son's duty to her.

36. LHS to MB, 15 Feb 1815, Bod MS 5758.

37. Compare this letter to the one to Leveson Gower many years before where she says that the only way she can cope is to avoid him altogether.

38. LHS to MB, 15 Feb 1815, Bod MS 5758.

Chapter 10

1. LHS to Barker, 2 Feb 1815, Mar Elias, Kent UI590.

2. Meryon, *Travels*, Vol. 3, pp. 96–7.

3. LHS to MB, 22 March 1815, Haifa Bod (NL p. 336).

4. LHS to Richard Grenville, BL Add 42057. This is also borne out by the conversation reported by Meryon in *Travels*, Vol. 3, p. 166. Lord Elgin's removal of the Elgin marbles early in the century was heavily criticized by the general public.

5. LHS to MB, 8 Feb 1815, Bod MS 5758.

6. *Lavalette Bruce*, p. 97.

7. *Ibid.*

8. LHS to MB, 24 June 1815, Bod MS 5758.

9. *Ibid.*

10. See *Lavalette Bruce,* Chapter 8.

11. See MacCarthy, p. 130.

12. *Ibid.*, p. 352.

13. See *Some Correspondence etc.* pp. 33–59.

14. LHS to Marquess of Buckingham, 22 April 1816, quoted in *Life and Letters*, p. 184.

15. See Bosworth, 1972.

16. Buckingham, *Travels among the Arabs*, pp. 336–7 (1827).

17. *Ibid.*, p. 423.

18. *The Nun of Lebanon* p. 372.

19. *Ibid.*, p. 375.

20. LHS to Grenville, undated, BL 42057.

21. LHS to MB, Bod MS 5758.

Chapter 11

1. *Memoirs*, see Vol. 1, pp. 3–4.

2. Lord Carrington to Lord Mahon, 11 Oct 1816, Kent UI590.

3. See Stanhope and Gooch, p. 267.

4. Lord Mahon to Lord Carrington, 31 Dec 1816, Kent UI590.

5. James Stanhope to Lord Mahon, 11 Oct 1816, Kent UI590.

6. See Stanhope and Gooch, p. 267.

7. LHS to Rose, 3 Sept 1807, Add 42774 f. 224.

8. LHS to Rose, 3 Sept 1807, Add 42774 f. 225.

9. *Ibid.*

10. See Eliade, p. 477.

11. Meryon, *Additional Memoirs*, UI590 S6/2, quoted on f. 267 from the Comte De Marcelles, *Souvenirs De L'Orient.*

12. Notes in *Additional Memoirs*, UI590 S6/2/6.

13. See Duchess of Cleveland, p. 210.

14. Meryon, *Additional Memoirs*, 21 May 1818, Kent UI590 S6/2.

15. *Ibid.*

16. Meryon, *Additional Memoirs*, July 1819, Kent UI590 6/4/2.

17. Transcript letter LHS to Meryon, 17 Oct 1817, Mar Elias, Kent UI590 S6/2.

18. *Ibid.*

19. BL 37016 V1, f. 4 recto and v2 ff. 68 and 69.

20. See Burty, 1879, p. 135.

21. Meryon to LHS, Brig Anna Cyprus, 1 April 1819, Kent UI590 S6/2.

22. Meryon to LHS, 5 April 1819, Kent UI590.

23. Meryon, *Additional Memoirs*, 9 April 1819, Kent UI590 S6/2

24. LHS to Canning, Joun, Mount Lebanon, 25 May 1827, PRO FO 352/19.

25. Meryon, *Additional Memoirs*, 9 April to 9 May 1819, Kent UI590 S6/2.

26. *Ibid.*

27. *Ibid.*

28. *Ibid.*

29. *Ibid.*

30. Meryon, *Additional Memoirs*, May 1819, Kent UI590 S6/2.

31. *Ibid.*

32. *Ibid.*

33. *Ibid.*

34. Meryon, *Additional Memoirs*, 28 May 1819, Kent UI590 S6/3.

35. In letter 1317 of *The Letters of John Greenleaf Whittier*, Vol. 3 (Cambridge, MA, 1975), reference is made to Harriet Livermore speaking of 'her stay with Lady Hester Stanhope' but there is no other evidence to confirm whether or when the meeting took place.

36. Meryon, *Additional Memoirs*, July 1819, Kent UI590 S6/4.

37. Transcript letter, LHS to Meryon, July 1819, Kent UI590 S6/4.

38. Meryon, *Additional Memoirs*, July 1819, Kent UI590 S6/4.

39. Meryon, *Additional Memoirs*, 24 July 1819, Kent UI590 S6/4.

40. Meryon, *Additional Memoirs*, July 1819, Kent UI590 S6/4.

41. *Ibid.*

42. *Ibid.*

43. *Ibid.*

44. *Ibid.*

45. *Ibid.*

Chapter 12

1. The dates in this section differ from those in other publications but are borne out by the contemporary manuscripts in Kent. Captain Loustennau stayed with Hester only a short time before he died. The date of his death was indisputably 1820 as a letter in a private collection, dated 2 October 1820, was sent by Hester to notify the French Consul at Rhodes of it.

2. LHS to French Consul, 2 Oct 1820. Private Collection.

3. Lady Caroline Lamb to Michael Bruce, undated in the Bodleian Bruce collection. Cited in *Lavalette Bruce*, p. 300.

4. *Ibid.*

5. See Emery & Emery 1955 and Wedmore 1879.

6. Pierre Narcisse to Meryon, 21 Dec 1821, BL 37016, f. 20.

7. Meryon, *Additional Memoirs*, Kent UI590 S/6/5/6.

8. Many of these letters are in the British Library, MS 37016.

9. *Memoirs*, Vol. 1, pp. 85–7.

10. Makdisi, Ussama, *The Culture of Sectarianism*, p. 47.

11. Salibi, Kamal S., *The Modern History of the Lebanon*, p. 27.

12. LHS to Meryon, 8 Jan 1825, cited in Cleveland, p. 239.

13. LHS to Captain Yorke, Mt Lebanon, 8 Jan 1825, Kent UI590.

14. These events are recounted in LHS to SC, 25 May 1827, PRO FO 352/19.

15. Madden, R. R., *Travels in Turkey, Nubia and Palestine*, pp. 236–7.

16. Salibi, Kamal S., *The Modern History of the Lebanon*, p. 27.

17. Makdisi, Ussama, *The Culture of Sectarianism*, p. 49.

18. Cleveland, p. 240.

19. LHS to Meryon, 6 Jan 1827, cited in Meryon, *Memoirs*, Vol. 1, p. 21.

20. LHS to SC, 25 May 1827, PRO FO 352/19.

21. *Ibid.*

22. MS letter LHS to John Webb, 30 May 1827, Kent UI590.

23. SC to LHS, 26 July 1827, PRO FO 352/19.

24. Hester was not unique in this; see Makdisi p. 21 – 'in the refuge of the Lebanon the ancient regime survived and even flourished'.

25. Madden, p. 247.

26. Madden, pp. 268–9.

27. Letter quoted in *Memoirs*, Vol. 1, p. 66.

28. BL 37015.

29. See the description given by an observer and cited in *Memoirs*, Vol. 1, p. 157.

30. Transcript letter Meryon to LHS, Jan 1829, Kent UI590.

Chapter 13

1. *Memoirs*, Vol. 1, p. 136.

2. BL 37016.

3. BL37016 ff. 54 and 96.

4. *The Modern History of the Lebanon*, pp. 28–9.

5. *Ibid.*

6. Letter LHS to Sir Francis Burdett, 20 Sept 1839, Chevening Library.

7. LHS – undated letter to unknown recipient – post 1830, Chevening Library.

8. Lamartine, p. 70.

9. *Ibid.*

10. Lamartine, p. 75.

11. Lamartine, pp. 70–1.

12. Kinglake, p. 84.

13. *Eothen*, p. 85.

14. Kinglake, p. 86.
15. Kinglake, p. 88.
16. Kinglake, p.102.
17. *Eothen* p. 136.
18. *The Modern History of the Lebanon*, p. 30.
19. *Ibid.*, p. 31.
20. Letter from Agent of the Viceroy to LHS, 7 July 1834, Kent UI590 C246/1.
21. Cleveland, p. 342.
22. LHS to Meryon, 21 Aug 1836. Cited in Memoirs, Vol. 1, pp. 240–46.
23. *Memoirs*, Vol. 1, p. 247.

Chapter 14

1. *Memoirs*, Vol. 1, pp. 251–2.
2. *Memoirs*, Vol. 2, p. 11.
3. Several previous books (cf. Haslip, Childs) have claimed that Hester did not make a public appearance until 1796 at Lord Romney's review. This is incorrect, as her grandmother Stanhope's letters and diaries recall several balls attended by Hester between 1793 and 1796, Kent UI590 C11.
4. Countess Grizel Stanhope to Lady Chatham, 12 Jan 1796, Kent UI590 C11.
5. A list of the food and wine ordered for banquets can be found in Kent UI590 C42.
6. *Memoirs*, Vol. 1, p. 299.
7. *Ibid.*
8. *Memoirs*, Vol. 2, p. 266.
9. LHS to Sir Edward Sugden, 12 Feb 1838, Kent UI590 C246.
10. LHS to Queen Victoria, *The Times*, 27 Nov 1838.
11. LHS to Puckler Muskau, cited in *Memoirs*, Vol. 3, pp. 18–19.
12. *Memoirs*, Vol. 3, p. 40.
13. For details of his visit see Puckler Muskau, 1846, pp. 230–93.
14.. Puckler Muskau, p. 257.
15. Lord Palmerston to LHS, 25 April 1858, cited in *Memoirs*, Vol. 3, p. 278–79.
16. *The Times*, 6 Dec 1838.
17. See *Memoirs*, Vol. 1, pp. vi–vii.
18. *Morning Herald*, 26 Nov 1838.
19. *Morning Chronicle*, 8 Dec 1838.
20. LHS to Meryon, 6 May 1839, quoted in *Memoirs*, Vol. 3, pp. 338–40.
21. *Ibid.*
22. Description based on that of the missionary: Thomson, W. M., *The Land and the Book*.

Chapter 15

1. Cited in Cleveland, p. 436.
2. *Ibid.*, p. 437.
3. Cited in Fama, P. G., 'Charles Meryon: A Biographical and Psychiatric Reassessment', in *New Zealand Medical Journal*, No. 28, 1973, pp. 448–55.
4. BL Add 37016 F 1,2.
5. CLM to MB, 27 May 1849. Cited in *Lavalette Bruce*, pp. 325–6.

Epilogue

1. See the article in the *Quarterly Review*, September 1845.
2. Strachey, Lytton, *Books and Characters: French and English*, p. 241 (London, 1924).
3. *Ibid.*, p. 249.
4. Auden, W. H., *The Complete Works of W. H. Auden: Prose Volume II 1939–1948*, Ed. Mendelson, E., p. 148 (London, 2002).
5. Begnal, M., 'Molly Bloom and Lady Hester Stanhope', in Kershner (Ed.), *Joyce and Popular Culture* (Florida, 1996).

Index

Figures in italics indicate captions; 'H' indicates Lady Hester Stanhope.

Abdullah Pasha of Acre 165, 177, 182–3, 184, 200, 202, 207
Abra 126, 128, 131, 164, 169, 214, 217
Abu Ghyas sepulchre 149–50
Acre 94, 96, 141, 151, 184
  siege of (1831-2) 202, 203, 204, 218, 222
Acre, Pasha of *see* Suleyman Pasha
Addington, Henry, Viscount Sidmouth 28
Aegean Sea 82, 86
Aga, Jacoub, Consul 186, 187
Ahmed Bey, Pasha of Damascus 106–9, 139, 159, 199
Aleppo 104, 105, 106, 109
Aleppo button 105
Alexander I, Tsar 7
Alexandria 81, 86, 121, 145, 146
Alexandria, Battle of (1801) 16
Ali, Captain Pacha Hafiz 71
Ali, Mehmet, Pasha of Egypt 87–8, 89, 91, 93, 94, 96, 121, 139, 183, 190, 195, 202, 206, 207, 208, 217
Amiens, Treaty of (1802) 10

Anazah tribes 108, 109, 116, 121
Anderson, Colonel 18, 19
Ansary 152, 153
Ansary mountains 152
Ansary trail 146
Anthony, St 133, 134
Antioch 128, 152
Arles, M. (French silk merchant) 72
Arles, Mlle 73
Arslan, Hubus 101
Ascalon, Israel 140, 142–3, 145, 233
Athens 61–4
Auden, W.H. xv, 232
Awali River 97
Ayubid sultan 87

Baalbek 129, 132, 133
Bankes, William 149–51, 153
Banks, Sir Joseph 158
Barker, Harissa 124
Barker, Consul General John 109, 110, 122, 124, 125, 131, 140, 144
Barker, Zabetta 124
Bashir Shihab II, Emir 124, 175, 200, 219

invites H as his guest 97
elected to the Emirate 102
his religion 102
travelling party 103
palace at Beittedine 104
appearance 104
personality 104
plague epidemic 128
H stays in his summer house 130
and letters of introduction 150
enmity between him and Jumblat
  164
cultivates support of Maronite
  Christians 164
uneasy truce with the Jumblats 165
forced into exile 177
retakes control of the region 182
his troops joined to those of Pasha of
  Acre 183
terrible revenge on the Jumblat
  children 184
consequences of H's defiance 185–6,
  189
strong alliance with Mehmet Ali 202
a puppet of his Egyptian masters 207
Puckler Muskau granted an
  audience 220
Bath 3, 30, 72
Bebec 74–5, 76
Bedford, Duke of 185
Bedlam asylum, London 90
Bedouin Arabs
  swathed in a mist of rumour and
    romanticism 105
  makeshift tents 110
  livestock 110–11

  tattoos 111, 116
  jewellery 111
  H named 'queen of them all' 111
  desert journey 115–16
Beirut 149, 154, 193, 209, 213, 216, 233
Beittedine 104, 175, 183, 202
Bekaa 132, 133
Belle Poule (a frigate) 56, 59
Berber, Mustafa Age 152
Bertrand, M. (dragoman
  interpreter) 107–8
Bessborough, Countess Harriet 5, 23,
  25, 26, 31, 179
Beyer, Professor 9
Black Sea 66
Bonaparte, Joseph, King of Spain 16
Bosphorus Strait 66, 69, 76, 233
Bourbons 144
Boutin, M. (French Consul General)
  128, 147, 149, 152, 154
Brandenburg-Bayreuth, Margravine of
  9
Brisbane, Captain 56, 59
British Library 228
Brothers, Richard 89–91, 92, 117, 161
Bruce, Crauford 54, 59, 60, 86
  correspondence 54, 59, 60, 66–8, 69, 84,
    92, 93, 102, 112–13, 123, 143
  receives anonymous letter from
    Dover 59, 67
  financial matters 102–3, 108, 148, 152
  told of Michael's proposal 112
  urges Michael to travel abroad
    without H 113
  very ill 123
  H's illness 130

H's last letter to him 131
and Michael's imprisonment 148
stops allowance to H 166–7
Bruce, Marianne (previously Parker) 179
Bruce, Michael 45
  on the 'Grand Tour' 48
  admiration for Moore 48
  and Meryon 49, 51, 52, 53, 55, 60, 69,
    93–6, 105–6
  education 51
  appearance 51
  relationship with H 51, 52, 54, 62–3,
    73, 82, 123, 124, 147–8
  tentative advances to Byron 64–5, 147
  writes to his father 68, 92, 143
  H refuses his proposal of marriage
    69, 112, 114
  James's challenge 69–70
  tour of Asia without H 70
  shipwrecked 82–5, 103
  visits the Pasha of Egypt 88
  fits of temper 93–4, 96
  and the ailing Barker 110
  disappointed in his father 113–14
  money issue 123, 134, 146, 166–7
  sets off home due to father's illness 123
  new lover 127–8
  H suspects he has met someone else
    129–30
  and treasure trove affair 140
  imprisoned on a charge of treason
    49, 148
  plays a careful game from his prison
    cell 152
  free from prison 154
  H writes for the last time 159

  and Lady Caroline Lamb 179
  marriage 179
  birthday wishes from Meryon 229
Brummel, Beau 40
Brusa 72–4
bubonic plague 122
Buckingham, Mr Silk 151
Builth Wells, Powys, Wales 30–31
Burckhardt, Johann 95–6, 108, 145, 148
Burdett, Sir Francis 8, 219, 221
Burrard, Sir Henry 16, 17, 18
Burton Pynsent, Somerset 8, 31, 205
Byron, George Gordon, Lord 206
  hatred of Lady Bessborough 26
  relationship with Caroline Lamb 26,
    147, 179
  in Athens 62–5
  liaison with Nicolo 63
  attitude to H 63–4
  rejects Bruce's tentative advances
    64–5, 147
  opposes robbery of ruins 121
  and Bankes 149

Cadiz 49
caiques 81
Cairo 86, 87–9, 91, 122
Calabria 49
Campbell, Colonel (British Consul
    General) 208, 217
Campbell, General 48
Canning, George
  and Pitt's death 4–5, 15
  H's rift with 15, 16, 17, 20
  and Moore's death 19
  Gower's friendship with 24, 26

and Addington 28

Canning, Stratford 71, 72, 75, 76, 77, 85, 186, 187, 191

Caroline, Princess of Wales *45*, 91, 141, 151–2

Carrington, Robert, 1st Lord 11, 158

Castlereagh, Robert Stewart, Viscount 19

Catafagio, Signor 94, 95, 141

Catholic emancipation 7, 16

Cavendish, Harriet 31

Cerberus (a ship) 50

Charlotte, Queen 4, 10, 26, 42, 43

Charlton, Louise (servant) 163, 164, 171, 173, 177, 178, 199

Chasseau (H's amanuensis) 193

Chatham, Lady (H's maternal grandmother) 8, 10, 27, 31, 35, 38, 39, 44

Chatham, Lord (H's maternal grandfather) 17, 19, 205

Chatham family 31

Chaucer, Geoffrey: 'The Monk's Tale' 115

Chevening Manor, Kent 7–8, 9, *21*, 38, 39, 41–4, 158, 159, 214, 223

Chios 81

Chouf, Lebanon xv

Christian revivalism 169

Christianity 160, 167

Church of England 160, 224

Cline, Henry 32

Colonna 62

Constantinople 53, 56, *57*, 64, 65–72, 74–7, 81, 102, 123

Constantinople, Pasha of 77

Convent, The, Gibraltar 48

Convention of Paris (1815) 147

Corfu 56

Corinth 60

Corinth, Bey of 60, 61

Corunna, Battle of (1809) 18, 48, 83

Coutts Bank 144, 152

Coutts banking family 8

Crete 190

Crump sisters 42–3

Cyprus 148–9, 154, 163, 189, 216

Dalrymple, Sir Hew 16

Damascus 105–11, 122, 132, 184, 199, 200, 202

Damascus, Pasha of *see* Ahmed Bey

Damiani, Signor (British agent) 91

Damietta 122

Datura 167–8

Dawkins, James 114, 121

Dayr-El-Kamar ('The House of the Moon'), Mount Lebanon 97, 102, 103, 202

dervishes 200

Devonshire, Duchess of 23

Didot, Firman 153–4

Djezzar 94

Dorset, Duke of 27

Dover, Kent 29, 59, 67

Downing Street, London (No.10) 23, 25, 29, 55, 222

Drovetti, Bernardino 121

Druse Jumblats 102, 104, 202

Druse sect xv, *79*, *155*, 169, 218
  a mysterious mountain sect 96
  location of 101
  costume 101, 103

a closed religion 101
means of subsistence 103
penalty for being unchaste 103
raw meat-eating 105
holy books 105
and the Mahdi 159–60
resentment of the Emir's rule 164
refusal to accept conscription 207, 220

Edgeworth, Maria: *Tales of Fashionable Life* 147
Egerton, Mr and Mrs 10
Egypt 77, 85
  Zenobia conquers 114
  Cairo 86, 87–9
  tour of the pyramids 88–9
  rules Syria 202, 206
Egypt, Pasha of *see* Ali, Mehmet
Egyptian army 207
Elba 143, 144
Elden, William 48–9
Elgin, Lord 121
Elias, St 169
Eniskillen dragoons 145
Erlangen, University of, Germany 9
Espagnet family 178
Essence of the First 105

Farquar, Walter 3, 32
ferigees 60, 73
Fernandez, Commissary-General 49, 50
Fid'an group 108, 121
firmans 139–40, 141
Flaxmer, Sarah 90
  'Satan Revealed' 90

Foreign Office 208
Fortuna (Italian frigate) 189
Fox, Charles James 5
France
  H's revenge for death of Boutin 152–3
  James wants H to live there 172
Frederick, Duke of York 31
'Free Franks' 54–5
French Revolution 7
Fry, Anne (H's maid) 56, 84, 161

Galilee 95
Gaza 88
George (Wynn's servant) 89
George III, King
  Catholic emancipation issue 7
  in Weymouth 9–10
  at Lord Romney's review 42, 43
George IV, King (as Prince Regent) 162
Germany 123
Ghosh, Abu 92
Gibraltar 37, 47–8, 50
Gloucester House, London 214
Gower, Granville Leveson 68, 135, 145, 179
  H's first serious romantic attachment 23–8
  personality 23
  affair with Countess Harriet Bessborough 23, 25
  friendship with Canning 24, 26
  appearance 25
  H's unrequited love for 21, 23, 25–9, 31
  ambassador to St Petersburg 26
  last exchange with H 26

returns from Russia 31
engaged to Harriet Cavendish 31
Greece 56, 189
Greek islands 53
Greek-Turkish war 189, 190
Grenville, General 153
Grenville, Sir Richard 37
Grenville, William Wyndham 17, 18
Grosvenor Square, London 37
Guildford, Lord 29
Gustavus IV, King of Sweden 16
Guys, M. 217

al-Hakim 101
Hamah 110–13, 121–2, 127
hamam 73, 133
Hardwicke, Lord 208, 211, 222
harems 60–61, 74
Hasanah tribe 108, 109
Haslip, Joan: *Lady Hestor Stanhope*
    232–3
Hayes Parish Church, Middlesex 38
Heathcote, Sir Gilbert 180, 185
Hems 110
Heraklion 65
hikma (Druse religious doctrine) 101
Hobhouse, John 64, 65
holowe (holy buildings) 105
Holy Land 86, 91
Homs 108
Homsy (moneylender) 217
Hope, Commander 86
horses 61
House of Commons 55, 90
House of Lords 55
Hume, Mr (Sligo's companion) 48

Ibrahim Pasha 190, 202, 203, 206, 207
Ionian islands 56
Ishmael Bey 93
Islam 160
Israel
    Druse sect in 101
    and Meshmushy 132
Italy: H and Mahon reunited in (1802)
    10–11

Jabr, Jamil 130
Jackson, Francis 8, 9, 10, 19, 28
Jackson, George 19–20, 24
Jackson, T.J. 45
Jaffa 91
Jason (frigate) 37
Jerusalem 90–95, 173
jewellery 111, *119*
Jordan, Druse sect in 101
Joseph (Mameluk servant) 95
Joun *188*, 190, 233
    location 132
    described 180, *181*, 182
    Captain Loustennau's body reinterred
        182, 223
    refugees in 183, 190, 202, 203
    Bashir II's orders 186
    accommodation for Meryon's family
        193, 216
    H's garden *195*
    H's living conditions described 197–8
    epicentre of political refuge and
        defiance 207
    view from the terrace 220
    regime of the household 215
    Loustennau settles in 222–3

H's ori...al grave *231*

162, 164,

Ki...
Eo...
Kings...
Lond...
Knights o...
kohl 61

Lackner, Walbu...
Lamartine, Alph... 3–5,
  206, 219, 220
Lamb, Lady Caroline 26, 179
Lascaris, M. 109–12, 122
Lascaris, Mme 109, 110, 111, 122
Latakia 122, 124–6, 127, 135
Laurella, Mr (a British agent) 149
Lavalette, Count 147
Layla (a foal) 159, 188, 220
Leander, Miranda 163, 165, 166, 169, 171,
  172–3, 178
Lebanon
  Druse sect in 101, 207
  Mehmet Ali threatens to invade 202
Leghorn 187, 190
Lepanto 60

Liston, Robert 140
Livermore, Harriet 169
London hangings 70, 71
Lonsdale, Lord 6
Louis (manservant) 163, 164, 170
Louis XVIII, King of France 147, 149
Loustennau, Captain 177–8, 182, 223
Loustennau, General ('the Prophet')
  142, 168, 170, 177, 178, 214, 222–3
Lowther, Fanny 163, 179
Lowther, Lord William 162–3, 179
Lulu (a chestnut mare) 159, 188
Lunardi, Dr 201, 202, 205

Madden, Dr 187–8
Mahdism 159–61, 168–9, 170, 198–9
Mahon, Lord *see* Stanhope, Philip
  Henry, 4th Earl
Malta 7, *35*, 49–56, 59, 60, 72, 93, 122,
  123
Mamelukes 87, 91, 92, 95, 96, 203
Mansfield, Lord 178
Mansfield Street, London 90
Mar Elias *99*, 124, 126, 132, 133, 134, 147,
  153, 169, 173, 216, 229
  rented by H 124
  described 126
  repairs 126–7
  heat starts to affect H's health 130
  arrival of a Zaim from Constantinople
  139
  arrival of European visitors 149–51
  besieged by locusts 151
  H's affair with Captain Loustennau
  178
  death of Captain Loustennau 177–8

H moves to Joun 182
General Loustennau remains 182, 214
Meryon family moves in 216
General Loustennau moves out
 222–3
Marie (servant) 163, 171
Marie Louise, Empress of the French
 49
Maronite Convent of St Anthony
 133–4
Maronites 102, 103, 105, 164, 202, 207
Marseille 154, 209
Mauburg, M. (French chargé d'affaires) 76
Mawali 108
Mayfair, London 5
Meryon, Charles 179–80, 190–91, 201,
 209, *225*, 227, 228–9
Meryon, Dr Charles Lewis *1*, 114
 background 32
 education 32
 appearance 32, *225*
 death of his wife 32
 his daughter 32, 33
 accompanies H on her travels xv, 32,
 33
 initial optimism 47
 and Michael Bruce 49, 51, 53, 55, 60,
 69, 93–6, 105–6
 in Malta 50–53, 55–6
 dalliances 55–6, 81, 112
 and Sligo 60, 62
 looks after H in Constantinople 68, 72
 and public executions 70–71
 establishes himself as a medic for
 wealthier families 71

discovers Bebec 74–5
persuades H of his true wish to
 accompany her 76–7
shipwrecked 82, 85
enjoyment of Rhodes 86
and the dancing girls in Egypt 89
on riding astride 91
and the Pasha of Acre 93
dislikes the palace at Beittedine 104
fascinated by the Druse 104
friendship with Lascaris 109
and the ailing Barker 110
journey with Lascaris 111–12
at work in Hamah 121–2
stays in Abra for nearly three years
 126
laments his new isolation 127
writes H a poem 129
tension between him and H 131
treasure trove affair 139–42
wants to go home 144, 153
H arranges leave for 145
trip to Alexandria 145
opposes removal of antiquities 150
and Bankes 149–50
Newberry takes over from him 153
returns home 154
two trilogies of books xv–xvi, 157
and Narcisse 162, 163, 179–80, 199,
 201, 209, 228
birth of his son Charles 179–80
brings new servants to H 163–4
terrified by severity of H's tantrums
 167
and H's theological concerns 168–9
looks after Mar Elias 169–70

told to take the servants back to
    Europe 171–3
correspondence with H 178
agrees to support his son 180
marries Eliza Gardiner 180
disasters at sea 189–90
his family not welcome at Joun 193,
    213
Ahmed Bey's request 199–200
promises to try to raise money in
    England 201
gift from H 201–2
final visit to Joun 213–21
small literary success 228, 231
and son's fate 228–9
the ultimate fan 229
Additional Memoirs 157
Memoirs of Lady Hester Stanhope 132,
    157, 227
Travels of Lady Hester Stanhope 214,
    227–8
Meryon, Eliza (née Gardiner) 180, 189,
    190, 193, 199–201, 213, 214
Meryon, Elizabeth 32
Meryon, Eugenia 213, 214
Meryon, Lucy Elizabeth 32
Meryon family 33
Meshmushy 130, 131–2, 146, 152, 169,
    170–71, 233
metempsychoses 101
Metta (a village doctor) 160–61
Minorca 49
Misset, Colonel 145, 146, 147
Montagu Square, Mayfair, London
    (No.4) xvi, 5, 15, 16, 18, 30, 31, 37, 83
Montague, Lady Mary Wortley 74

Moore, General Sir John
    appearance 15, 177
    relationship with H 15–16
    Pitt impressed with him 16
    failed diplomatic mission in
        Sweden 16–17
    sent to Portugal 16
    at Salamanca 17, 18, 48
    writes a letter full of foreboding 17
    death at Corunna 18–19
    H keeps his blood-stained gauntlet
        until her death 19, 83
    fails to receive honours 31
    Bruce's admiration for 48
Moore, Thomas: 'Lalla Rookh' 99
Morning Chronicle 222
Morning Herald 222
Moukhtara 104
Mount Cenis 11
Mount Lebanon 96, 97, 124, 128, 202
    home of the Druse 96
    climate 96
    feudal cantons (muqata'at) 102
    described 103, 126
    possible yellow fever 191
Mount Olympus 72
Mudania 72
Muhana Al Fadil, Muhana 108, 110, 111,
    121, 150, 168
Mukhtara 13
Murat, Joachim, King of Sicily 49
Muslims 105
mystics 167, 168

Napier, Sir William 222
Napoleon Bonaparte 17, 18, 49, 87

defeat of 1798 7

coronation 162

establishes brother as King of Spain 16

marries Marie Louise 49

H plans an intrigue 53, 76, 77

his armies sweep across mainland Europe 56

exiled to Elba 143

escapes and reaches Paris with a new force 143, 144

abdicates for the second time 146–7

H admires 149

Narcisse, Pierre (Narcisse Gentil) 162–3, 179–80, 199, 201, 209, 221, 228

narghileh (long water pipe) 164, 166, 168

Navarino, Battle of 190, 202

Navarino (now Pylos) 190

Nazareth 94–5

Needham, Colonel 208

Nelson, Admiral Lord Horatio 7, 47

New Testament 198

Newberry, Dr 153, 157, 159, 161–2, 173, 178

Newgate Prison, London 48, 166

Ney, Madame 143, 144, 147, 154

Ney, Marshall 143, 144, 147

Nicolo 63

Nile, Battle of the (1800) 87

Nile barques 86–7

Nile River 88, 89

Oakes, General 53, 151

  governor of Malta 50

  his banquets 50

country residence in San Antonio 52

H's farewell gift 56

correspondence with H 56, 70, 73, 75, 85, 122

and Sligo 70, 75, 112

urges H to reconsider Michael's proposal 75

Opera Ballet, London 179

Orontes River 113

Oswald, Major General 59

Ottoman Empire 65, 87, 139, 189, 202

Ovenden dower house, Kent 41

Oxford and Cambridge Gentleman's Club 222

packhorses 61

Paddington Street, London 90

Palmerston, Lord 217, 220–21, 222

Palmyra 106, 108, 109, 111, 113–17, 121, 122, 142, 150, 153, 233

Paris 53, 143, 144, 148, 162

Paris Opera 162

Parthenon Marbles 121

Patras 60

Pauline (servant) 163, 164, 171

Pera, Constantinople 66, 68, 74, 127

Picasso, Pablo xv, 233

piracy 189–90

Piraeus 61, 64

Piraeus (a yacht) 48, 60

Pisa 189

Pitt, William, the Younger (H's uncle) xv, 19, 27, 31, 222

  sister Heather's illness 39

  begins to take an active role in H's life 42

at Lord Romney's review 43
resigned to H's stubbornness 24–5
intervenes on Griselda's behalf 44
makes provision for H and her sisters
  5
alcoholism 3
Mahon's promise 6
Catholic emancipation issue 7, 16
estranged from H's father 8
supports Mahon's escape 8, 9
and H's efforts to protect Mahon's
  inheritance 8
nursed by H in 1802 10
Warden of the Cinq Ports 16
and H's affair with Gower 25
H intercedes on Canning's behalf 28
and Elizabeth Williams 31
impressed with Moore 16, 18
H's box of mementoes 83
death of 3–5, 15, 158, 208
Plymouth 47
Portman Estates 5
Portman Square, London 5
Portsmouth 33
Portugal, Moore in 16–17
Price, Mrs 30
Price, Reverend 30, 31
Prince's Island 81
Prison de la Force, Paris 148
public executions 70–71
Puckler Muskau, Prince Hermann
  219–20, 222
Putney, south-west London 3, 4, 23, 29

Quarterly Review 228

Raby (a Bedouin girl) 112

Ramadan 107
Revelations, book of 198
Rhodes 82, 84–6, 148
Romans: Palmyra taken 114–15
Romney, Lord 42, 43
Rosetta 86
Rousseau, Jean-Jacques 30
Royal College of Medicine 180
Royal Navy 37
Royal Oak inn 31

St Anne Street, London 37
St Antonius 133
St Thomas's Hospital, London 162
Salamanca 17, 18, 48
Salsette (a frigate) 86
San Antonio, palace of, Malta 52, 53
Sayda 126
Sba'ah group 108, 116, 121
Sea Castle, Sidon 97
Selim (a Mameluke) 92
senna 191
shamans 167
Shia Muslims 159
Shihab family 102
Shiite minority 102
Shorncliffe barracks, Kent 16
Sicily 49, 50
Sidon 96–7, 122, 125, 126, 128, 170, 172,
  177, 183, 185, 187, 202, 204, 207, 213,
  216, 219
Signora L 215–16
Sligo, Howe Peter Browne, 2nd
  Marquess of 72, 113
  travels round the Mediterranean in a
    yacht 48

entices a seaman to desert and help
  navigate 48–9
yacht remanded in Malta 60
and Meryon 60, 62
his Albanian servants 61
and Byron 62
tour of Asia 70
and General Oakes 70, 75, 112
tells Crauford of the Michael-H
  liaison 112
Smyrna 85
Somerset 7, 10, 44
Song of Solomon 119
Stanhope, Catherine, Countess (née
  Smith) 11–12, 27
Stanhope, Charles, 3rd Earl (H's
  father) 214
first marriage to Hester Pitt 7, 39
makes changes at Chevening 7
obsession with science and politics 7,
  8, 38, 39
second marriage to Louise Grenville
  7, 40
Mahon escapes from 9
becomes Lord Stanhope 41
rages 41, 42, 44
reconciliation with Mahon 11
rejects his aristocratic heritage 8
wants Mahon to agree to the sale of
  Chevening 8
eccentricity 42, 158
anti-war stance 42
stalked by Sarah Flaxmer 90
taken to court by Mahon 158
and Mrs Lackner 158, 159
reunion with H 158–9

death 158–9
'Principles of Electricity' 38
Stanhope, Charles Banks (H's half-
  brother) 5, 15–18, 19, 83, 167
Stanhope, Griselda see Tickell, Griselda
Stanhope, Lady Grizel (née Hamilton;
  H's paternal grandmother) 35, 214,
  215
brings up the children after their
  mother's death 39, 111
H's birth 38
and daughter-in-law Heather's death
  39
husband's death 41
careful schooling of H 24
H's horsemanship 35
Stanhope, Hester, Countess (née Pitt;
  H's mother)
choice of St Anne Street home 37
marriage 38
pregnancies 38–9
personality 39–40
death 39, 40
Stanhope, Lady Hester Lucy
birth (8 March 1776) 38
relationship with Griselda 39, 40
eye inflammations 40, 41
education 40
appearance 6, 24, 40, 43
horseriding 35, 41, 73, 74, 91, 111
childhood 39–42
plans to move to Wales 20, 23
in Wales 30–31
European tour with the Egertons
  10–11

relationship with Mahon 6–7

schemes to protect Mahon's inheritance 8

attends Lord Romney's review 42–3

stays with her maternal grandmother 44

Pitt makes financial provision for her 5

and Pitt's death 3–5

rift with Canning 15, 16, 17, 20

settles in Montagu Square 5

departs on travels (1810) 47

social obligations in Gibraltar 48, 49–50

unrequited love for Gower 21, 23, 25–9, 31

her will 32

in Malta 49–53

relationship with Michael Bruce 51, 52, 54, 62–3, 73, 82, 123, 124, 147–8

plans an intrigue with Napoleon 53

correspondence with Oakes 56, 70, 73, 75, 85, 122

opinion on Byron 64

in Constantinople 65–72, 75–6

refuses Bruce's proposal of marriage 69, 75, 112, 114

attends public executions 70

first dresses as a man 72

attitude to lesbianism 74

refuses Pasha's proposal 77

shipwrecked 82–5, 86, 123

box of mementoes 83

Eastern costume 85, 86, 88, 91, 106, 114, 205, 219

begins to travel the tourist trail in earnest 86

shaves her head 88

relationship with the Pasha of Egypt 88

and Brothers' 'Queen of the Jews' prophecy 90–91, 92, 117, 161

revels in freedom and respect found in the East 92

riding accident 96

fascinated by the Druse 104

delighted enthusiasm from crowds 106–7

obsessed with Zenobia 114–15

named 'queen of them all' by the Bedouin 111, 115

desert journey with the Bedouin 115–16

financial problems 123, 144, 151, 159, 166–7, 168, 185, 201, 202, 208, 217, 218, 220, 222

very ill in Latakia 125–6

plague epidemic at Abra 128

suspects Michael has met someone else 129–30

reconciliation with James 130

stays in Bashir II's summer house 130

last letter to Crauford 131

and Lucy's death 132

promise to Crauford 131, 135

feels that Michael is seeing someone else 135, 145

treasure trove affair 139–43

briefly given great power in the Turkish Empire 139–40

opposes removal of antiquities 150

vengeance for Boutin's death 152–3

Meryon leaves after seven years 154
learns Arabic 157
reunion with her father 158–9
death of her father 157–8
and Mahdism 159–61, 168–9, 170, 198–9
attempts to become Lebanese 160
and eastern mystics 168
criticism of Christianity 160, 167
smokes the narghileh 164, 166, 168
criticism of her new servants 165–6, 171
affair with Captain Loustennau 178
sends help to Sheikh Bashir
　Jumblat's family 183–4
brother James' death 184, 185
consequences of her defiance of
　Bashir II 185–6, 189
and Lamartine 203–5
saviour of the Druse reputation 208
supposed inheritance 208, 209, 216
deteriorating health 208–9, 217
death and burial 223–4
personality
– acerbicness 24, 220
– aloofness 24
– courage 82–3, 111, 135
– cruelty xv, 131, 215, 233
– dress sense 24
– generosity 31, 56
– independence 24
– intelligence 6
– political acumen 6
– rages 42, 130, 131, 167, 168
– religious delusions xvi
– strong-mindedness 24
– stubbornness 24
– tyranny xv, xvi, 27, 161

– volubility 24
– wit 6, 24, 64
Stanhope, Iowa xv
Stanhope, James, 1st Earl (H's paternal
　great-grandfather) 7
Stanhope, James Hamilton (H's half-
　brother) 32, 50, 166
and Moore 17, 18–19
returns home from Corunna 19
settles in Montagu Square 5, 15
debt repayment 6
and Pitt's death 4, 5
his horse 30
visits H in Wales 31
travels on the *Jason* 37
rejoins his regiment in Cadiz 49
disapproval of Michael 69–70, 75
reconciliation with H 130
H refuses his financial help 144
developing friendship with Michael 146
worried about H's spending 153
wants H to live in France 172
H wants him to visit her 172
marries daughter of Lord
　Mansfield 178
death 184, 185
Stanhope, Louisa, Countess (née
　Grenville; H's step-mother) 7, 40,
　41–2, 158
Stanhope, Lucy *see* Taylor, Lucy
Stanhope, Lucy, Countess (née Pitt;
　H's paternal great-grandmother) 7
Stanhope, Philip, 2nd Earl (H's paternal
　grandfather) 37, 41
Stanhope, Philip Henry, 4th Earl (Lord
　Mahon; H's half-brother) 27, 75, 225

birth 41
relationship with H 6–7
education 8, 9
becomes Lord Mahon 41
father tries to persuade him to agree
    to sale of Chevening 8
avoidance of London society 27
visits Griselda at Walmer 43
reneges on promise to Pitt 6
escapes to Europe 9, 19
takes his father to court 158
reconciliation with his father 11
inherits Chevening 8
marriage to Catherine Smith 11–12
reunited with H 10–11
Stewart, Miss (dressmaker) 19
Strachey, Lytton 232
Sugden, Sir Edward 218
Suleyman Pasha, Pasha of Acre 93, 94,
    96, 139, 141, 164, 165
Sussex, Duke of 185
Sutton, Nassau 50
  visits H with James 31
  travels on the *Jason* 37
  goes to Minorca 49
Syria 91
  H sends Lord Lonsdale a statue 6
  plague epidemic 122
  governors of 139
  Ali demands 190, 202
  under Egyptian rule 202, 206

Tartars 61
Taylor, Lucy (née Stanhope; H's sister) 6
  birth (1780) 38–9
  appearance 39

childhood 39
  marriage 42
  death, leaving seven children 132
Theophanie 127–8
Therapia, Constantinople 66, 72, 74, 75
Tickell, Griselda (née Stanhope; H's
    sister) 6
  birth (1778) 38
  relationship with H 39, 40
  stays at Walmer 43
  relationship with Tickell 43–4
  marriage to Tickell 44
  and Lucy's death 132
  writes to H 184–5
Tickell, John 43–4
Times, The 222
Trafalgar shoals 47
transmigration of the soul 101
Trianda 71, 85
Tripoli 133, 134, 152
Tunbridge Wells: Pantiles 215
Turkey 56
Turkish army 87
Turkish Empire 139, 140
Turkish fleet 71–2
Turner, William 145

uqqal ('the knowing') 101, 105

Vale of Brusa 72
Valletta, Malta 49, 52, 55
Valley of the Tombs 116
Van Gogh, Vincent 228
Victoria, Queen 217, 220
Vienna 131, 134

Wales, H stays in 30–31

Walmer Castle, Kent *13*
  living accommodation 27
  Pitt's role while living there 16
  Pitt's orders to H 24
  H retreats from London society 26–7
  guests 27
  H nurses Pitt (1802) 10
  H creates a garden 23, 28, 29–30
  Griselda stays at the cottage 43
Wedmore, Frank 229
Wellington, Arthur Wellesley, 1st Duke
  of 16, 17, 77, 208, 217
Weymouth, Dorset 9–10
Whitby, Captain 50
Whittier, John Greenleaf 169
Williams, Elizabeth 154
  educated by Pitt and retained as his
    maid 31
  spends most of her life with H 31
  travels on the *Jason* 37
  in Malta 49, 56, 122, 125, 148
  H's generous marriage gift 56
  dreadful journey to Mar Elias 148–9
  opts to stay with H 161
  and H's financial difficulties 168, 185
  pleased with the arrival of the Swiss
    maids 170
  becomes H's amanuensis 185, 190
  illness and death 191–2, 193
Wolfe, Charles: 'The Burial of Sir John
  Moore after Corunna' 13
Wood, Robert 114, 121
Wye River 30
Wynn, Henry (H's cousin) 88, 89

Yusuf, Emir 102

Zaims 139, 140
Zante 59, 190
Zenobia, Queen 114–15
Zezefoon 198